BREADLINE BRITAIN

'Inequality is the biggest challenge of our time. This important book exposes the real causes of poverty in modern Britain and makes a powerful case for the radical change we need to build a fairer and more equal society.'

Margaret Hodge MP – Chair of the Public
Accounts Committee

'The big debates about social and economic policy in Western countries are shifting from concerns about poverty to a recognition that growing inequality is our fundamental problem. Stewart Lansley and Joanna Mack, who have been working in this field for a generation, offer a massively convincing analysis of this problem and the policies it calls for.'

David Donnison – Emeritus Professor in Urban
Studies, University of Glasgow, and former chair
of the Supplementary Benefits Commission

ABOUT THE AUTHORS

Stewart Lansley is a visiting fellow at Bristol University. He has written extensively on poverty, wealth and inequality for specialist journals as well as the *Guardian* and the *Independent*. His book, *The Cost of Inequality*, was shortlisted for the Spear's business book awards for 2012.

Joanna Mack was the Open University's lead on the 2012 Poverty and Social Exclusion study, including the research resource www.poverty.ac.uk. She was the Principal Investigator of the 1983 *Breadline Britain* research which pioneered poverty measurement based on publicly determined needs, now widely used internationally.

They are co-authors of *Poor Britain*, 1983, and have collaborated on work on poverty from the Breadline Britain surveys to www.poverty.ac.uk. They are both award-winning television producers.

Stewart Lansley
Joanna Mack

BREADLINE BRITAIN

THE RISE OF
MASS POVERTY

ONEWORLD

A Oneworld Book

First published in North America, Great Britain &
Australia by Oneworld Publications, 2015

ISBN 978-1-78074-544-2
eBook ISBN 978-1-78074-545-9

Typesetting and eBook design by Hewer Text UK Ltd

Printed and bound in Great Britain by Clays Ltd, St Ives plc

Oneworld Publications
10 Bloomsbury Street
London WC1B 3SR
England

Stay up to date with the latest books,
special offers, and exclusive content from
Oneworld with our monthly newsletter

Sign up on our website
www.oneworld-publications.com

CONTENTS

FIGURES

PREFACE
For richer, for poorer

What thoughtful rich people call the problem of poverty,
thoughtful poor people call with equal justice a problem
of riches.
R. H. Tawney, 1913[1]

In 2012, nearly three out of every ten people in Britain fell below the minimum living standard set by society as a whole, twice as many as did so in 1983. One-in-ten households lived in a damp home, a thirty-year high. The number of those who could not afford to heat their home adequately had trebled since the 1990s, rising from three to nine percent. The numbers of those who had skimped on meals from time to time over the previous year had doubled since 1983 – up from thirteen to twenty-eight percent.[2]

The reality for people on low incomes today is one of a constant struggle to get by, of endless worry about how to pay the next bill, of parents cutting back for themselves to prioritise the kids, and of young people left with few hopes for the future. Person after person tells a similar story: 'I only tend to eat one meal a day and that does me, 'cos I like to make sure I've got enough for my children'; 'I try to keep the heating on for a couple of hours and then turn it off – I'm afraid of the bill coming in, to tell you the God's truth'; 'It's just in your head ... you have to constantly think about money, constantly think about it'; 'By the time the bills have been paid, we're left with little to nothing, we're living below the breadline.'

These experiences echo those of the poor in 1983, when we first researched poverty in Britain. Then, as now, people told us: 'I can't cope on the money'; 'It's very difficult to manage from day to day'; 'I make sure the kids have enough for them and if there's enough, I have just what's left'; 'You're going down and down, it's very hard to get back on your feet.'

So, in an affluent country such as Britain, why is such a high and growing proportion of its citizens left with an inadequate standard of living, one considered unacceptably low by a majority of the population? Why, with the country twice as rich as it was thirty years ago, have poverty rates doubled? What are the forces that have turned Britain into one of the most unequal and socially fragile countries in the rich world?

Poverty is now one of the hottest political topics of the day. The explosion in the number of foodbanks and other forms of charitable support has sparked ongoing controversy. As in the 1980s, high-profile church leaders have publicly clashed with the government over the impact of its policies on the poor, while leading charities are under fire for the nature of their anti-poverty campaigns. Underlying these clashes are a number of key issues. Should poverty be measured by the standards of today or those of the past? How low a standard of living is too low in contemporary Britain? Is lack of income the root of the problem or is it just bad money management? Do people fall into poverty because of personal inadequacies or because of a lack of jobs and opportunities? Just what is the link between poverty and inequality?

In 2010, just before the general election, the last Labour government passed the Child Poverty Act enshrining in law ambitious targets for the reduction of poverty by 2020. The Act was an unambiguous statement, perhaps the most significant of the post-war era, of the societal obligation to tackle poverty. Significantly it was passed with all-party support, apparently showing that a new political consensus on poverty had finally emerged. However, within weeks of coming to office, the 2010 coalition government moved to distance itself from the Act, effectively abandoning its targets and disowning the principles on which it was based. The same highly charged debates that have dogged policy since the early Victorian age are back. Any consensus now lies in ruins.

The view promoted by government ministers and much of the media is that rising poverty is largely self-inflicted and a matter of individual failure – 'a lifestyle choice', as ministers like to call it. In the name of austerity and the need to shrink the state, the coalition government imposed a series of ongoing cuts in benefit levels, and in welfare services, leading to rising numbers turning to charitable help for the most basic of needs.

The evidence presented in this book challenges this individualistic view of the causes and nature of poverty. Rising vulnerability cannot conveniently be dismissed as the result of personal failings. The real cause of the growth of deprivation is to be found elsewhere, in the great interlocking social and economic upheavals of the last thirty years, many of them politically driven.

Today's working population faces not just a hardening political climate but a much more treacherous jobs market, one that has brought greater joblessness, the spread of low pay and deepening insecurity at work. These problems have been compounded by other changes: from the shrinking of housing opportunities, especially for the young, to a deliberate shift in the burden of economic and social risks from the state and employers to the individual. People have increasingly been left to cope by themselves at the very time when insecurity and uncertainty have been on the rise.

This book draws throughout on the two surveys – and a range of qualitative research – conducted by the largest ever research project into poverty in the UK, the Economic and Social Research Council–funded 2012 *Poverty and Social Exclusion* project. It also draws on its predecessors; the *Breadline Britain* surveys of 1983 and 1990, the 1999 *Poverty and Social Exclusion in Britain* surveys, and the series of detailed case studies conducted in conjunction with each.

Based on face-to-face interviews, these large-scale surveys identify those who are deprived as judged by the standards of the day. This method, which we developed in 1983, establishes a minimum standard based on what the majority of people think are the necessities of life, which everyone should be able to afford and no one should have to do without. The list of necessities chosen by the public covers a wide range of items and activities, from a basic diet and a minimum level of housing decency, to a number of personal and household goods and leisure and social activities. Next, the approach investigates people's actual living standards, identifying those who cannot afford the items and activities classed by the public, at that time, as necessities. These four surveys enable a detailed comparison of trends in the extent and nature of deprivation – as defined by public consensus – in the UK over the last thirty years.

Those in poverty are then identified as people whose lack of necessities – and the extent of their deprivation – together has a pervasive and multiple impact on their lives. This is a group which is much more likely to experience a range of problems, ones closely correlated with other indicators of poverty, such as poor health and financial stress. We've referred to this group as being in 'deprivation poverty' and it is used as our measure of poverty throughout. It is a measure based on people's actual living standards, rather than on an indirect measure, such as income. While there is room for debate about the terminology – though the public does use the word poverty in this way – that is essentially a diversion. Whatever the situation facing those deprived in this way is called, it is one which most people, across all parts of society, think their fellow citizens should not have to endure.

Some may argue that this definition of poverty is too broad. Others, that it is too narrow. But the standards used are those of the public and thus provide a measure that not only has resonance with the people affected but also has societal backing and political leverage.

The latest 2012 survey finds more and more families in Britain face little more than a hand-to-mouth existence, missing out on a range of the most basic of contemporary needs. Their children lack the leisure and educational opportunities that others have, their health is damaged by poor housing and inadequate food, and their self-esteem is harmed through being unable to participate in routine aspects of daily life. In the UK, in 2013, because of lack of money:

- one-in-four children didn't get an annual holiday away from home;
- one-in-five children lived in a home which was cold or damp;

- one-in-ten children lacked an essential clothing item like a warm coat or two pairs of shoes;
- one-in-twenty households couldn't afford to feed their children adequately.

There has, in particular, been a rise in acute deprivation since the 1999 survey. While this reflects in part the impact of the 2008 financial crisis, it is also the product of a number of deep-seated, longer-term trends.

Not only have the numbers of poor been rising, but a growing proportion of the population is at risk of falling into poverty. Many are clustered precariously close to the poverty line, only just above the living standard defined as the minimum necessary in Britain today, and often struggling financially. The proportion of households in arrears on at least one of their household bills – rent and mortgage payments, gas, electricity charges or council tax and loan repayments – has risen from fifteen percent in 1983 to twenty-one percent in 2012. Increasing numbers of people do not have the financial reserves to cope with emergencies and are unable to save for a rainy day. While not all those facing financial insecurity are in poverty, this lack of financial reserves makes many families vulnerable.

Of course poverty amid plenty is nothing new. But in the UK (and in a number of other countries including the United States) poverty has been growing as affluence has spread. In the first two decades after the Second World War, as Britain got richer, poverty fell. During the 1950s and 1960s, sustained economic growth was used to close the income gap and pay for a more effective war on poverty and improve levels of social protection. Since the late 1970s, that relationship has reversed: Britain has got richer, but poverty rates have gone up not down. Far from providing the means to tackle poverty, the growth of prosperity has been associated with a doubling of the numbers of poor.

Growing economic wealth over the last thirty years has brought greatly improved choices and opportunities for the majority – those near or in the top half of society – but increasingly restricted ones for a significant minority. At one level, Britain is a society of mass abundance. But while the size of the cake has continued to grow, creating a pretty good party for many and a very good one for some, it is one to which entry is increasingly restricted.

A bigger economy has become associated with the spreading of disadvantage and a growth of barriers to individual, social and economic progress. While most are better off than in 1983 – better fed and with better quality lifestyles and living for longer – the gap in living standards between those at the bottom and the rest has been widening sharply, leaving growing numbers not just left behind but in some key respects worse off.

Poverty matters for all groups in society, not just the poor. It brings poorer health, lower levels of educational achievement and fractured social cohesion, and thus wider costs for all. As poverty rates have risen in recent decades, aspirations have been capped and life chances eroded. This has wasted talent, stifled opportunity and lowered economic performance. High levels of poverty are a sign of democratic and political failure. Growing numbers now live on incomes that are not much higher than those of their parents, or in some cases lower, breaking one of the central trends of the post-war era – that successive generations would be better off.

One hundred years ago, the eminent historian and social reformer Richard Tawney attributed the question of poverty to 'a problem of riches'. He could equally have been writing about today. Britain is a rich nation, historically and internationally. Over the last thirty years and longer, the prevalent view has been not just that poverty is unrelated to what is happening at the top but that allowing the rich to get richer would benefit everyone, including the poor, as their wealth 'trickles down' to those on lower incomes. It is a view that has suited those at the top very well.

We argue that this view is fundamentally wrong, that the issue of poverty is intimately linked – socially and economically – to what is happening across the income range, and especially to what has been happening at the very top of society. Indeed, over the last thirty years, in the name of economic dynamism, a small group at the top has been able to colonise a growing proportion of economic output, leading not just to a widening gap in incomes and living standards, but to a deepening divide in life chances. It is, we will argue, this rising inequality, especially towards the very top, that lies at the heart of the spread of deprivation, the reversal of housing gains, and the blighted lives and fragmented communities of recent decades.

Britain has created an economic model that is incapable of delivering a decent publicly determined minimum standard of living to all its citizens. It is the model that is wrong, not the citizens. Other countries of comparable wealth have much lower levels of poverty. The last decade has seen two alternative approaches to tackling poverty, both based on significant adjustments to the welfare system. The first, under Labour, offered improved benefits, especially through more generous tax credits. The second, the strategy of the coalition, was to impose tougher sanctions and lower benefits in the name of 'making work pay'. Both have had a significant impact – for better or worse – on the lives of the poor but neither attempted to tackle the real root causes of the problem. To do so requires a fundamental change in course, one that constructs an alternative model of political economy, which reduces inequalities, enhances opportunities across society and, in particular, enables people to obtain a decent standard of living from work, by raising wages and improving job security at the bottom end. Without such a change, Britain will continue to live with levels of poverty that are much higher than those of the past and of other comparable nations.

There is nothing inevitable about condemning such a large proportion of the population to a life with few opportunities and low incomes. Rather, the historically and globally high levels of poverty in the UK can be traced directly to the political choices taken by successive governments over the last three decades. Levels of deprivation and poverty are, ultimately, down to decisions on the way the economic cake is divided, and how the fruits of economic growth are shared. Other choices are possible.

Stewart Lansley
Joanna Mack
November, 2014

1

To live or to exist: Defining poverty in an age of plenty

It's not unfair and it is unfair, 'cos like other people get
to have their houses, all the money and sometimes
people don't have the money even if they save up.
Eleven-year-old, London 2012[1]

Jennie lives in temporary accommodation in Redbridge, north London. She is a single mother with three sons over the age of ten, all of whom have disabilities. While she tries to make sure her sons are properly fed, she struggles: 'Chicken drumsticks, which I am going to do today for the kids for their dinner, with some chips, beans and spaghetti. They mainly have fruit and veg over the weekends and then usually if I do get fruit, 'cos [there's] three sons, they tend to eat it as soon as I get it. I can't go and get any more because I don't have the money. I have to budget.'

She sometimes gets offered food by friends and neighbours, but in order to ensure that her children are properly fed, she regularly goes without herself. 'I only tend to eat one meal a day and that does me, 'cos I like to make sure I've got [enough] for my children.'

Jennie worked as a hairdresser when she left school, but her middle son, Mark, contracted meningitis as a baby leaving him visually impaired. Jennie, now forty-one, left work to care for him. Having separated from her husband when the children were young, she moved to a women's refuge and has lived in a variety of temporary accommodation for the last ten years.

Most of the family's benefit income goes on food, fuel, school clothes and local travel, with rent paid by housing benefit. They rarely socialise and have never had a holiday. They do have a television set, a fridge and a washing machine. Jennie often runs out of money: 'But I have to stay strong for myself and for my children, and I hate being in the situation that I'm in now.'

Despite their situation, the family don't necessarily see themselves as poor. Thirteen-year-old Mark: 'We've got this house; we've got friends and stuff like that. So I don't think we are actually poor. Sometimes I think we're poor, because like we can't get money to spend on like things we want, so I kind of think and I kind of don't think we are poor.' And eleven-year-old Michael, the youngest: 'We're not actually poor like in a living on the streets way. We ain't got the perfect clothes in the world, clothes that other people's kids have, but we're happy with what we've got as long as we can live.' 'I don't like the word poor,' is how Jennie puts it. 'I mean, in a way, yes, I am poor. Poor – it means you can't afford anything. You can't afford what you need.'

So are Jennie and her family in poverty? Their standard of living is well below that of most people in the UK, and they experience deprivation in a variety of ways – but are they too poor? The family recognise that their situation could be worse, even drawing some comfort from this. They have a roof – however insecure – over their head. They just get by on food – even if they run short quite regularly. They have a higher standard of living than the poor of a century, or a half century ago – they have access to health services and education. They are not starving.

This question of how to define poverty has long divided opinion between those who see it in more relatives terms and those who see it in more absolute ones. This is not just some academic debate. Definitions of poverty matter. They set the standards by which we determine whether the incomes and living conditions of the poorest in society are acceptable or not and are essential for assessing questions of fairness. From these definitions follow actions to help the poorest. Which approach is adopted has different implications for the scale of and trends in poverty. The narrower the definition, the less action is needed and the more the problem can be swept away. Conversely, too broad a definition will not chime with people's experiences and risks alienating the wider public.

Absolute measures have traditionally been seen in terms of minimal, subsistence standards, sufficient to secure the barest of living standards. More recently, they have also been used as a measure fixed at a particular point in the past and updated only in line with rising costs. This can provide a useful measure of progress – or lack of progress – over short periods of time. Typically, though, absolute measures, with their emphasis on situations such as hunger and homelessness, have often been employed as a way of underplaying the extent of poverty.

Relative measures, on the other hand, are based on contemporary norms and social standards, and are higher than absolute standards. They change over time, not just in relation to the cost of living but also in relation to changing incomes, needs and social habits. For a period, the debate seemed to have been settled in favour of a relative approach, but in the last few years, just when levels of hardship have become more wide-spread, these questions have become, once again, more and more hotly disputed.

Apart from the question of whether to take a more absolute or relative approach, there are two main ways of tracking poverty: by looking at income, or people's actual living standards. Both income- and living-standards-based measures can be either absolute or relative.

Using income to measure poverty

In 1999, when invited to give the 'Beveridge revisited' lecture, the Labour prime minister, Tony Blair, stunned his audience by promising to halve child poverty within a decade and 'eradicate' it within twenty years. The promise came out of the blue and, while widely welcomed, raised the eyebrows of almost all the leading social policy academics, advisers and journalists in the lecture hall. The move was as ambitious as it was unprecedented. The scale of the task and the timetable laid down were certainly daunting but, as a result, tackling poverty was turned into a central political aim and was never going to be far from the headlines.

The goal set by Blair was based on a clearly defined relative income measure: the proportion of the population with incomes falling below sixty percent of the household income at the mid-point of the income range (known as the median income). This was the first time such a measure had been formally adopted by government and was, in effect, being made the official measure of poverty in Britain.[2] It is one that has also become widely used internationally. A year earlier, the Statistical Program Committee of the European Union agreed that such a threshold should be used when making international comparisons of poverty across its member nations. Based on data which is readily available, it allows comparisons between countries and of trends over time.

That poverty should be defined in this relative way also came to be endorsed across the political spectrum. 'All forms of poverty – absolute and relative – must be dealt with,' Iain Duncan Smith, the Conservative lead on welfare, wrote in 2006. 'We should reject completely the notion that poverty can be defined in absolute terms alone. Relative poverty matters because it separates the poor from the mainstream of society.'[3] It was a commitment echoed by the Conservative party leader, David Cameron, in the same year: 'I want this message to go out loud and clear: the Conservative Party recognises, will measure and will act on relative poverty.'[4]

Just over a decade after Blair's speech, with some, clear progress made towards the goal,[5] Labour – now under a new prime minister, Gordon Brown – introduced the 2010 Child Poverty Act. Backed by all the major parties, the Act made reducing the numbers of children living in families below sixty percent of the median household income a legal duty for the government of the UK.[6] A statutory recognition that poverty is relative, it was a significant turning point in the long debate on how to measure poverty.

In the agreement to form a coalition government signed by the Conservatives and the Liberal Democrats in May 2010, the two partners specifically committed themselves to its aims: 'We will maintain the goal of ending child poverty in the UK by 2020.'[7] Yet, within weeks of taking office in 2010, in a swift political U-turn, senior ministers launched a number of attacks on the Act's central poverty measure. The new government now wanted to shift the emphasis in tackling poverty away from income. They were also uncomfortable with the target itself. Iain Duncan Smith, the new Work and Pensions secretary, recruited Frank Field – Labour MP for Birkenhead, former director of the Child Poverty Action Group and one of the country's leading authorities on welfare – to review the case for reform. Field's task was to examine whether there should be a shift away from income-based measures to ones that included 'non-financial elements'. [8] The setting up of the review was soon followed by a series of statements dismissing the income-based target as just 'poverty plus a pound'.[9]

Initially, it seemed that this might be a move to tackle the deeper causes of poverty. In November 2010, Nick Clegg, the deputy prime minister, wrote: 'Poverty plus a pound is simply not an ambitious enough goal.'[10] He argued that instead we needed to invest in 'mobility'. In December 2010, the then children's minister, the Liberal Democrat MP, Sarah Teather, reiterated the government's new approach: 'The Government is clear that tackling child poverty requires more than simply treating the short-term symptoms of poverty or moving families across an arbitrary income line.' [11]

In fact it soon became clear that senior ministers were seeking a fundamental change in direction on the poverty question, in definition as well as policy, in ways that directly challenged the principles at the heart of the 2010 Act. Iain Duncan Smith increasingly dismissed the income target itself, arguing that 'increased income and increased wellbeing do not always follow the same track.'[12] Taking this a step further, Frank Field argued that some of the money used to support children should be redirected from benefits to improving 'life chances'.[13]

As well as questioning the importance of income in tackling poverty, the government also set out to challenge the relative nature of the sixty percent of median household income measure, claiming inherent problems with the way the target worked. 'You get this constant juddering adjustment with poverty figures going up when, for instance, upper incomes rise,' was how Duncan Smith put it shortly after the election.[14] Frank Field expanded on this idea arguing that a target based on relative income was impossible to achieve. 'Any candidate sitting GCSE maths should be able to explain that raising everybody above a set percentage of the median income is rather like asking a cat to chase its own tail. As families are raised above the target level of income, the median point itself rises. Not surprisingly, therefore, no country in the free world has managed to achieve this objective.'[15]

In fact, these particular criticisms of the relative income measure appear to misunderstand some basic statistical concepts. The median is the mid-point of the income range. That is, if you lined up the population in order of their income, the person halfway along would have the median income. So, if 'upper incomes rise', as Duncan Smith put it, and just those on top incomes get richer – with incomes elsewhere unchanged – there is *no* effect on the median income. Thus, a poverty line set at a fixed proportion of the median stays exactly the same. Similarly, raising the incomes of those below the target of sixty percent of the median to just above the target, for example, by raising the generosity of a means-tested benefit for those on the lowest incomes, does not raise the median point. If all households below sixty percent of the median were to rise above this threshold but stay below the median income, the median – and therefore the target – would stay the same and poverty would be eliminated.[16]

It is a widespread misconception that poverty based on a relative income measure cannot be abolished and will always remain high. A few years ago on the BBC's *Today* programme, John Humphrys was interviewing a leading social policy expert on the question of the definition of poverty. But surely, asked Humphrys, if you define poverty as relative, it will never be abolished?[17] Or take this leader in *The Scotsman* on 14 June 2013: 'Given this is a relative, as opposed to absolute, measure, then we can say with mathematical certainty that the poor will always be with us.' Such statements are simply incorrect – the mathematics does not work like this. While some people, no doubt, will always be poorer than others, this is not the same as saying they are in relative poverty. A distribution where no one has less than sixty percent of the median is perfectly possible without complete equality. But despite a wide number of websites and commentators highlighting such misunderstandings, they keep coming back. Iain Duncan Smith, in a joint piece with George Osborne for the *Guardian* in February 2014, returned to his earlier critique. 'For far too long, a fixation on relative income led the last government to chase an ever elusive poverty target.'[18]

Cutting relative income poverty may not be easy but it is perfectly possible. Figure 1 shows how the level of child poverty in the UK compares with other countries, using the common sixty percent of the median measure. The child poverty rate in the UK (at twenty-one percent in 2009) stands at around double that of the most successful countries, Iceland, Slovenia, Norway and Denmark, and is also significantly higher than in Germany, Belgium and France. Relative income poverty targets are not, by definition, elusive.

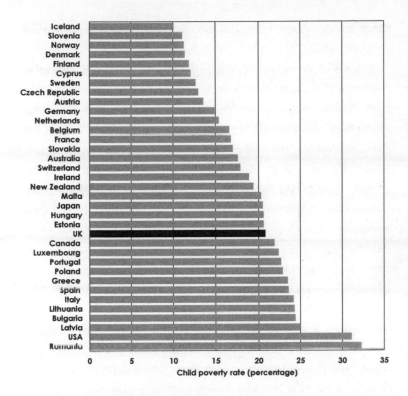

**Figure 1: How relative child poverty rates
vary across countries: 2009/10** [19]
(poverty line at 60% of median income in each country)

In the UK, an explicit relative approach to the measurement
of low income was first introduced in the late-1980s as part of a
new official annual series – Households Below Average Incomes
(HBAI).[20] Enabling trends in the numbers at the bottom whose
incomes were falling behind to be tracked, it proved to be politically explosive ensuring that, from its inception, this relative
approach was highly controversial. During much of the Thatcher

era, officials were even banned from using the 'poverty' word. This was also true in the United States during the Reagan years, a position popularised in a striking cartoon by the American satirist Jules Feiffer. This portrayed two 'down-and-outs' philosophising: 'We used to be poor, then disadvantaged, then deprived, then discriminated against, then socially excluded. We have not got any more money, but we do have a lot of labels.'[21]

The HBAI findings, however, put the issue of low income and poverty firmly onto the UK political map. They exposed a sharp rise in relative income poverty during the first half of the 1980s, more than reversing the gains of the immediate post-war era.[22] Caught on the back foot, the government's response was to dismiss the concept on which the figures were based. In May 1989, John Moore, the social security secretary, one of Margaret Thatcher's favourite ministers and once tipped to succeed her, launched a high-profile and public attack on the very idea. Relative poverty was, he argued, 'simply inequality' and could therefore be ignored: what the 'relative definition of poverty amounts to in the end is that ... however rich a society it will drag the incubus of relative poverty with it up the income scale. The poverty lobby would in their definition find poverty in Paradise.' 'Acknowledge British capitalism's true achievements', he continued, which had been to wipe out the 'stark want of Victorian Britain'.[23]

Moore was, if robustly, merely expressing the view common across the Conservative party in the 1980s, that what mattered was not the position of the poor relative to those who were better off, but whether the poor were getting better off absolutely, even if they were slipping further behind those above them.

There would of course have been a big political dividend from switching from a relative measure – one that reflected the standards of the day – to a past, absolute one. Such a switch would have enabled the government to claim that poverty had fallen and not soared during the 1980s. Though the living standards of the poor were rising more slowly than those of people higher up the income ladder, the poorest were, on average, getting absolutely better off (the John Moore criterion for success). Nevertheless, such a move would have been a clear public statement that those on low incomes did not have a right to participate fully in growing prosperity.

In the event, Moore's speech was badly received. It was at odds with the visible evidence, ignoring a stream of reports showing the very real problems of hardship facing a growing proportion of the population. It would have been difficult politically to have dropped the relative poverty measure even for a government so ideologically uncomfortable with the concept.

From then on, relative income remained central to the measurement of poverty in the UK. At least for a while, during the 2000s, it came to receive the official backing of the Conservative party with its deep-seated reservations only becoming public on forming a government.

None of this means that the sixty percent of the median income measure does not have important limitations. The official measure, for example, is based on net household incomes (that is, total income, including benefits, minus direct taxes) and as such fails to take account of other financial resources, changes in the cost of living or debt repayments. It is also based on household income *before the deduction of housing costs*. But because of the hike in the cost of housing over the last decade, the use of an income measure *before* the deduction of such costs gives a significantly lower poverty count than when they are deducted, along with a much shallower upward trend.[24] A study by the Joseph Rowntree

Foundation into these alternative measures concluded: 'Not taking this [housing costs] into account significantly underestimates the risk of poverty and material deprivation for workless households, minority ethnic groups, single people, renters and Londoners.'[25]

One of the most important issues is the choice of sixty percent of median income as the threshold. Why not fifty or seventy percent? In the 1980s, there was a good deal of discussion – in the UK and across Europe – about the merits of various percentages, and the first HBAI analysis used a number of alternatives.[26] The eventual choice of *sixty* percent of median income as the threshold in the UK was essentially a convenient statistical compromise, with officials preferring a single rather than a multiple of indicators each showing somewhat different trends.

It was not, however, a measure based firmly on evidence about exactly where to draw the line.[27] Which threshold is chosen certainly makes a substantial difference to the numbers. In 2012/13, relative income poverty (after housing costs) was twenty-one percent using the sixty percent threshold but, for example, twenty-nine percent using a seventy percent threshold.[28]

Income matters in that it is the key determinant of living standards, but it is an indirect measure, and without validation from direct measures of people's living standards is essentially arbitrary.[29] Without some external justification as to why one target has been chosen rather than another, it is not always clear as to why what it is measuring matters. The question 'how poor is too poor' is therefore better answered by examining people's standard of living – their actual ways of life.

Using actual living standards

In the early studies, poverty in Britain was viewed in terms of a minimum standard of living rather than income. The pioneers of poverty research – Charles Booth and Seebohm Rowntree – based their attempts to measure poverty on how people actually lived. Rowntree, a wealthy Quaker and influential member of the confectionary family, undertook three surveys of poverty in York – in 1899, 1936 and 1951. These aimed at establishing a measure of poverty based on the idea that there is some minimum subsistence level of consumption necessary for the maintenance of physical health.

Rowntree, whose aim was to draw attention to the plight of the poor, set out to establish an 'absolute' measure of poverty, based only on subsistence needs. But even concepts such as physical health, minimal shelter or having enough to eat are essentially relative, reflecting the standards and expectations of the time. Because perceptions of what is good health or an adequate diet change, Rowntree found that his standard had to be adjusted upwards over the fifty-year time span of his studies to reflect changes in social norms in the intervening years. Despite setting out to find an objective measure of subsistence, he ended up making concessions to the idea of 'relativity'. His 1936 and 1951 studies were an explicit acknowledgment that poverty standards would have to reflect improvements in economic and social conditions from the turn of the century. Significantly, they revealed just how difficult it is to apply an absolute standard in the real world and that any conception of a minimum will inevitably reflect the society of the time.[30]

This idea that needs are socially determined has a long pedigree. Adam Smith, the founding father of modern economics, recognised the importance of custom and expectations – and how they change – when setting out his views on 'the necessaries of daily life' in his seminal book, *The Wealth of Nations*, published in 1776.

> By necessaries I understand not only the commodities which are indispensably necessary for the support of life, but whatever the customs of the country renders it indecent for creditable people, even the lowest order, to be without. A linen shirt, for example, is, strictly speaking, not a necessary of life. The Greeks and Romans lived, I suppose, very comfortably, though they had no linen. But in the present times, through the greater part of Europe, a creditable day-labourer would be ashamed to appear in public without a linen shirt, the want of which would be supposed to denote that disgraceful degree of poverty ... Custom, in the same manner, has rendered leather shoes a necessary of life in England. [31]

Karl Marx, writing in 1849, observed, similarly, that, 'our needs and enjoyments spring from society; we measure them therefore by society'.[32] A century later, the highly influential American economist, J. K. Galbraith, wrote in his global bestseller, *The Affluent Society*, published in 1958, that:

> People are poverty-stricken when their income, even if adequate for survival, falls markedly behind that of their community. Then they cannot have what the larger community regards as the necessary minimum for decency, and they cannot wholly escape therefore, the judgment of the larger community that they are indecent. They are degraded for, in a literal sense, they live outside the grades or categories which the community regards as acceptable.[33]

During the second half of the twentieth century, however, the person who led the way in the development of poverty as a relative concept was the social scientist Professor Peter Townsend. 'Society itself is continuously changing and thrusting new obligations on its members,' he wrote in 1962. 'They, in turn, develop new needs.'[34]

So how should we determine what are needs, or new needs as Townsend put it, and what aren't? To translate his idea that poverty is about the ability to participate in society, Townsend conducted a major survey in 1968–9, in which he drew up a list of sixty indicators of living standards ranging from diet and clothing to home amenities and recreation. From this he devised a 'deprivation index' limited to twelve of these items and used this to identify a poverty line determined by the point at which people's risk of lacking these items sharply increased.

In the findings of the study, published in *Poverty in the United Kingdom* in 1979, Townsend argued: 'Individuals, families and groups in the population can be said to be in poverty when they lack the resources to obtain the types of diet, participate in the activities and have the living conditions and amenities which are customary, or at least widely encouraged or approved in the societies in which they belong.'[35] The 1,200-page book was to have a huge influence on the development of our understanding of poverty.

Townsend's work, however, had several limitations, the most important of which was that the items chosen were essentially arbitrary. Why these twelve and not others? Personal value judgments – in this case those of Townsend and his colleagues – had been applied in selecting the items for inclusion in the poverty standard, as they had been in the previous history of poverty research.

For Townsend, it was sufficient that the items represented common activities and were widely practised and that deprivation fell as incomes rose. But in selecting these indicators, he had failed to take account of, or relate to, any generally accepted view of 'need' or how one might determine it.[36] Critics, such as David Piachaud, professor of social policy at the London School of Economics, argued that this was a fundamental weakness that left the term poverty devoid of any 'moral imperative that something should be done about it'.[37]

Indeed, without evidence of this 'imperative', the relativists risked losing the political argument. Harking back to the earlier attempts at the turn of the century, Sir Keith Joseph, Margaret Thatcher's first education secretary and one of her main ideological soulmates, argued in 1979 that the needs of the poor should be defined in terms of subsistence needs only. 'An absolute standard means one defined by reference to the actual needs of the poor and not by reference to the expenditure of those who are not poor. A family is poor if it does not have enough to eat ... By any absolute standard there is very little poverty in Britain today.'[38] It was an influential view and widely held on the political right. To move these arguments on, there needed to be a more robust and defensible method of determining what the 'actual needs' of the poor were.

'The necessary minimum for decency' – the public's view

The *Breadline Britain* methodology – developed for a 1983 ITV television series – set out to establish a firmer basis for deciding what should be seen as 'needs', or in Galbraith's phrase, 'the necessary minimum for decency'. It did so by setting out to measure the public's, rather than social scientists', perception of contemporary needs. This was the first time this had been attempted and meant that public opinion was made the central determinant of a minimum living standard in contemporary Britain. Instead of choosing deprivation indicators, as Townsend had, based simply on what was typical or widespread, this approach sought the views of society as a whole. It asked people to distinguish between items and activities that are 'necessities' and 'those that may be widespread and may be desirable but are not necessities'.[39]

A nationally representative sample of the population was asked in detail about their views on what constituted an unacceptably low standard of living in that year. Respondents were asked to distinguish which of a list of thirty-five items, broadly representative of living standards, they thought 'were necessary and which all people should be able to afford and should not have to do without', and which of them 'may be desirable but are not necessary'.

The 1983 list was drawn up on the basis of focus group discussions of what is and what is not essential. It included items which covered a cross section of social and personal life, from food, heating and clothing to household goods, transport, leisure and social activities.[40] It did not include items which, though likely to be core parts of any conception of poverty, are, in the UK, free at the point of delivery (notably health care and schooling).[41] In the survey, twenty-six of the thirty-five items were defined as necessities by more than fifty percent of respondents.

This approach was then developed in the subsequent surveys – *Breadline Britain* 1990, and the 1999 and 2012 *Poverty and Social Exclusion (PSE)*. Following focus group discussions, a number of new items and activities to be tested were added to reflect new and changing priorities. For example, a question on fresh fruit and vegetables was added in 1990 and one on being able to take part in sport or exercise in 2012, both reflecting changing emphases on maintaining good health.

Among the later additions have been several questions concerned with household finances. In 1983, perhaps because of a lower dependence on borrowing, these matters were not raised by focus groups participants. In 2012, with growing levels of personal debt, the growing insecurity of earnings, and less support from local and national government for emergencies, the focus group research found 'that long-term financial security, insurance against risks, and hazard prevention, were key priorities for participants, often reflecting pessimistic assessments of the prospects for future public welfare provision including during retirement'[42] Additional questions on financial security were therefore added to the 2012 survey of attitudes to necessities.

The public's view on the necessities for living in Britain for *adults* is shown in Figure 2 for each year – 1983, 1990, 1999 and 2012. A more detailed list of child items was first included in the 1999 survey and Figure 3 shows the results for children in 1999 and 2012.[43] In both these figures, items above the bold line were classed as necessities in 2012.

The findings show that the public accept that minimum living standards need to reflect contemporary and not past styles of living. They believe that needs do not stand outside society as some kind of timeless given. They not only give high scores to items essential to basic survival such as food and shelter; they also give majority scores to a long list of items beyond these physical needs, from a 'washing machine' to, from 1990, a 'telephone'. Many items chosen as necessities enable people to play a wider social role, including 'celebrations on special occasions' and 'a hobby or leisure activity'.

In all the surveys, the most heavily supported items do relate to what traditionally have been seen as basic needs – shelter,

Items and activities	% thinking item to be a necessity			
	1983	1990	1999	2012
Heating to keep home adequately warm	97%	97%	95%	96%
Damp-free home	94%	98%	94%	94%
Two meals a day	64%	90%	91%	91%
Visit friends or family in hospital or other institutions			92%	90%
Replace or repair broken electrical goods			86%	86%
Fresh fruit and vegetables every day		88%	87%	83%
Washing machine	67%	73%	77%	82%
All recommended dental work/treatment				82%
Celebrations on special occasions	69%	74%	83%	80%
Warm waterproof coat	87%	91%	87%	79%
Attend weddings, funerals and other such occasions			81%	78%
Telephone	43%	56%	72%	77%
Meat, fish (or vegetarian equivalent*) every other day	63%	77%	81%	76%
Curtains or window blinds				71%
Hobby or leisure activity	64%	67%	79%	70%
Enough money to keep your home in a decent state of decoration		88%	80%	69%
Household contents insurance		92%	83%	69%
Appropriate clothes for job interviews			70%	69%
A table, with chairs, at which all the family can eat				64%
Taking part in sport/exercise activities or classes				56%
To be able to pay an unexpected expense of £500				55%
Two pairs of all-weather shoes	67%	74%	67%	54%
Regular savings (of at least £20 a month) for rainy days**		68%	67%	52%
Television	51%	58%	58%	51%
Regular payments into an occupational or private pension				51%
Replace worn-out clothes with new not second-hand clothes	64%	65%	50%	46%
Presents for family or friends once a year	58%	69%	58%	46%
Friends or family around for a meal or drink at least once a month	32%	37%	65%	45%
Car	22%	26%	36%	44%
A small amount of money to spend each week on yourself, not on your family			61%	42%
Holiday away from home, not staying with relatives	63%	54%	56%	42%
Internet connection at home			6%	41%
Home computer		5%	11%	40%
Mobile phone			8%	40%
Roast joint or equivalent once a week	67%	64%	58%	36%
Hair done or cut regularly				35%
Going out socially once a fortnight	36%	42%	41%	34%
Attend place of worship			44%	29%
Visit friends or family in other parts of the country four times a year***		39%	41%	27%
Meal out once a month		17%	27%	25%
Holidays abroad once a year		17%	20%	18%
Drink out once a fortnight			22%	17%
Going to the cinema, theatre or music event once a month				15%
Dishwasher		4%	7%	10%

Notes:
* Source of protein
** £10/month in 1990 and 1999
*** Coach or train fares to visit family once a quarter in 1990 and 1999

Figure 2: Attitudes to necessities for adults, Britain: 1983, 1990, 1999, 2012

Note: See appendix for sample sizes.

Child items and activities	% thinking item to be a necessity	
	1999	2012
Warm winter coat	95%	97%
Fresh fruit or veg at least once a day	93%	96%
New, properly fitting shoes	96%	93%
Three meals a day	91%	93%
Garden or outdoor space to play in safely*	68%	92%
Celebrations on special occasions	92%	91%
Books at home suitable for their ages**	90%	91%
Meat, fish or vegetarian equivalent at least once a day***	76%	90%
Place to study	n/a	89%
Hobby or leisure activity	88%	88%
Toddler group or nursery or play group at least once a week for pre-school-aged children	89%	87%
Indoor games suitable for their ages (building blocks, board games, computer games, etc.)	n/a	81%
Enough bedrooms for every child aged 10+ of a different sex to have their own room	76%	74%
Clubs or activities such as drama or football training	n/a	74%
Computer and internet for homework	38%	66%
Some new not second-hand clothes	67%	65%
Day trips with family once a month	n/a	60%
Outdoor leisure equipment such as rollerskates, skateboards, footballs etc	n/a	58%
At least four pairs of trousers, leggings, jeans or jogging bottoms	74%	57%
Going away on a school trip at least once a term	73%	55%
Money to save	n/a	55%
Pocket money	n/a	54%
Holiday away from home for at least one week per year	63%	53%
Construction toys (like Lego, Duplo etc)	66%	53%
Child has friends round for tea or a snack once a fortnight	53%	49%
Bicycle	54%	45%
Clothes to fit in with friends	n/a	31%
Mobile phone	n/a	27%
MP3 player such as an iPod	n/a	8%
Designer/brand-name trainers	n/a	6%

Notes:
* Garden in 1999
** Books of their own in 1999
*** Twice a day in 1999

Figure 3: Attitudes to necessities for children, Britain: 1999 and 2012

food and clothing. For adults, the top three items in 2012 – 'heating to warm living areas of the home', a 'damp-free home' and 'two meals a day' – all received over ninety percent support. For children, the top three – 'a warm winter coat', 'fresh fruit and vegetables once a day' and 'new, properly fitting shoes' – also all gained more than ninety percent support.

But there were also very high figures in 2012 for a range of social items, including 'visiting friends/family in hospital' (ninety percent) and 'being able to afford to attend a wedding/funeral or other such occasions' (seventy-eight percent). For children, a wide range of activities rank highly, including 'child celebration on special occasions' (ninety-one percent) and a 'child hobby or leisure activity' (eighty-nine percent). A number of items relating to financial security now and in the future, such as savings and meeting unexpected costs, also gain majority support. The public accept that measures of poverty should enable people to participate, at least to a degree, in the society in which they live and that they should be able to afford some degree of financial security. They are also more generous towards children than adults: on a like-for-like basis, child items get higher levels of support.[44]

There are clear limits to this process. The public are highly selective. Only fifteen percent of adults think going to the cinema, theatre or music event once a month is a necessity and only ten percent select a dishwasher. And for children, only eight percent choose an MP3 player or iPod and only six percent designer or brand-name trainers.

The public also endorse the idea that needs change over time. While there is a core group of items and activities considered necessities across all the surveys, a process of revision, deletion, substitution and addition has taken place with some items being replaced by others as tastes and fashions change and as perceptions evolve. As societies get richer, yesterday's luxuries – from telephones to washing machines – enjoyed first by the few, come to be enjoyed by the many, largely because of rising incomes but also because of falls in their comparative prices. As ownership becomes more widespread, the way we live changes until there comes a point when it is difficult to manage without them. For the most part, such items eventually come to be seen – by the public – as essential to contemporary life.

In 1983, the personal computer was only just becoming available to the everyday consumer. In 1990, it was added to the list of items tested and received only five percent support. In 1999, eleven percent thought it a necessity for adults, though thirty-eight percent thought it necessary for children to have access for homework. By 2012, support for a home computer with internet access for an adult had risen to forty percent, but for children to sixty-six percent – a clear majority. As a single parent from Belfast explained in one of the focus group discussions: 'I do see it as relative, I mean I'm in the situation at the moment where the twins, they're both doing their GCSEs . . . What they really need is a laptop each, and ten years ago, fifteen years ago, people would have laughed at you if you said I think I'm poor because I can't afford laptops for my girls.'[45]

Some items also drop out as tastes and customs change. The 'roast joint', for example – once an important family meal on a Sunday – has become less and less popular: the percentage seeing this (or its vegetarian equivalent) as a necessity has sunk from sixty-seven percent in 1983 to thirty-six percent today.

While there has been a shift in perceptions, sometimes up, sometimes down, the overall trend has roughly followed that of wider living standards.[46] Between 1983 and 1999, levels of support for most of the items common to all four years went up, though, because of changing tastes, some fell. However, in the tougher economic climate of the 2012 survey, this upward trend came to a halt with a slight decline in support across a range of items, especially in relation to social and leisure activities. This fall in expectations is in part down to changes in tastes and customs. But it also reflects the harsher economic conditions in 2012, with a significant proportion of the population experiencing a sharp decline in incomes during the economic crisis. According to the Office for National Statistics, median income was no higher in 2012 than in 2001.[47]

Since 1999 some former necessities have become 'non-necessities', notably presents for family and friends once a year and a holiday away from home for adults (though this is still seen as a necessity for children). This slight fall in the minimum standard compared with 1999, reflecting a lowering of public generosity, is an indication of the strength of this approach to setting standards, one that is sensitive to wider changes in prosperity.

This approach of finding out what the public think are necessities has also been widely applied internationally. In 2007, the European Union conducted a survey on attitudes to necessities across its twenty-seven member states to determine the deprivation indicators to be used to measure poverty.[48] Surveys have also been carried out in a large number of countries, from Japan, Australia, Finland and Hong Kong to South Africa, Vietnam and Bangladesh.[49] As in Britain, these surveys, in poor, middle-income and rich countries, also show that the public are committed relativists. Take Benin, in West Africa, a country with a gross national income per capita of $1,570 in 2012. A 2006 survey of attitudes in the country found that the standards set were far wider than the subsistence-based indicators conventionally used by the World Bank and others. The population of Benin took a clear relative view of poverty, with a majority endorsing, for example, being able to buy a television as essential.[50]

While there has been much debate about the absolute versus relative question, relativism in fact turns out to be a core, embedded principle, across time and across developed and developing economies alike. It is an idea that gels with public perceptions – both nationally and globally – of what it means to be poor.

In the UK, one of the key findings of these surveys is that people perceive that needs extend beyond the basics of food and shelter; that poverty is dependent on the society in which they live. This finding is not without its critics.[51] Other, mostly less comprehensive, surveys have found the public taking a plurality of views on what poverty means, from austere to generous.[52] But once investigated in depth, a clear relative view of poverty emerges. The focus group discussions conducted for the 2012 Poverty and Social Exclusion project found that: 'Participant understandings of poverty tended to broaden spontaneously as discussion developed, moving from subsistence definitions focusing on deprivation or "basic" needs, to discussions of relative deprivation and its effects on social participation, social networks and support, living conditions, health, quality-of-life and wellbeing.'[53]

'If a person hasn't got a vast or sufficient income then they can't participate in activities. They're excluded from communities if you like. They're frightened to get involved with neighbours in case the neighbours say well let's go down the pub tonight, and then they've got to open up and say sorry I can't, I can't afford it. So they're excluded ... If you've got children going on school exchanges or trips, they can't really afford it,' is how a pensioner from Bristol put it.

And this is what a single parent from Belfast said: 'There's the psychological, emotional wellbeing thing . . . You may be covering your basic needs, but there's this underlying sense of low self-esteem, you know, guilt.' And a young owner-occupier in Cardiff said: 'If you were on the breadline and you were invited to a wedding or a christening, you wouldn't be able to go, because you wouldn't be able to afford an outfit for yourself, your children and presents . . . Birthday parties, if the children were invited to birthday parties they wouldn't be able to go.'[54]

Is there a consensus?

The strength of this method depends on the extent to which we *all* sign up to what constitutes a minimum living standard. This is important, for otherwise the views of the majority could be imposed on minorities. The evidence from across the successive surveys – in the UK and elsewhere – is that there is a strong consensus across social and income groups, across gender, education levels and ethnicity, about what is necessary to enjoy such a minimum. In the 1983 survey, for example, twenty-three of the twenty-six items classed as necessities by a majority were classed as a necessity by every social class. In the 2012 survey, twenty-four of the twenty-six items and activities for adults classed by the majority as necessities were classed as necessities by all occupational groups.[55]

In the 2012 survey, there were very few instances where the majority of one group in society considers as a necessity an item which is not also seen as a necessity by all other groups. If the majority of women, young people and those on high incomes think something is a necessity then, with only a few exceptions, so do the majority of men, older people, and those on lower incomes. There are also very few differences between Scotland, Northern Ireland and England and Wales.[56]

Of course, there are some differences in views. Women, for example, are less likely to pick 'going out socially once a fortnight' as a necessity than men. But the majority of these differences are among items where a minority of both groups think the item to be a necessity. The greatest variation is by age. Indeed, there are four items which older people believe are necessities but the majority do not (namely, being able to give presents to the family once a year, a holiday, a regular haircut and a small amount of money to spend on themselves).[57]

Of all the items and activities tested, the television is the one that causes most disagreement. It is also the item most often singled out for particular indignation among critics of the poor. Time and again, commentators suggest, as Jamie Oliver did when interviewed in August 2013 for his television show *Jamie's Money Saving Meals*, that spending money on a television is incompatible with being in poverty.

Although a television has been a near-universal possession for decades, it only just scores as a necessity overall (fifty-one percent in 2012 as it was in 1983). This is in sharp contrast with other items with such high levels of ownership. A television, it seems, is exceptional in dividing opinion and does so along particularly revealing lines: sixty-five percent of those in manual or routine work think it is a necessity compared to forty-eight percent in non-manual work, and seventy-one percent of those with no qualifications against forty-three percent of those with a degree. And for those groups who face restrictions in going out – whether from old age, disability or a lack of income – having a television ranks highly; chosen, for example, by seventy percent of the elderly. Thus, whether one sees a television as a necessity or not says more about the person concerned than any other item.

This is what Pamela, a young lone parent with a nine-month-old baby living in a damp and decaying attic in London told *Breadline Britain* in 1983: 'I watch TV from first thing in the morning till last thing at night, till the television goes off. That's all I've got: to watch television. I can't afford to do other things at all. I can't go out and enjoy myself or nothing. I should be able to take my daughter out somewhere. I would take her to the zoo and things like that. Places she's never been, or seen, and half the places I haven't seen in London myself.'[58]

But overall differences are small and significantly are found to be extremely small across one of the most important social dividers: how people vote. Figure 4 shows, for 2012, attitudes to the adult items by political affiliation. On this scatter plot, each point represents an item, and its position is determined by the percentage of Conservative supporters and Labour supporters thinking that item is a necessity. The points on this graph run closely together along a straight line at an angle of 45° showing very similar percentages supporting each item across the two political affiliations. Statistical tests showed no significant differences for any of the forty-six adult items between Conservative and Labour supporters.[59] The same applies to other breakdowns, such as coalition supporters (Conservative and Liberal Democrats) and all others. Moreover, this similarity of views across the political divide has been found in all previous surveys.

The international surveys have also found a high degree of consensus between different groups on what is a minimum standard. Take the study conducted in South Africa in 2006. This found that, in spite of the extreme inequality across different social, racial and economic groups, a surprisingly common view exists about what is required for an acceptable standard of living.[60] The international and domestic surveys all find a clear public consensus about what should be in a minimum acceptable living standard, one shared by different groups in society. It is a finding that applies across nations and time, confirming the conclusion of the first 1983 survey in Britain that: 'People from all walks of life, from across the generations ... and with fundamentally opposed political beliefs, share the same view of the kind of society Britain should be in terms of the minimum standards of living to which all should be entitled.'[61]

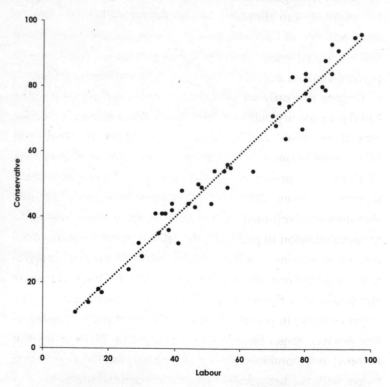

Figure 4: Percentage thinking item a necessity, by political affiliation, Britain: 2012

The 1983 survey was, at least initially, met with a good deal of cynicism, especially from within political circles. Dr Rhodes Boyson, minister for social security, and thus theoretically in charge of assessing the poor's needs, dismissed the idea that poverty had anything to do with consumer items such as refrigerators, washing machines and carpets on the basis that, '50 years ago, or even 25 years ago, people merely aspired to have such things.'[62] The minister seemed to be saying that if the poor of yesteryear managed without goods – some of which had yet to be invented – so should today's poor. Yet such views were a long way out of line with public opinion. In the 1983 survey, seventy-seven percent said that a fridge was a necessity, seventy percent a carpet and sixty-seven percent a washing machine.

Despite this early scepticism, the 'consensual' method one based on majority public opinion – has come to be adopted for official purposes. In 2002, the Department of Work and Pensions drew on the 1999 PSE study to develop key indicators of material deprivation for inclusion in official government surveys.[63] From 2004/5 the government's annual Family Resources Survey, used for purposes ranging from helping to measure inflation to providing the official poverty count, added a question relating to a list of twenty items of material deprivation.[64] Further, one of the four targets in the 2010 Child Poverty Act (along with the relative income target, a 'persistent poverty' target of being in poverty for three years or more and an 'absolute poverty' target based on sixty percent of 2010/11 median income) is a combined low-income and material deprivation target, with the latter drawing on the consensual method.

None of this means the debate on the nature of poverty and how to tackle it has been finally settled. While the partners in the coalition government soon turned cold on the goals of the legislation, others continue to see the standards set by using public opinion as too generous.[65] The 2012 results brought out, as for previous surveys, those committed to a narrow view of poverty. The journalist and commentator Carole Malone, writing in *the Mirror*, and based on a complete misunderstanding of the method, dismissed the idea that poverty had anything to do with the standards of contemporary Britain, insisting on seeing it in absolutist terms: 'It's about not having a roof over your head, living hand-to-mouth, wearing hand-me-down clothes, walking around in shoes full of holes.'[66] The LBC broadcaster Nick Ferrari similarly ridiculed the idea that it had anything to do with things like having a minimum of four pairs of trousers or leggings for children.[67] The views of such commentators are, however, out of line with wider public opinion. The UK public are expressed relativists. Time and again, respondents choose items that would not be present in a subsistence or 'absolute' standard. They are endorsing the idea that, in a wealthy country such as Britain, no child should have to manage without a decent minimum of essential clothing, or be prevented from going on a school trip because their parents cannot afford to pay for it.

Poverty is about falling below a minimum standard of living, and the standard laid down in the *Breadline Britain* methodology is the nearest we have to a publicly endorsed poverty line in the UK. It is a democratically defined standard, free of value judgments by experts, officials or the government. It is supported by all groups in society, young and old, rich and poor, in and out of work – and perhaps, most significantly, across the political spectrum.

It is a relative standard in that it reflects the time and place of the society in which it applies. It is also dynamic, adjusting over time according to wider changes in living standards, though not in the precise mathematical way that the official sixty percent measure adjusts automatically to changes in median incomes. The shift in the standard over time does reflect changes in incomes and prosperity, but also wider shifts in social norms and ways of living, though not in some simple, deterministic way. Notably, the public's perception of what is a necessity adjusts over time as the impact of going without comes to be perceived by society as unacceptable. And, having set the standard, how many – and who – fall below?

2

Going backwards: Poverty then and now

I absolutely hate it. I hate it. When I have to put a brave face on for everybody. It's demoralising. There's been many times I've picked the children up from school and oh Mum can we go out — and I'm no, I've got no money. Okay.

Lone parent, Birmingham 2012[1]

In recent years, examples of acute deprivation have become much more commonplace. When a couple with two children approached the children's charity Barnardo's in South Wales looking for help, the case worker reported: 'The family struggled with food, and the children eat first and the parents eat the leftovers. The mother says she is always tired and feels unwell. The family also cut back spending on other essentials, including heating and lighting. Family activities are rare. School holidays are particularly difficult as the children need breakfast and lunch. The children also want to attend school trips/activities but are unable to go.'[2]

Although Britain has become a richer nation since 1983, growing numbers have been falling behind the wider growth of prosperity. From well before the 2008 crash, incomes started to fall for a significant proportion of the population leading to a sustained slip in their living standards.[3] But how many now fall below society's minimum standard? And in what ways? And are more falling below than in the past?

The four Breadline Britain and Poverty and Social Exclusion surveys allow trends in people's actual living standards to be tracked against the minimum standards set by society over the last thirty years. Having established a consensually agreed minimum, those falling below it because of lack of money can then be examined. Respondents are asked which items they have, which they don't have because they 'don't want them', and which they 'want but cannot afford'. This question allows for choice and personal tastes to be taken into account. In Peter Townsend's pioneering survey of 1968–9 a distinction was made only between those who had or did not have an item.[4] But for some items on his list – such as a 'Sunday joint' and a 'cooked breakfast' – whether people had them or not was likely to be determined by taste as well as lack of money. The *Breadline Britain* methodology allows for taste to be discounted by giving respondents the option of saying they don't want the item.[5]

This approach gives both the public at large, and the individual, control over the concept of necessities. For an item or activity to be seen as a necessity it must first gain majority public support. But to count as deprivation, the individual must also want the item, or want to partake in the activity, and be unable to do so for lack of money. A person is only deprived when they want but cannot afford a necessity. Deprivation is thus defined as an 'enforced lack of socially perceived necessities'.[6]

A bare existence

In 2012, the proportion lacking a number of the most basic of the publicly defined necessities was higher than in 1983. The proportion of households unable to heat their home adequately – the top necessity, supported in every survey by over ninety-five percent of people – is now almost double the rate found in 1983. Then, as seen in Figure 5, five percent of households could not afford to heat their homes. This dropped to three percent in the 1990s but by 2012 had jumped to nine percent.

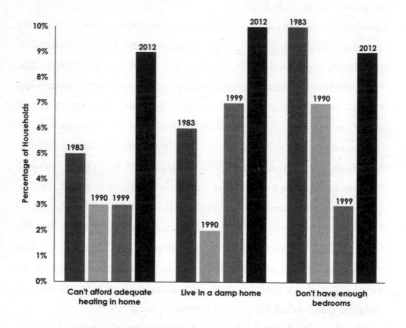

Figure 5: The return of poor housing and inadequate heating, Britain: 1983 to 2012

Proportion of households who cannot afford the minimum housing and heating standards set by the public

With fuel costs rising and incomes shrinking, the numbers taking out loans during recent winters to cover the cost of heating has gone up.[7] Others simply turn the heating off. 'I can't afford to heat my home sometimes,' said a single parent in Gloucester, 'and we have had times when we've had to sit with no heat because that's how bad things are.'[8] Children living in a cold home are more than twice as likely to suffer from breathing problems as those who live in warm homes while long-term exposure to such conditions increases hospital admission rates. For babies and infants it can affect weight gain.[9] For the elderly, it increases the risk of death.

The winter of 2012–13 saw the number of 'excess winter deaths' – the additional numbers that occurred from December to March compared to the average for the rest of the year – rise by twenty-nine percent compared to the previous year. That winter was relatively harsh, partly explaining the sharpness of the rise. But the number of such deaths – most of which are among the elderly – had been in long-term decline from the 1960s, and had already started to rise again from the mid 2000s.[10]

Not being able to afford heating is a constant worry for older people on low incomes. At the John Vianney Senior Citizen's Club in south Belfast, the pensioners are all anxious about the 'big bills': 'I think we need to [campaign] now because if this weather gets any colder we'll not be around next year to do anything and we'll all be dead,' comments an elderly pensioner. 'Maybe that's what they want,' remarks another.[11]

Homes which are inadequately heated are also more likely to be damp. One housing association, Aragon, has reported that the number of cases of damp and mould was up threefold in 2013 compared to the previous year. The figures had been rising each winter for the previous four years, roughly in line with rises in energy bills. 'This is about poverty,' said Aileen Evans, the Association's managing director. 'It is about people who cannot afford to use their heating system.'[12]

Although 'living in a damp-free home' has gained the support of around ninety-five percent of the population in each of the Breadline Britain and Poverty and Social Exclusion surveys, again, the proportion of households living in such conditions is on the rise. Figure 5 shows that, in 1983, around six percent of households lived in a damp home. This dropped to just two percent in 1990 but now stands at ten percent. In 2012, nearly one-in-five children – 2.5 million – lived with damp while over half a million children lived in a home that was *both* damp and cold.

Children who live in damp and mouldy homes are up to three times more likely than those in dry homes to suffer from coughing, wheezing and respiratory illness.[13] And this has long-term effects beyond childhood: children experiencing multiple housing deprivation are twenty-five percent more likely to become seriously ill by the age of thirty-three than the rest of the population.[14]

Renée, who works full-time as a mental health support worker, lives with her four children and her mother, Edith, in a third-floor, three-bedroom council flat in the north London borough of Hackney. The largest bedroom has been uninhabitable for the last eighteen months because of severe damp, so the family of six has only two functioning bedrooms between them. 'No one sleeps in the back room because of the damp. The damp in this room is right in the corner of the room and there is damp at the sides and on the window sills. If we did sleep in there, we would get sick,' explains eight-year-old Tyrone.

Tyrone shares one small room, with two bunk beds, with his eighty-year-old grandmother and sixteen-year-old brother Girvain. Because of the overcrowding, Girvain has been sent, reluctantly, to live with his uncle in Lewisham in south London in order to study for his GCSEs. But that still leaves Edith and Tyrone sharing: 'There is no room for a wardrobe,' Edith explains. 'There's nowhere to put the clothes.' Renée shares the other bedroom, and one bed, with her two daughters, Cheyrice, aged fifteen and, Zennisha, four.

Although the council treated the damp in early 2013, it quickly returned, infecting clothes, bedding and wardrobes. Renée is often ill, as are the children. 'Damp and overcrowding are killing us; as we've got older things have got worse and not better.'

Edith, whose husband died in 2005, came to England from Barbados in 1959, first doing manual work in a factory and then working as a hospital domestic. 'The last thing I expected was to end up living like this.' Although Renée does shift work and takes as much overtime as she is offered, including some evenings and nights, making ends meet is difficult.

When Girvain comes back home Edith and Tyrone end up sharing a bed. Edith explains: 'Tyrone sleeps back there and I sleep at the front. If Renée could have a bigger home I might be able to have a room for myself, it would be a lot easier.' The proportion of households without enough rooms for children aged ten or over of different sex to have their own room, which is another key housing necessity, dropped during the 1990s, from ten percent in 1983 to a low of three percent in 1999 (see Figure 5). It is now back at around the 1983 level with nine percent of households (eleven percent of children) living in overcrowded conditions. This means that, in 2012, 600,000 children were sharing bedrooms in a way considered unacceptable by the vast majority of people. In 2013, Steph Harrison, a member of the Chartered Institute of Environmental Health, told the *Guardian* newspaper: 'In thirty years working as an environmental health officer I've never seen so many cases of overcrowding as I am seeing now.'[15]

Having enough food is another core aspect of a minimum standard. The Department of Health has defined food poverty as 'the inability to afford, or to have access to, food to make up a healthy diet'.[16] The proportion of households unable to afford two meals a day – one of the top three necessities in 2012 – stood at three percent in 2012, back to the levels found thirty years earlier, having dropped to negligible levels in the intervening period. These households are clearly in food poverty.

There has also been an increase in the numbers struggling to maintain a diet of sufficient quality. The need to be able to afford fresh fruit and vegetables every day has been a consistent health message of recent years and is seen as a necessity for adults by over eighty percent. Yet the percentage of households where adults go without has risen from five percent in 1999 to seven percent in 2012. Being able to afford 'meat, fish or vegetarian equivalent every other day' (a measure of adequate protein in the diet) gains over seventy-five percent support as an adult necessity. Again the proportion of households where the adult goes without is up – from two percent in 1999 to five percent in 2012. On the basis of the three adult food necessities (two meals; fruit and vegetables; and meat, fish or vegetarian equivalent), 3.5 million are not properly fed.

In addition to those who, week in and week out, cannot afford two meals a day, far more are cutting back on food in less severe ways. The numbers who have 'skimped on food over the previous year' has risen sharply. In 1983, thirteen percent had missed out on meals at times during the year because of lack of money. By 2012, twenty-eight percent skimped 'often' or 'sometimes' on food for themselves, with nearly eight percent doing so 'often'. People only end up skimping like this when there is no choice, when they have run out of money at the end of the week or are faced with a pressing bill, both increasingly common for low-income households.

Many of these are parents who are cutting back on food for themselves to try to make sure their children have enough. It has been a constant finding over the years that parents prioritise their children's needs. 'I don't eat in the day so I know I've got enough money at the end of the week to buy food,' explained a single parent from Gloucestershire. 'My boy eats all the time. I have dinner with him but I can't not eat with my child. It's not fair.'[17]

The result is that children have been more protected.[18] The proportion missing out on food is lower than that for adults. Those going without three meals a day – the standard set for children – was below one percent in 2012. But despite being prioritised, three percent of children in the UK in 2012 went without fresh fruit and vegetables every day and three percent without meat, fish or its vegetarian equivalent. Overall, half a million children are not adequately fed in the UK today. In these households, the vast majority (ninety-three percent) have at least one adult who 'skimps' on their own food to try to protect the children.

The Magic Breakfast charity, which provides a free breakfast to British schoolchildren in need, reported in August 2014 that teachers in the schools they worked with were expecting a dramatic decline in the health of their pupils as they returned after the holidays: 'Teachers tell us they know even with free school meals it will take two to three weeks to get their kids back up to the weight they were at the end of the last school term because their families cannot afford the food during the holidays.'[19]

Families employ a range of strategies to try to cope. 'On a bad day, I have to go up to the shops at ten in the evening, before they shut, to get the cut-price food that is about to go out of date,' one mother comments. 'You look for nearly out-of-date or out-of-date items but obviously it's not good for your health but that is all you can afford,' is how an unemployed man from Glasgow manages.[20] And a couple from Perth, both with disabilities: 'Sometimes we eat the wrong thing – 'cos you go for what's cheap and that isn't always the healthy option. You eat beans and toast for your tea some nights, egg and chips or egg and tatties. It's not a healthy meal but it's a cheap meal.'[21]

The healthy diet messages of recent years have been widely spread but to follow them is expensive. A study by Cambridge University's Centre for Diet and Activity Research found that healthy food, such as lean salmon, yoghurts and fresh vegetables, now costs three times more than unhealthy alternatives, including fast food.[22]

Poor diet is a risk factor for the UK's major killers. In a review of the evidence, the Royal College of Physicians reports that it contributes to almost half of coronary heart disease and a third of cancers.[23] For growing numbers it leads to diabetes, for older people it increases the risk of fractures, and for pregnant mothers there is a greater chance of a baby of low birth weight. For children there are a range of associated problems, from increased levels of obesity and bad dental health to poorer concentration at school.

At the end of 2013, a group of experts wrote to the *British Medical Journal* warning that UK food poverty 'has all the signs of a public health emergency that could go unrecognised until it is too late to take preventive action'.[24] The public face of growing food insecurity is most clearly seen in the escalating numbers turning to foodbanks, up fifteen-fold in 2013 over 2010, prompting the Department for Environment, Food and Rural Affairs (DEFRA) to commission research in early 2013 into the sudden rise in 'food aid'. The resultant report, published in February 2014 and written by experts at Warwick University, found that people turn to foodbanks when all else has failed: 'It is only after other key strategies have been employed (including increasingly extreme changes to shopping and eating habits, cutting back on other outgoings and turning to family and friends for informal help) that the most food insecure households may turn to food aid.'[25]

Going without

More and more families in Britain are unable to afford some of the most basic of needs – ones that have been at or near the top of people's priorities consistently over the last thirty years, and ones that would form part of any subsistence-based view of poverty. Those who lack such items are also likely (and much more likely than others) to lack other necessities. But the downward pressure on living standards is also having a much wider impact. Many who live above the level of bare existence are still missing out on key aspects of a decent life. Figure 6 shows, for 1999 and 2012, the percentage of households who could not afford each of the items

...ities seen as necessities; those above the bold line were ...s necessities in both 1999 and 2012, those below in 1999 but not 2012. (There were no adult items that moved from being non-necessities in 1999 to being necessities in 2012.[26])

Adult Items and activities	% of households who lack/can't afford	
	1999	2012
Heating to keep home adequately warm	3%	9%
Damp-free home	7%	10%
Two meals a day	1%	3%
Visit friends or family in hospital or other institutions*	3%	3%
Replace or repair broken electrical goods*	12%	26%
Fresh fruit and vegetables every day	5%	7%
Washing machine	2%	1%
All recommended dental treatment*	n/a	17%
Celebrations on special occasions	2%	4%
Warm waterproof coat	4%	4%
Attend weddings, funerals and other such occasions*	3%	3%
Telephone	2%	2%
Meat, fish or vegetarian equivalent every other day	2%	5%
Enough bedrooms for every children aged 10+ of a different sex to have their own room [3]	3%	9%
Curtains or window blinds	n/a	1%
Hobby or leisure activity	7%	8%
Enough money to keep your home in a decent state of decoration	15%	20%
Household contents insurance	10%	12%
Appropriate clothes for job interviews*	4%	8%
Table and chairs at which all the family can eat	n/a	5%
Taking part in sport/exercise activities or classes*	n/a	10%
Two pairs of all-weather shoes	7%	8%
Regular savings (of at least £20 a month) for rainy days****	27%	33%
Television	0%	0%
Regular payments to an occupational or private pension**	n/a	30%
Replace worn-out clothes with new not second-hand clothes	6%	15%
Presents for family or friends once a year	4%	7%
Friends or family around for a meal or drink at least once a month	6%	11%
Holiday away from home, not staying with relatives	18%	25%

Notes:
* These items and activities give percentage of adults not households
** Percentage of working age adults: taken as men aged 18-65, women aged 18-60
*** For households with children only
**** In 1999 the criterion was 'regular savings (of at least £10 a month) for rainy days or retirement'
n/a: not asked in 1999

Figure 6: Households going without, Britain: 1999 and 2012
Items are in descending order of the percentage
seeing each item as a necessity in 2012.[27]
See appendix for sample sizes.

In nearly all cases, the proportions lacking items have either risen or remained the same. For some, the increase has been large: those without the money 'to keep their home in a decent state of decoration' is up from fifteen to twenty percent over the period; those unable to afford to 'replace broken electrical goods that have broken down' up from twelve to twenty-six percent; and those 'unable to afford clothes for a job interview' – a particular problem for the young unemployed – up from four to eight percent.

Marc, 21, lives in Redcar on jobseeker's allowance. For most of the time since he left college and began his long search for work he's been unable to afford new clothes: 'Buying new ones for me, I'm not really bothered about them. I'll take second-hand ones passed down from family and charity shop ones and stuff like that. I'm not bothered about them you know they're clothes, clothes, clothes.' But it has been a problem when he has been offered a job interview, as all he has that is suitable to wear is a suit he had at school: 'This is my prom suit that still fits me. It's nowt special. Most people my age usually get a new suit when they go out job hunting but I haven't. As you can see this is the only one I have got so I have to bear with it and live with it really ... wish me luck.' [28]

The trends are not all negative. One area in which people's living standards have improved is in consumer durables. In 1983, eleven percent couldn't afford a phone and six percent a washing machine; these had dropped to two and one percent respectively by 2012. This partly reflects the relative drop in the price of such goods and partly the changes in the way we live which makes them a greater priority. There are now, for example, few laundrettes in which you can wash and dry your own clothes (though more services for those who are well off, where your clothes are washed and ironed for you).

Between 1999 and 2012, there was also a rise in the proportion of children missing out as shown in Figure 7 (as for Figure 6, those below the bold line were necessities in 1999 but not 2012). The main exception relates to a computer and internet access for homework – not a necessity in 1999 but now seen as one – where the proportion lacking one dropped sharply from thirty-six percent in 1999 to six percent in 2012. But for the majority of items common to 1999 and 2012 there were rises in the percentages of children going without because of their families' lack of money, in some cases more than doubling. In 1999, two percent of children couldn't afford a school trip once a term; by 2012 it was eight percent. In 1999, twenty-two percent missed out on one week's holiday a year; by 2012 it was twenty-six percent.

In 2012, four million children (one in three) missed out on one or other (or more) of the family activities of holidays, day trips, and celebrations on special occasions. Nearly one in five school-aged children (1.6 million) lacked one or other (or more) of the necessities seen as crucial to children's education and development, that is, books, a space to study, indoor (educational) games, construction toys (such as Lego), a PC and internet for homework, and school trips.

Significantly, these material and social deprivations are also associated with other disadvantages. In particular, those unable to afford necessities are also more likely to be in poor health. PSE analysis shows that those who cannot afford meat, fish or its vegetarian equivalent every other day are over seven times more likely to be in poor health than those who can. Those who cannot afford to heat their homes adequately are over six times more likely to be in poor health. This applies to *all* of the necessities even those for which a possible link to health is not so direct. Thus, those who can't afford household insurance are five times more likely to be in poor health. Poor health is intimately interlinked with poverty both as a cause and a consequence.[29]

Child necessities	% of children who lack necessity 1999	2012	Number of children who lack necessity 2012	What age children?
Warm winter coat	2%	1%	100,000	0 to <18
Fresh fruit or veg at least once a day	2%	3%	400,000	0 to <18
New, properly fitting shoes	2%	4%	500,000	0 to <18
Three meals a day	1%	1%	100,000	0 to <18
Garden or outdoor space to play in safely	4%	5%	600,000	0 to <18
Celebrations on special occasions	4%	1%	100,000	0 to <18
Books at home suitable for their ages	0%	2%	200,000	>2 to <18
Meat, fish or vegetarian equivalent at least once a day	4%	3%	400,000	0 to <18
Suitable place at home to study or do homework	n/a	5%	500,000	>5 to <18
Hobby or leisure activity	3%	6%	500,000	>5 to <18
Toddler group or nursery or play group at least once a week for pre-school-aged children	n/a	4%	100,000	<5
Indoor games suitable for their age	n/a	1%	200,000	0 to <18
Enough bedrooms for every child aged 10+ of a different sex to have their own room	3%	11%	600,000	>10 to <18
Children's clubs or activities such as drama or football training	n/a	9%	1,000,000	>2 to <18
Computer and internet for homework (not a necessity in 1999)	36%	6%	500,000	>5 to <18
Some new not second-hand clothes	3%	4%	500,000	0 to <18
Day trips with family once a month	n/a	21%	2,500,000	0 to <18
Outdoor leisure equipment, such as roller skates, skateboards, football, etc	3%	6%	700,000	0 to <18
At least four pairs of trousers, leggings, jeans or jogging bottoms	3%	5%	600,000	0 to <18
Going away on a school trip at least once a term	2%	8%	600,000	>5 to <18
Money to save	n/a	32%	2,800,000	>5 to <18
Pocket money	n/a	16%	1,300,000	>5 to <18
Holiday away from home for at least one week per year	22%	26%	3,200,000	0 to <18
Construction toys (like Lego, Duplo etc)	3%	5%	500,000	0 to <18
Child has friends round for tea or a snack once a fortnight	4%	8%	1,000,000	0 to <18

Those affecting less than 200,000 children (the percentages and numbers marked in italics) are based on small sizes and should be treated with caution.

Figure 7: Children going without, Britain: 1999 and 2012
Note: Items are in descending order of
the 2012 necessities' count

This can also be seen in the relationship between deprivation and mental health which, like poor health, is both a cause and consequence of poverty. Half of those who lack three or more necessities suffer four or more of the standard twelve indicators of stress, anxiety and depression used in government surveys, a cut-off widely taken as an indicator of poor mental health.[30] This compares with fifteen percent of those lacking no necessities and thirty-one percent among those who lack two necessities. Those who lack control over their lives, and sense this lack of control, pay the cost in poor mental health.

Those lacking any one of the necessities are also much more likely to see themselves as poor. Adults who cannot afford two meals a day are twenty times more likely to feel poor all the time than those who can afford them, and those who don't have enough money to replace electrical goods fifteen times as likely. Even those items for which many more go without are still strongly associated with feeling poor. For example, those who cannot afford a holiday for their children are six times more likely to feel poor all the time. This measure makes sense not just to the public at large but to those experiencing hardship.

The 'deprivation poverty' count

The total numbers in 'deprivation poverty' depend on the way these deprivations cluster. In 2012, nearly forty-seven percent of adults lacked *none* of the items seen as necessities, fourteen percent lacked one, a further nine percent lacked two necessities and thirty percent lacked three or more. Thus, a majority of the population go without at least one necessity.[31] So what level of deprivation constitutes poverty? Where do we draw the line?

Many people, at some point in their life, may, for various reasons, cut back in the short term on one, or even two, key items. For a person to be in 'poverty' – as opposed to suffering one particular deprivation at a given point in time, important as that might be – their level of deprivation needs to have a more pervasive effect on their lives.

What is clear, as shown in Figure 8, is that even those with moderate levels of material deprivation, those who lack one or two items, in fact face a range of other disadvantages. Thus, a fifth of those lacking one item, and a fifth of those lacking two, say their health is affected in some way (from 'slightly' to 'a lot') by low income. Twenty-seven percent of those lacking one item and thirty-nine percent lacking two say they feel poor sometimes or all of the time. A quarter of those lacking one item and forty-one percent of those lacking two have one or more financial problems (that is, they are 'constantly struggling to keep up with their bills or have fallen behind'; they have during the last year 'borrowed to meet day-to-day needs' or have 'been in arrears on one or other of their household bills').

For those who lack three or more items, the level of disadvantage rises further: fifty-nine percent of this group have health issues, seventy-three percent have at least one financial problem and three-quarters feel poor. In sharp contrast, those lacking none of the necessities are much less likely to experience other disadvantages. There is a clear gap between the experience of the forty-seven percent of the population who have *all* the necessities and the fifty-three percent who lack at least one and especially those who lack three or more.

These results reveal a clear downward spiral whereby those

who are deprived are more likely to suffer poorer health or incur financial problems which in turn increase the chances of becoming further deprived.

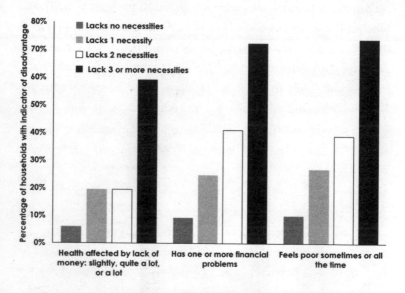

Figure 8: The wider impact of going without, UK: 2012
Those who lack none, one, two or three or more of
the necessities because they cannot afford them
by three other indicators of disadvantage

Nevertheless, what Figure 8 also shows is that, among those lacking necessities, there is not a distinct jump at different levels of deprivation. Wider disadvantage – on these measures – rises broadly in line with deprivation levels. There is more of a continuum than a clear dividing line. This is significant. The results paint a picture in which a majority of the population, even those with moderate levels of material deprivation, face other forms of hardship that make them vulnerable to poverty.

Figure 9 looks at the relationship between deprivation levels and more *severe* levels of disadvantage: those whose health is affected 'quite a lot or a lot' by lack of money (that is, excluding 'slightly'), those with *three* or more financial problems and those who feel poor 'all the time' (that is, excluding 'sometimes'). Here there is a much clearer distinction between those lacking one or two and those lacking three or more necessities. The latter are much more likely to constantly feel poor and have more financial problems and are strikingly more likely to feel their health has been more seriously affected.

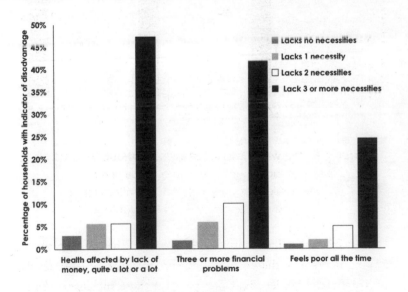

Figure 9: The relationship between going without and severe disadvantage, UK: 2012

Those who lack none, one, two or three or more of the necessities because they cannot afford them by three other indicators of *severe* disadvantage

This suggests that those lacking three or more necessities form a distinct group; that this level of deprivation affects their lives in a more fully embracing way leading to severely restricted lifestyles and opportunities. Other measures and tests – in particular of the relationship between income and deprivation level – show that, at this level of lack, a small fall in income is also associated with a sharp rise in deprivation.[32]

There is room for debate about the level of deprivation that constitutes poverty. There is a scale of disadvantage in Britain. Those lacking four or more items face even greater levels of disadvantage while even those who lack one or two items have problems that affect their lifestyles and wider life chances. But there does come a point on this scale at which the level of deprivation reached has an all-pervasive impact on people's lives. This is at three or more necessities for adults and is the level we take as our measure of poverty.

This is a group whose deprivations are both overwhelmingly enforced (by lack of income) and whose lives are affected in deep and multiple ways. We refer to this group as in 'deprivation poverty'. For the child items, not being able to afford two or more is found to provide the distinguishing threshold.[33] With very few exceptions, children who lack necessities live in households which, on the household and adult measures, are multiply deprived. As the adults have already cut back on their own living standards, the result is that the distinguishing point at which even small falls in household income lead to rapidly increasing levels of child deprivation is, at a lack of two necessities, lower than for adults.

Taking these cut-off points, thirty percent of adults cannot afford three or more of the necessities for adults, and thirty-one percent of children live in households that cannot afford two or more of the child necessities. These high levels of child 'deprivation poverty' come despite the fact that children are being protected from the impact of deprivation by their parents. Indeed, there are many other children who, while they themselves do not lack two or more child necessities, do live in households where adults are in poverty, lacking three or more necessities.[34]

High levels of deprivation are found in all parts of the UK, though there is some regional variation. Deprivation poverty rates for both adults and children are slightly higher in London, the North-East and North-West of England, the West Midlands, Wales and Northern Ireland, and slightly lower in Scotland and southern and eastern England (excluding London).

Multiple hardship is primarily caused by lack of income and resources. In every Breadline Britain and PSE survey, for every single necessity, households who cannot afford that necessity had a *much* lower average household income than households of the same size and composition who did have that necessity. Taking any two necessities, households that lack both of them have lower household incomes than households who lack just one of them, and much lower incomes than those who *have* both. And so it goes on. While some (at whatever income level) manage their finances better than others, it is lack of money not bad money management that is the overwhelming reason why people go without.

However, a small number of those who lack three or more necessities do have higher incomes. This is in part because incomes fluctuate. Some may have only recently obtained a higher income (through, for example, an additional household member finding employment) and may in time be able to raise their living standard. On the other hand, some may only be enjoying a temporary increase in income (for example, as a result of a one-off piece of overtime or temporary job), while others may have taken on additional financial commitments and debts. For some there will be caring responsibilities (looking after elderly parents or a disabled relative, for example) that impose extra financial strain. Excluding high deprivation, higher income households would slightly reduce the 'poverty' count (for details, see appendix). But their deprivations – whatever the cause – are real and they are included in this measure of deprivation poverty.

Similarly, some of those who lack three or more necessities will possess some items that are seen as non-necessities. They might need a car to get to work or have household durables bought a number of years back. Some may, on occasion, prioritise an item classed as a non-necessity, such as giving presents to family or friends. But they are also *much* less likely to have items and do activities that are non-necessities than others.[35] And those that they do possess are much more likely to be of low value or poor quality.[36] It would be some kind of Orwellian dictatorship that allowed no individuality or choice – and one that ended up taking away goods people acquired when times were better – if the only possessions the poor were allowed were the necessities.

There has been a long-running debate on whether it is possible to draw an objective, scientific poverty line that distinguishes the poor from the non-poor.[37] We do not claim that the deprivation threshold used in this book is an exact, scientific measure of poverty. Rather that it draws on the public's standards, not ours or anyone else's, and that households who fall below his threshold face multiple problems. All measures of poverty, in our view, involve judgments as to what should be the main focus and where to draw a line. In 1983 and 1990, a similar range of analysis found that this level of three or more necessities formed a distinguishing point.[38] The 1999 survey suggested that the line could be drawn at a lower level – lacking two or more necessities - but for consistency across time, we have used a lack of three or more necessities (see appendix for details).

Figure 10 shows the trends in household poverty since 1983 using this deprivation measure of poverty; those who cannot afford three or more of those items and activities seen, in each year, to be necessities.[39] On this basis, poverty, as measured by the standards of the time, has been steadily rising over the last thirty years. The proportion of households lacking three or more necessities stood at thirty percent in 2012, double the level of fourteen percent found in 1983. In 1990, the figure stood at twenty percent and, in 1999, twenty-four percent. There has also been a rise in the level of deep deprivation: twenty-three percent of adults lacked four or more necessities and eighteen percent lacked five or more in 2012 compared to seventeen and fourteen percent, respectively, in 1999.

The percentages of children lacking multiple necessities have also increased. In 2012, thirty-one percent of children lacked two or more necessities in that year compared to eighteen percent in 1999. And again more were suffering deeper levels of deprivation in 2012.

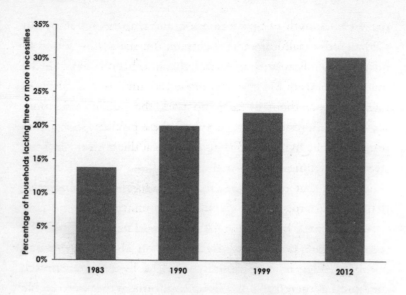

Figure 10: Poverty levels using the deprivation measure, Britain: 1983 to 2012

These results, it should be noted, are before a succession of changes to the benefits system came into effect in 2013. These changes will have further reduced the incomes for most of those in receipt of benefits – in or out of work – and are likely to have increased levels of deprivation.

Why has poverty doubled since 1983?

Over most of the period since 1983, the living standards of the poorest groups in society have been rising. Virtually everyone has their own bath and indoor toilet today and few lack essential consumer goods – from a washing machine and a fridge to a telephone. These are significant improvements. However, the material gains enjoyed by the poorest have not kept pace with the wider growth of prosperity. Moreover, as the economy has grown, the socially determined minimum standard – found to be an essentially relative measure – has also been rising. But the living standards of the poor have failed to improve at a sufficient rate to enable them to keep up with the public's minimum standards. As a result the gap between these publicly determined norms and the living conditions of those at the bottom has been steadily widening.

It is not that the public's minimum has been rising faster than general prosperity. Indeed, the minimum has been rising broadly in line. It is that living standards across a significant section of the population have not been keeping pace. The numbers living in deprivation, as judged by the standards of the time, has therefore been rising over time, and is now double the 1983 level. While the poor today are in many respects (though far from all) better off than those in the early 1980s, and certainly those of the 1930s or the 1960s, they are less a part of the society in which they live.

Moreover, overall levels of deprivation have not only risen over the shorter period since 1999 on a relative basis – that is, as measured by the standards of the day – they have also risen using a *fixed* 1999 standard. Figure 11 shows the percentage of adults in 2012 and 1999 unable to afford the items and activities seen as necessities in 1999. That is, the 2012 count excludes items and activities not asked about in 1999 while all the items and activities seen as necessities in 1999 are included (even if in 2012 some were no longer seen as necessities). This count gives us a like-for-like comparison of levels of deprivation between the two years.[40] This is, in essence, a measure of the change in absolute deprivation between the two years in that it takes a fixed standard (the 1999 standard) and compares both years on that standard.

The comparison shows that more are falling below the 1999 standard in 2012 than in 1999 with higher percentages lacking multiple numbers of items. So, fifty-three percent lacked one or more in 2012 compared to forty-two percent in 1999, through to twenty-one percent lacking five or more items in 2012 compared to fourteen percent in 1999, and so on all the way up to eleven or more items. Not only are more falling below 1999 standards but those who are deprived are being forced to go without across a wider range of their lives.

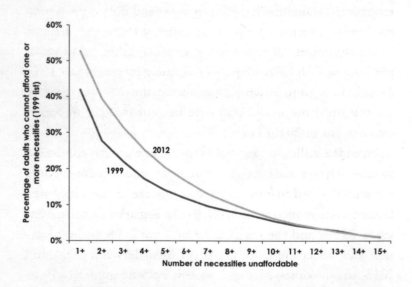

Figure 11: Rising absolute deprivation, Britain: 1999 and 2012
Percentage of adults who couldn't afford multiple items and activities in both 1999 and 2012 using the 1999 list of necessities

The sharp rise in deprivation poverty over the last thirty years reflects a number of significant trends that have put downward pressure on the living standards of an increasing number of households. The overriding change has been the sharp increase in inequality over the period. From the late 1970s the steady march towards greater equality that had taken place since the 1930s went into reverse. This earlier shift to greater equality had helped transform the lives of those on low and middle incomes, while millions of families at the bottom were lifted nearer to contemporary standards.

But the 'great levelling', as it is known, was not to prove a permanent revolution. Instead, in little more than the span of a single generation, it gave way to the 'great widening', returning the income gap between top and bottom closer to the level last seen in the pre-war era. As a result, the share of total net income (after taxes and benefits) taken by those in the bottom fifth of households fell from ten percent in 1979 to eight percent in 2010/11. In contrast, the share received by the top fifth rose from thirty-five percent in 1979 to forty-two percent in 2010/11.[41]

From the millennium, while top-income groups continued to take a larger share of the cake, low- and middle-income households faced an ever-tightening squeeze on their incomes. Indeed, average incomes for this group began to stagnate from around 2004 and then started to fall from 2008 as the recession and wider austerity began to bite. Between 2004 and 2013, the incomes of those in the bottom quarter fell by around nine percent and, overall, were no higher in that year than in 2000.[42]

This income squeeze has been further tightened by

differential changes in the cost of living. Not only have low incomes been contracting in recent years, but they buy fewer things. While the Consumer Price Index (CPI) – an official measure of inflation – rose by just under a third between 2002 and 2013, food prices rose by over fifty percent, the price of electricity and gas more than doubled, and rents also rose more steeply than general prices.[43] As low-income households spend a higher proportion of their income on these basics than other households, these price changes have hit them particularly hard, forcing more families to cut back on necessities, including, in a rising number of cases, on food or heating or, increasingly, both.

On top of these trends, and the wider impact of inequality, a number of other deep-seated long-term changes – from an increasingly bleak jobs market to more uncertainty about pay and income – have brought greater economic insecurity and greater uncertainty over incomes. By making it more difficult to build the reserves and resilience necessary to cope with harder times, these trends will have raised the overall vulnerability to poverty in society,

In 2012, a third of households could not afford to put aside even a small sum for savings for a rainy day resulting in sharply increasing proportions unable to cope, for example, with emergencies such as repairing electrical equipment. Levels of personal debt have also been rising. Figure 12 from the PSE findings shows that between 1999 and 2012 the numbers having to borrow just to get by rose sharply, with, in particular, a growing dependence on help from the family.

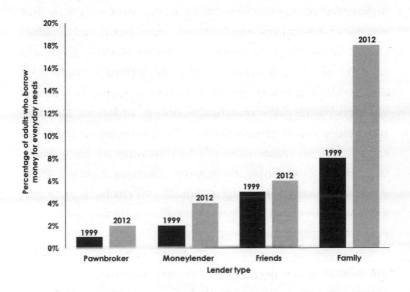

Figure 12: Borrowing for everyday needs, UK: 1999 and 2012

Those forced to borrow are heavily concentrated among those who lack three or more necessities. Virtually no one who has all the necessities borrows from pawnbrokers, moneylenders or friends, while only four percent of this group borrows from their family. In contrast, forty-three percent of those lacking three or more necessities borrow from their family and seventeen percent from friends, while eleven percent borrow from a moneylender and six percent from a pawnbroker.

These pressures have been brewing for decades, but accelerated from the mid 2000s. The size of the loan industry doubled between 2009 and 2013. Its high-street stores are also disproportionately concentrated in impoverished communities such as Glasgow, Harlow in Essex and Halton to the east of Liverpool.[44] A remarkable 400,000 payday loan commercials for companies such as Wonga were broadcast on UK TV channels in 2012, up almost 400-fold from 2009, many of them on children's television. There are now over 240 lenders operating in the UK. Wonga, the market leader, saw its loans soar to £1.2 billion in 2012, up sixty-eight percent on the previous year, and pre-tax profits rise by thirty-five percent.[45] While some borrowers have been able to repay their loans quickly, growing numbers have been trapped in a debilitating cycle of debt and poverty.

'I have seen first-hand experience of all these loans and the difficulty people get themselves into . . . they start off with something small and it ends up massive and they're hounded,' commented one participant in the Communities in Action project run with the PSE in Northern Ireland. 'You've used all the things that you've turned to in the past, like your store cards, Credit Union, and you're at the point now where you're not allowed any more money, so what's next?' added another.[46]

There has also been a steady rise in the numbers in arrears on at least one core household bill – from rent and mortgage payments to utility bills.[47] With levels of personal borrowing at record highs in the UK, and with interest rates likely to rise at some point, financial pressures on cash-strapped borrowers can only intensify.[48]

One of the consequences of this growing squeeze is that the official poverty measure, based on relative income, understates the degree of contemporary hardship. In 1983, 1990 and 1999, the level of relative income poverty was fairly similar to the deprivation rate – and the trend for both was upwards. Using the sixty percent of median threshold, the level of poverty for the whole population reached a low of just over twelve percent in 1977. It then started to rise reaching fourteen percent in 1983 and a high of over twenty-five percent in 1992. During the 1990s, it stabilised at around this level, then dropped to twenty percent in 2005 largely as a result of Labour's anti-poverty measures, which were targeted to bring relative income poverty down. The latest official rate – at twenty-one percent in 2012/13 – is lower than its peak in the mid 1990s but remains considerably higher than in the early 1980s and indeed much higher than in the 1960s and 1970s.[49]

But, at twenty-one percent, the level of relative income poverty for 2012 is notably lower than the deprivation poverty rate. This gap is in part down to differential changes in the cost of living which means that to achieve a minimum living standard has required a higher and higher income.[50] It is also because rising levels of debt will have spread lower living standards up the income scale.

But the gap also reflects another of the inherent weaknesses of the official relative measure. As critics (including the government) have argued, it can lead, in some situations, to seemingly perverse trends. During recessions, for example, relative poverty can appear to decline even if real incomes among the poor fall and absolute poverty rises.[51] The median income benchmark is a measure of the gap between low and middle incomes, showing how those at the bottom fare in relation to the middle. If the incomes of the poorest fall, but by less than the median so that this gap narrows, relative income poverty will decline even though the actual living standards of the poor are lower. If everyone takes a step down the ladder, it is only those at the bottom who fall off. This is what happened after the 2008 crash, when real wages (after adjusting for inflation) fell while, at least initially, benefit levels were protected. This led to a relative narrowing of the gap between those at the bottom and those higher up and thus a slight lowering of the level of relative poverty from 22.5% in 2007/8 to 21.0% in 2012/13.[52]

Since the late 1970s, Britain has built a high propensity to poverty into its economic and political system, one linked, in essence, to the increasingly unequal division of power, opportunities and rewards. Not only are increasing numbers living in deprivation poverty, but a growing proportion of the population is at risk, facing a range of disadvantages that increase their chances of falling below the living standard defined as the minimum necessary in Britain today.

Over the last thirty years, the precise nature of the deprivations that the poor face has changed. But while the poor of today do, in some respects, have more possessions than they had in the past, they share with the poor of previous times a fundamental inability to fully participate in the society in which they live. Despite rises in overall prosperity over time, far greater numbers have become unable to meet the requirements for living in contemporary society.

The experience of those who fall below society's minimum standard therefore remains remarkably similar over time. There remains a constant juggling to get by, worry over the future and widespread awareness of falling short of social expectations. In 1983, a visually impaired pensioner described her life thus: 'This isn't a standard of living, this is existence.' 'You are just about existing. It's from hand to mouth or from hand to bill,' is how a single parent described her situation in 1990. And, in 2012, a young jobseeker saw his situation in these terms: 'I'm not living, I'm surviving ... it's like rationing on food, rationing on electric and gas, it's not a life at all.'

Yet, despite these trends and the widening barriers faced by the poor, the post-2010 coalition government promoted a very different view of the nature and causes of poverty. For them, the blame for poverty lies with the poor themselves.

3

The loaded dice:
Who becomes poor?

*It's a struggle. It's an effort. I get up in the morning
and it [money] is the first thing I think of and I go to
bed at night and it is the last thing I think of. That's
the impact it has.*
Lone parent, female, Birmingham 2013[1]

A few months after the riots that spread through parts of
urban Britain in the summer of 2011, the prime minister
launched the government's 'Troubled Families' strategy.
'Troubled families', David Cameron argued, lay at the heart
of the problem of poverty. 'Let me be clear what I mean by
this phrase,' he explained. 'Officialdom might call them
"families with multiple disadvantages". Some in the press
might call them "neighbours from hell". Whatever you call
them, we've known for years that a relatively small number
of families are the source of a large proportion of the problems in society. Drug addiction. Alcohol abuse. Crime. A
culture of disruption and irresponsibility that cascades
through generations.'[2]

Central to the coalition government's broader social strategy were two recurring themes: that many social problems lay at the door of people in poverty and that the poor themselves were largely to blame for their situation. In November 2012, the government published a much promoted consultation document, *Measuring Child Poverty*, which set out to measure poverty by people's individual behaviours and characteristics as opposed to their circumstances.[3] The new 'multidimensional' measure they were seeking to develop aimed to downgrade the importance of income and living standards and instead concentrated on criteria such as parenting skills, parental health, drug and alcohol dependency and family stability. The approach proposed bore no relation to any previous method of measuring poverty in this country or worldwide, either historical or present day. But the consultation document, like the 'Troubled Families' programme, gave a clear insight into the government's central understanding of the causes of poverty – namely that it was down to individual behaviour.

There are essentially two schools of thought over the question of what causes poverty and how to tackle it. The first is what might be called the 'individualistic' school. This holds that poverty is mainly the product of individual failings and thus primarily a matter of personal responsibility. The role of the state should therefore be limited to changing the behaviour and aspirations of those who fail and providing some, limited, support to enable them to change their prospects. Poverty in this approach tends to be seen in minimalist terms, reflecting more of an 'absolute' approach than one that is more inclusive. It is more difficult to write off a large percentage of the population as failures than a small one.

The second, 'societal' view, while acknowledging some role for the individual, primarily sees poverty as a structural problem, stemming from a failure of social and economic policies, and factors such as a lack of jobs, low wages and rising living costs. It tends to take a more generous, relative view of individual needs that acknowledges the importance of everyone being able to participate in society. Tackling poverty is seen as a central social responsibility requiring strong collective intervention. Without creating a society that offers decent opportunities for all, individual endeavour, however strong, will for many not be enough to prevent a life of low income.

So why is it that some people fall below society's minimum standards? Is it primarily down to their personal behaviour, or are they essentially the victims of circumstances beyond their control? Who becomes poor?

'Dipstick' policymaking

In practice, policy has always been something of a compromise between these two views, though with shifts in emphasis over time. While the creation of the post-war welfare state was a strong expression of the societal view that sought to tackle the structural causes of poverty, the last thirty years – from Margaret Thatcher's governments onwards – have seen a shift in emphasis towards individual responsibility. The three post-1997 Labour governments shifted the balance again – with an acceptance of the central role of government in reducing poverty through changes to benefits. But the emphasis was still on enabling the individual to lift themselves out of poverty rather than tackling structural economic inequalities.

The 2010 coalition government marked a return to a more fully fledged individualistic approach, singling out people's behaviour – and not wider social and economic forces – as the key driver of poverty. This is clearly seen in their controversial 'Troubled Families' strategy. These families were labelled as flawed and anti-social individuals and as bad parents. While the broad aim was to help some of the most disadvantaged families in England, the publicity around the policy, quite deliberately, had the effect of making the actual problem of poverty seem small and, moreover, confined to a group of dysfunctional families. 'Facts and evidence were bent to meet the needs of policymakers', concluded *The Lies We Tell Ourselves*, a report from the Baptist Union of Great Britain, the Methodist Church, the Church of Scotland and the United Reformed Church on the policy's implementation and impact. 'The reputations of society's most disadvantaged families became collateral damage in the rush to defend a new policy. Perhaps we are not surprised by this but we should at least be appalled.'[4]

In a much-criticised estimate, this group of 'troubled families' was initially said to total 120,000, a figure later increased – in August 2014 – to 500,000. The original number had been plucked out of wider research that used seven deprivation indicators (from living in overcrowded housing to having a long-standing illness) to identify households which were multiply disadvantaged. These families were then redefined by ministers first into families that are 'troubled', and then into families that *are* or *cause* trouble. Yet there is no evidence that the families identified are involved in crime or anti-social behaviour. Ministers had misrepresented official statistical analysis to support their political philosophy on poverty. 'If we interrogate the research behind the imputed existence of 120,000 troubled families', wrote Ruth Levitas, professor of sociology at Bristol University, 'this turns out to be a factoid – something that takes the form of a fact, but is not. It is used to support policies that in no way follow from the research on which the figure is based. The problem is not the research itself, but its misuse.'[5]

Despite the evident misrepresentation of official research, the government pressed on with its flagship strategy, backed by a number of policy initiatives. In July 2012, the first report into its progress presented sixteen case studies with harrowing stories of drugs and alcohol use, disruptive behaviours and child sexual and physical abuse. The report insisted this was 'a good starting place to inform our thinking and policy development'.[6] Confronted by an extensive backlash from experts and academics, the Department for Communities and Local Government, which published the report, was eventually forced to admit that this did not constitute research and was no more than 'dipstick' information gathering.[7]

But by then the policy had served its purpose in presenting behavioural shortcomings as central to the problem of poverty. It was part of an overall strategy to change people's thinking. This was explicitly stated in the *Measuring Child Poverty* consultation document. 'It cannot be right', wrote Iain Duncan Smith, the secretary of state responsible, in the foreword, 'that experiences so vital to childhood, like seeing a parent go out to work or growing up in a stable family, are not reflected in our understanding of child poverty.'[8] Factors such as family breakdown, poor parenting, and drug addiction were to be prioritised, instead of family income or the lack of job opportunities, in the government's strategy to tackle poverty and in its attempt to devise a new measure.

To support this view, the Department for Work and Pensions published the findings of an online poll. Respondents were asked how important a number of factors were in deciding whether someone is growing up in poverty. The items included: 'A child having parents who are addicted to drugs or alcohol', 'A child living in a home that is damp or cold', 'A child's family not having enough income' and 'A child experiencing family breakdown'. The item that came top of the public's list – chosen by ninety percent - was 'drug or alcohol addiction'. A lack of income, in contrast, was picked by seventy-nine percent.[9]

The DWP's poll was widely dismissed by leading social policy experts as highly misleading, amateurish and deeply flawed.[10] Yet the ninety percent figure was seized on by the government: 'Interestingly, having a parent addicted to drugs or alcohol was thought to be the most important factor of all ... above and beyond other dimensions such as going to a failing school or living in a cold damp home,' Iain Duncan Smith told the charity Kid's Company in January 2013. 'It is striking that so many people pick out as central to a child's experience of poverty, a factor that so rarely features in the poverty debate.'[11]

That drug and alcohol addiction can lead to poverty is indisputable, and for single homeless people sleeping rough, or in hostels, it is a common cause of death.[12] But the evidence is clear – neither play more than a very minor role. A study for the Joseph Rowntree Foundation found that under one percent of adults are problem drug users (heroin/crack) noting that the scales of the problems of drug addiction and poverty are of an entirely different order.[13] While signs of drug dependency are higher among men (though not women) in the lowest income groups, most of this use relates to cannabis, and the percentages relating to harder drugs are small.[14] Addiction to harder drugs is a serious problem in its own right, but is spread across incomes, a problem for a tiny minority of the rich as well as a tiny minority of those living in poverty.

Similarly alcohol abuse is serious and a cause of childhood neglect but research has failed to demonstrate a correlation between alcohol dependence and income levels. Indeed, government data shows that higher income groups for both men and women drink substantially more per week than lower income ones.[15]

The *Measuring Child Poverty* consultation document became the subject of widespread criticism. Professor Jonathan Bradshaw of the University of York described the document as the worst paper setting down government policy direction he had ever read, questioned whether it was written by civil servants and described it as reading as if it had been 'plagiarised from a right-wing thinktank tract'.[16] He dismissed its approach as 'conceptually completely inept and confused', failing to recognise the fundamental distinction between '**measures** of poverty, the **characteristics** of poor children and the **associations** and the **consequences** of poverty'.[17]

The government's approach also came under fire from the Social Mobility and Child Poverty Commission, the independent watchdog chaired by the former Labour cabinet minister Alan Milburn and created by the 2010 Child Poverty Act. The Commission expressed concern that the different dimensions set out in the consultation risked conflating the causes and existing experience of poverty in a way that was highly confusing.[18] There was also a lack of agreement between the coalition partners. The Liberal Democrat MPs Sarah Teather, children's minister until 2012, and Steve Webb, pensions minister, both let it be known that they had reservations about the convoluted measurement ideas that were circulating within Whitehall.

In the event, the government's attempt to devise a new multidimensional measure, to be launched in a long promised Green Paper, never materialised. The Treasury, nervous of the political implications of abandoning existing measures, and doubtful that the DWP's multidimensional measure was 'methodologically sound', vetoed change.[19] Such proposals were also going to struggle to pass through the UK's devolved governments in Scotland, Wales and Northern Ireland where there remains robust support for the importance of relative poverty and attempting to achieve the goals of the Child Poverty Act. When the government published its final consultation document on its child poverty strategy in February 2014 the proposed new measure had been dropped.[20] Not that the government was backtracking on its view that poverty was the fault of the individuals affected. In a joint comment piece for the *Guardian* in the same month, George Osborne and Iain Duncan Smith talked, yet again, of 'worklessness, family breakdown, educational failure, addiction, or debt' as the causes of poverty.[21]

'A destructive cycle of poverty'

In addition to the poor being blamed for their own poverty, poor parents were also being accused of creating the poor adults of the future, of transferring poverty between generations. 'A destructive cycle of poverty', passing down from parent to child, is how the government described the process.[22]

The idea of an intergenerational cycle of poverty and delinquency founded on the supposed personal and moral failings of families themselves has a long pedigree. The 'problem of poverty' was blamed on 'bad' genes before the Second World War and then, after the discrediting of the eugenics movement by the end of the war, on 'bad' culture. It was then resurrected by Sir Keith Joseph, who ran the massive Department of Health and Social Security in Edward Heath's Conservative government of 1970 to 1974. In a highly provocative speech in Edgbaston in October 1974, one that echoed some of the arguments of the pre-war eugenics movement, Joseph warned that 'our human stock is threatened'. 'A high and rising proportion of children are being born to mothers least fitted to bring children into the world,' he claimed. These were young women, he added, many unmarried, many 'of low intelligence, most of low educational attainment' producing 'problem children, the future unmarried mothers, delinquents, denizens of our borstals, sub-normal educational establishments, prisons, hostels for drifters'.[23]

The same ideas keep coming back. Boris Johnson, the London mayor, in a throw back to the social Darwinist theories of the turn of the last century, talked in a speech in 2013 to the Centre for Policy Studies think-tank of how in a competitive society 'some cornflakes get to the top'. 'It is surely relevant to a conversation about equality,' he continued, 'that as many as sixteen percent of our species have an IQ below 85, while about two percent have an IQ above 130.'[24] The corollary being that, on this analogy, success and failure in life is all in the genes.

But generally such biologically deterministic views hold less sway. More prevalent is the linking of a 'cycle of disadvantage' to a culture of poverty. However, none of dozens of detailed studies – domestic and international – has found any large group (of more than 1.5% of the population) with behaviour patterns that could be ascribed to a culture or genetics of poverty.[25] In evidence to the government's consultation on social mobility and child poverty, Professor David Gordon, head of the Townsend Centre for International Poverty Research at the University of Bristol, dismissed the idea of such a 'culture' as an 'old libel'. 'Poverty is not like syphilis or a biblical curse across the generations – poverty is not a disease and it cannot be caught and all creditable evidence shows that it is not "transmitted" to children by their parents' genes or culture.'[26]

But the idea persists that poverty is handed down from parent to child. Central to the coalition government's thinking was a version that put the emphasis on the quality of parenting, while greatly downgrading the impact that lack of money has on children's prospects. The argument runs that parents who are poor are more likely to be poor at parenting and that such parents produce poor adults. A report for the government on the impact of early intervention for children, conducted by the Labour MP Graham Allen and published in 2011, claimed that 'the right kind of parenting is a bigger influence on their [children's] future than wealth, class, education or any other common social factor'.[27] David Cameron went further: children born in poverty and those born in wealth achieved similar outcomes as long as they were brought up by "confident and able" parents. [28] It is, it seems, a very comforting thought for well-off parents – their children do well, not because they are wealthy, but because they are better parents.[29]

There is, of course, a link between parenting and outcomes for children: children who are abused or maltreated are at long-term risk; strong parent/child relationships are associated with higher cognitive abilities, and academic outcomes and social competencies.[30] Positive parenting – undertaking activities with children and having positive interactions with them – contributes to a child's school achievement regardless of any family disadvantage.[31] But it is not the case that poverty and wealth do not matter independently of parenting. Kathleen Kiernan, professor of social policy and demography at the University of York, and colleagues, have examined the extent to which positive parenting mediated the effects of poverty and disadvantage. She concludes: 'Children's achievement can be adversely affected by poor parenting; it can also be adversely affected by poverty . . . despite the best efforts of their parents, children living in poverty and relatively disadvantaged circumstances still remain behind their wealthier, well-parented peers.'[32]

Better educated parents have access to a range of resources that enable them to support their children; they have books around the home, may be better placed to help with homework and have what's called 'cultural capital'. Early years interventions, like Sure Start, are important for counterbalancing some of these advantages. But there is little or no evidence that parents who are poor are poor at parenting and none that they are the 'wrong kind' or 'not able' parents.

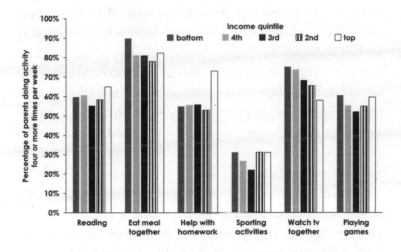

Figure 13: Activities undertaken by parents with child four or more days a week, UK: 2012

PSE 2012 looked at a range of parenting activities, from doing things together to playing games and support with education. Figure 13 shows the pattern by income group. Households – after adjusting for household size and composition – have, starting from the top down, been divided into five equal groups or quintiles (each quintile then representing a fifth of the population). In the case of three of these activities – reading, playing games and sport – there was little difference in such parent-child activity across the income range. On the other hand, poorer parents are more likely to watch TV and eat meals with their children than better-off groups. Significantly, parents in the top fifth by income are more likely than other groups to help with homework, with seventy-three percent of this group helping with homework four or more days a week compared to between fifty-three and fifty-six percent for all other groups. Indeed, highly educated parents (graduate or above) are even more likely to help with homework. This could suggest that this group place a higher value on education but equally it could suggest that they have a greater confidence that their help will be useful. Overall these figures suggest that any divide in parenting practices is between higher income groups and the rest rather than the poor and the rest.

Poor life chances

While there is no evidence here that it is untypical parenting practices among poor families that affects their children's life chances, it is certainly true that children born in poorer households are more likely to experience poverty as adults than those born into higher income families.

The PSE surveys have asked people about their experiences of poverty over their life, including childhood. In 2012, fifty-three percent said they had never experienced poverty, a slight fall on the fifty-nine percent who had never experienced poverty in 1999. However, as shown in Figure 14, there is a clear division in society. Most of those in the top three income groups say they have never experienced poverty at any point in their lives – rising to sixty-six percent of those in the top fifth. Insignificant numbers at this income level feel they have experienced poverty during their lives 'often' or for 'most of the time'. For those in the bottom fifth, in contrast, twenty-two percent feel they have been in poverty either 'most of the time' or 'often' throughout their lives.

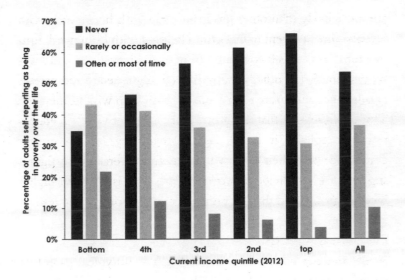

Figure 14: Subjective poverty across a lifetime, by income, UK: 2012
'Looking back over your life, how often have there been times in your life when you think you have lived in poverty by the standards of the time?'

That poor children are more likely to become poor adults, the evidence suggests, is primarily rooted in societal causes. The UK has a particularly bad recent record of intergenerational mobility. In all countries, to some extent or other, children's earnings correlate with those of their parents, but the variation between countries is large. The Paris-based Organisation for Economic Co-operation and Development (OECD) – the club of rich nations – looked at a son's earnings compared to his father's earnings across all the organisation's thirty-four member nations.[33] The UK (along with the USA) had the highest correlation with fifty percent of the economic advantage that high-earning fathers have over low-earning fathers passed on to their sons; by contrast, in the Nordic countries the advantage passed on from father to son is much lower, dropping to fifteen percent for Denmark. In the UK, inequalities of opportunity are deeply entrenched.

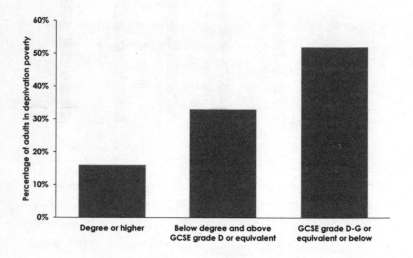

Figure 15: Educational level and risk of poverty, UK: 2012

A key explanation for this is the strong relationship found in the UK between the income of families and educational outcomes for children. The OECD found that socio-economic background had a considerable influence on educational attainment. Again the UK (along with the US) was among the countries where socio-economic background had the largest impact on educational performance with the Nordic countries showing a weaker relationship. Education level is a strong determinant of people's risk of being in poverty. As Figure 15 from the PSE study shows, those who have higher educational qualifications are much less likely to be in poverty; of those who have few or no qualifications just over half are in poverty (as measured by lack of three or more necessities).

But education does not explain all of the variation between poverty in childhood and the additional risk of poverty in adulthood. A study by the London School of Economics for the Joseph Rowntree Foundation has looked at the links between child poverty (using the official income measure) and poverty later in adult life through the experiences of two groups: one aged sixteen in 1974, followed up at the ages of thirty-three and forty-two, and the other aged sixteen in 1986, followed up at the age of thirty. The study found a significant persistence of poverty from teens to adult life and that a large proportion of the link between child and adult poverty could not be put down to any parental characteristics other than low income. The study also found that the link between teenage and adult poverty strengthened over this period. 'Financial resources in the teens seem to matter on top of any other driving background factors, and came to matter more between the 1970s and the 1980s.'[34] Those who did *not* experience poverty as a child increasingly had life's dice heavily weighted in their favour. The built-in advantage obtained from being born to higher income parents was even stronger for the 1980s than the 1970s group of teenagers. The apples had been falling even closer to the tree.

This was not because the 1980s group were ending up with poorer educational qualifications than their 1970s counterparts.

While poor teenagers in the 1970s who had similar educational and employment outcomes to their non-poor contemporaries were no more likely to be poor twenty years later, this was not the case for the 1980s group. For teenage men in the 1980s, teenage poverty linked through to adult poverty even when adults have similar education outcomes. Of course, we cannot know whether this will hold true for the teenagers of today as their future earnings are yet to be determined. But today's diminishing labour market opportunities are hardly encouraging.

A study of education and social mobility based on in-depth interviews with eighty-eight children in two high-performing academies, but with socially mixed intakes, found that despite the high quality of teaching and exam success in the schools, the chances and prospects of individual students were heavily shaped, and often constrained, by a mix of family background and wider economic forces. 'Our data suggests that academies are most unlikely to overcome family background or much increase social mobility. On the contrary, they seem to embed differences in family wealth, with successful students invariably describing advantages transmitted through their parents.'[35]

This will be down, at least in part, to the differing school experiences of children from poorer and better-off backgrounds. Evidence gathered by the Children's Commission on Poverty, established by the Children's Society charity in 2013, showed that there is a widening gulf in school experience between low and high-income families, with parents on low incomes struggling to pay for school uniforms, study equipment, after-school clubs and the other costs associated with school. More than half of families who are 'not well-off at all' have borrowed to pay school costs. As a result increasing numbers of children face social isolation and bullying, contributing to the narrowing of academic opportunities.[36]

There are always exceptions that run counter to general trends. Some children from poor backgrounds have high degrees of educational success and upward social mobility. Equally the life chances of some children from poorer backgrounds are weakened because of neglect or the chaotic lives their families lead. But to jump from this to assume that poverty is overwhelmingly a product of individual shortcomings is quite wrong. For that to be true the doubling of poverty in the last thirty years would have to be down to an intensification of such problems.

The changing face of poverty

Being brought up in a poor family *does* carry disadvantages for future life chances – and *does* increase the risk of poverty later in life – but these disadvantages can be heavily traced to wider societal factors, such as the condition of the labour market or educational access, rather than to a supposed culture of poverty.

Indeed, one of the most significant trends over the last thirty years has been a sea change in the groups most at risk of poverty. Despite the claims about the lack of personal responsibility, and a weak work ethic, the most striking shift has been the rise of poverty among those *in work*. In 1983, just over a third of those in deprivation poverty (lacking three or more necessities) were in a household where the 'head' was in full- or part-time work.[37] Today the equivalent figure is just above sixty percent.[38]

Employment status	Percentage of all the poor
In full-time work	39%
In part-time work	13%
Unemployed	12%
Permanently sick/disabled	11%
Looking after family/home	10%
Retired	9%
Student	6%
All	100%

Figure 16: Who are the poor? UK: 2012[39]
Adults lacking three or more necessities
by their employment status

Figure 16 shows the composition of those in deprivation poverty by the work status of the *individual* (as opposed to the work status of the household). Over half of individuals in poverty are in employment, thirty-nine percent in full-time and thirteen percent in part-time employment. The next largest group are the unemployed, constituting twelve percent of adults in poverty, closely followed by those who are sick or disabled (eleven percent). Those who are looking after the family/home make up ten percent of those in poverty. Most in this category will be in households where someone else in the household is in work (for example, one parent working while the other stays at home to look after the children or another relative). Similarly some of those who are sick and disabled, unemployed, retired or students will be in households where someone else in the household is in work. As a result the proportion of individuals in poverty living in *households* where at least one member is in work is higher than the percentages of individuals who are themselves in work. The overall figure rises from just over fifty percent to over sixty percent. Being in work, or being in a household where someone is in work, is increasingly not sufficient to keep members of that household out of deprivation poverty.

An equally striking change is the fall in poverty among those who are retired. In the 1960s, around a third of the poor were elderly.[40] Today less than a tenth of those in poverty are in households where all adults are retired.[41] Nevertheless, deprivation in older age continues for some, reflecting the inequalities experienced during their lifetimes. Today's poor pensioners are a group who were unable to build up resources during their lives and rely purely on the state pension and, when they take them, means-tested top-ups. Those most at risk of poverty are single pensioners – around twice the risk of pensioner couples. Among single pensioners, women are more vulnerable than men, because they are more likely to have been in low-paid work, to lack an occupational pension and to have paid insufficient national insurance (though the rules have improved in recent years) to get a full state pension.

However, the overall picture is one of a steady switch of fortunes away from those of working age and in favour of pensioners. Despite continuing problems for a minority of pensioners, the falling *rate* of poverty among the elderly is the only success story of the last three decades. Just over fourteen percent of all those who are retired today are poor, about half the overall poverty rate. This is down to a number of trends, from the spread of generous occupational pension schemes to the introduction of the means-tested pensioner credit from 2003, along with a range of free universal benefits such as the free bus pass and annual winter fuel allowance. These measures have boosted the incomes of most, if far from all, pensioners and enabled today's elderly population to enjoy a significantly better standard of living than that of their predecessor generations.

Nevertheless, today's pensioners are likely to be a special case. The likelihood is that their rate of poverty will rise in the future, overturning the gains of recent decades. PSE results show that of those who are not retired, fifty-four percent of the poorest fifth, and forty-one percent of the next fifth, could not afford to make any payments into a private or occupational scheme in 2012 and only fifteen percent and twenty-three percent respectively could make regular payments. (Though this was before the new automatic enrolment into workplace pensions unless employees opt out.) In contrast, sixty-two percent in the top fifth are making regular payments and only thirteen percent make none.

Further, while occupational schemes have offered good pensions for those receiving them in the past, employers are nearly all offering much less generous schemes which will pay out a good deal less in retirement in the future. The new rules allowing the cashing in of pension pots to spend now are likely to lead to even lower returns for those wishing to purchase annuities while leaving those who have cashed in with the prospect of shortfall in the future. Even with recent improvements to state pension provision – with a more generous system of annual uprating and the new higher flat-rate state pension from 2016 – the basic pension will remain below European standards. While more are likely to enrol in company schemes through auto-enrolment, the scheme will be inadequate for the growing army of low-paid workers who are not paid enough to build a decent fund. As Alex Brummer, city editor of the *Daily Mail*, has summed it up, 'The UK now has one of the meanest and most complex systems of state pension provisions in the world.'[42]

Poverty during working life greatly raises the risk of poverty in retirement. Of those of working age, while the largest percentage of those in poverty are those *in* work, the greatest *risk* is among those most excluded from the labour market. Figure 17 shows – for 2012 – those groups with the greatest *risk* of poverty compared to the average across all households. At the top are those who are unemployed, sick or disabled and lone parents.

	Percentage of each group in poverty
Household type	
No workers in household – unemployed	76%
No workers in household – permanently sick and disabled	72%
Lone parent	67%
Two adults with three or more children	48%
Two adults with one or two children	40%
Ethnicity	
Asian – Pakistani/Bangladeshi	42%
Black – Black Caribbean/Black African	56%
All	**30%**

Figure 17: Adults most at *risk* of poverty, UK: 2012

Overall, adults in households with children have an above-average risk of being poor. Forty percent of couples with one or two children are in poverty, rising to forty-eight percent for those with three or more children. While large families are at greater risk of poverty, the numbers of families with more than two children have dropped sharply, despite government claims that large families are a major cause of the problem. Among households with children in poverty, under one in five have more than two children. Most children in poverty live with both parents, are in families with one or two children and have at least one person in the household in full-time work.[43]

Couples with children are nearly twice as likely to be in poverty as those without children. Despite many new measures to help parents since 1997 – more investment in childcare, better support in early years and improved income support through tax credits – families remain at significant risk of poverty. The extra help provided by child benefit and child tax credits does not match the cost of raising a child. At the same time, maintaining an income is harder. It is more difficult to work extra hours and the costs associated with childcare, have been rising. Around half of all children live in households where there are adults who are deprived.

One of the most significant changes to family structure of recent decades has been the rise in the number of lone parents. The proportion of children living in single-parent households has risen from eight percent in 1971 to a fifth today.[44] Although lone parenthood is mostly a temporary situation lasting an average of five years, and there has been an improvement in lone-parent employment rates, their vulnerability to poverty remains high at sixty-seven percent. Nevertheless, lone parents represent a small proportion of the population as a whole and account for only nine percent of all those in poverty while families with two (or more) adults account for forty percent.

While the majority of lone parents are in work, managing full-time work and childcare is increasingly problematic. Childcare is increasingly expensive and the help through the benefits system is tapered. Lone parents who work more than fifteen hours a week have to contribute to costs. The charity Barnado's found that a lone parent on the national minimum wage using a childminder priced at the English average would in 2012 actually gain nothing from increasing their hours.[45] As a result, earning extra money from work depends heavily on the availability of family to cover their childcare. In countries which provide childcare services that are either free at the point of delivery or heavily subsidised – such as Norway and Sweden – rates for female participation in the labour force are much higher.

Over seventy percent of people who are sick or disabled are poor (Figure 18). This is partly because poverty and ill health are closely intertwined: those in poverty are especially likely to *become* sick or disabled. A study by Tania Burchardt in 2003 found that people in the poorest fifth of the income spread are two and a half times more likely to become disabled during a year than those in the top fifth.[46] Equally, ill health and disability *lead* to poverty.[47] In the last twenty years, there have been significant attempts to break the link between poverty and disability. The 1995 Disability Discrimination Act and its 2005 successor – though not as comprehensive as many would have liked – have helped to outlaw discrimination in employment and service provision. In 1992, the Disability Living Allowance (DLA) – a non-means-tested cash payment in recognition of the additional costs resulting from impairment – was introduced. Though the current social security changes are limiting some of these benefits (and replacing DLA with Personal Independence Payments), these moves recognised that 'disability' was the result of the barriers that people face including discriminatory attitudes, inaccessible environments, and lack of enabling support.

Nevertheless, many barriers remain. Despite the discrimination legislation, a person with disabilities with a degree is more likely to be wanting to work but unable to find a job than a non-disabled person with no qualifications.[48] Further, disability benefits underestimate the costs of living with disabilities. Children in families with a disabled adult are more likely to be deprived. For example, children who do not have new, properly fitting shoes or only have second-hand clothes, are over seven times more likely to live in a household where one of the adults has a long-standing illness or disability.[49]

One of the most striking findings of the 2012 PSE research is the high risk of poverty among certain ethnic minorities. As seen in Figure 17, over half of Black or Black British households and forty-two percent of Pakistani or Bangladeshi households are in poverty. There are many deep-seated reasons for this, including the greater prevalence of lone-parent households (with their higher poverty risk) among the African/Caribbean community.[50] But, most importantly, unemployment rates for certain ethnic minorities have been consistently higher than for white groups: in June 2012 the rates were 7.3% for white people, 15.5% for Black (African or Caribbean) people, 16.6% for Pakistani and 13.5% for Bangladeshi.[51] About one in four black Caribbean and Bangladeshi households did not have a family member in employment. Those from ethnic minorities are also likely to earn less: African/Caribbean and Pakistani men still earned on average up to £6,500 less a year than white men with similar qualifications.[52] Black African/Black Caribbean boys continue to underachieve at school and hence enter the market-place with lower qualifications.

The doubling in the poverty rate and its changing character over recent decades is the product of many different, sometimes conflicting economic and social trends, rather than changes in individual and personal characteristics. Some of these societal changes, such as improved incomes for pensioners and better support for parents, have been positive. But these gains have been more than outweighed by a range of corrosive forces that have, in particular, greatly increased the risk of poverty among those of working age. Especially significant has been decades of upheaval in the market for jobs.

4

Inopportunity Britain:
The work crisis

The things I am missing the most are just going out,
spending time, having a decent meal with my family or
taking my girlfriend out. Or even going for an ice
cream on the beach, sometimes you can't even afford
that. They're the times I really do miss . . . Christmas
presents! Last year I couldn't even afford to get my
mum a Christmas present and I felt really guilty.
Young unemployed, Redcar 2013[1]

In February 2013, Costa Coffee opened a new branch in Mapperley, Nottingham. It advertised eight positions – just three of them full-time. According to the high-street chain, 1,701 applications were received for the posts – over 200 per job. For 95 out of every 100 applicants, the process proved to be futile. Those chasing the posts, offering wages of between £6.10 and £10 an hour, ranged from new graduates to former retail managers (from chains such as HMV and Clinton Cards that had been forced into administration). Many, according to Costa, 'were clearly overqualified for the positions'.

It is a familiar story. In 2010, the retail giant Argos received fourteen thousand applications for seven thousand positions nationwide – twenty chasing every post. Its Longford store in the Midlands received 1,300 applications for just 20 temporary posts to cover the busy Christmas period. That's sixty-five for every job. In 2012, Jaguar announced a thousand vacancies at its plant in Castle Bromwich. There were twenty thousand applicants. Nine out of ten were out of luck. Then, in the summer of 2013, two thousand applied for thirty part-time, minimum-wage jobs in a cinema in West Bromwich.[2]

Marc, from Redcar, knows the pattern all too well. Redcar is a former industrial town based around steel and chemicals, but is now an unemployment black spot. Marc left college in 2009 with two A-levels and a BTEC. But, despite applying for hundreds of mostly low-skilled jobs – from catering to bar work – and apart from a temporary four-month Christmas job in a supermarket depot, he has been out of work more or less continuously since college. He lives off jobseeker's allowance with his rent paid on top. Like many in the same situation, it is barely enough for subsistence.

His mother, who is also struggling financially, provides a little help when she can but that is only occasionally. 'I'm not living, I'm surviving ... it's like rationing on food, rationing on electric and gas, it's not a life at all.' Receiving his benefits fortnightly, he plans his spending with precision: 'At the beginning of the week I put my money into two piles just so I don't overspend: £53 in each pile. It works out at £106 a fortnight. £15 for bus fares, £10 for gas which if you use wisely will last a fortnight and £15 for food.'

Marc suffers from periodic bouts of depression. 'It does take a lot out of you. I may not show it but it does. It's not physically, it's just in your head … 'cos you have to constantly think about money, constantly think about it. Last year I had a mental break-down in my mum's back garden 'cos I couldn't hack it. I couldn't do it. I just couldn't … with all the stress and worrying about money and everything, worrying about money, food on the table, heating, bills, I just couldn't do it.'

The hunt for work

Hunting for work in Britain, especially in areas of high unemployment, has become an increasingly demoralising and often demeaning process. For many it means a life of low income, repetition and constant strain all in the ever-present shadow of an increasingly intrusive Department for Work and Pensions.

Unemployment has a deadening impact on people's lives. 'I think it's scary what lies ahead. If we really sit down and think about it, what lies ahead of us? There's no jobs out there, you know … there's nothing to look forward to,' is what one woman said in a community focus group in County Derry held in late 2013 and supported by the PSE project. 'My husband has been dealing with depression. He's fed up being in the house, he's exhausted looking for work, he feels useless,' is how another woman in the same group described the effect of the lack of hope on her husband. 'He's at the point where he won't take the children to school or lift them because he doesn't want anybody to see him not working.' [3]

In the autumn of 2014, just under two million people were unemployed in the UK – a rate of six percent. Although the jobless rate rose by less than expected from 2008, compared with earlier recessions, and has been falling, from a peak of 2.7 million (8.3%) at the height of the recession towards the end of 2011, it remains high by immediate post-war standards. In the first quarter of 2014, it was also still higher in every nation and region of the UK, and among every age group, than at the start of the recession in 2008.[4]

In the golden days of the 1950s and 1960s, the best economic brains used to debate whether the unemployment rate that was consistent with capping inflation was two or three percent. Since 1980 the rate has averaged over seven percent. Figure 18 shows that in the two immediate post-war decades, the problem of the mass unemployment of the 1930s had been largely cracked. The unemployment rate averaged 1.6% and few people were out of work for long.

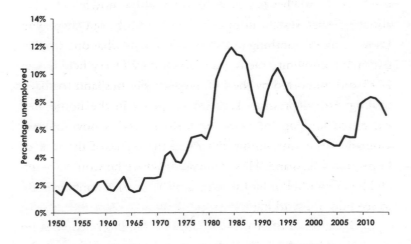

Figure 18: The lengthening dole queue, UK: 1950–2013[5]

Today, the headline unemployment figures also understate the scale of the modern jobs crisis. Workless levels are not just higher than in the immediate post-war decades – the unemployed are typically out of work for longer while the long-term unemployed are especially likely to face blighted futures. In the 1950s, the proportion of the unemployed out of work for more than a year stood at nine percent. Today it is over a third.[6] There has also been a steady rise in the level of enforced 'underemployment' – people working shorter hours than they would prefer – mainly because of the growing prevalence of part-time jobs. While many of those working part-time do so by choice, large numbers would prefer full-time work.[7]

A clear sign of growing fragility has been the big rise in the numbers classifying themselves as self-employed, a figure that now stands at above 4.6 million, with the numbers growing by 700,000 since the start of the financial crisis. This group now accounts for more than fifteen percent of the workforce compared with nine percent in 1975.[8] While some in this group are self-starting professionals and entrepreneurs, and many are going down this route by choice, its growth is another sign of lack of opportunity, with many forced to take this option because of growing desperation at failing to find work. There is also evidence of rising pressure from Jobcentres on the jobless to become self-employed in an attempt to reduce the unemployment count, similar to the strategy of the 1980s of switching unemployed people to incapacity benefits. Moreover, many of the newly self-employed earn very little indeed. This is especially so with self-employed women, who earned forty percent less than self-employed men in 2012.[9]

Over the last forty years, rising numbers of the workforce have been denied access to secure, decently paid work with reasonable prospects. A sizeable proportion of the jobs available today are part-time, poorly paid, temporary and offer very limited opportunities for further progress.

Figure 19 from the 2012 PSE survey shows that, on average, around a fifth of those currently employed or self-employed do not think that 'their job is secure'. Although those who are most worried are those with the lowest incomes, the insecurity spreads up the income scale, with many of those in middle-income and higher-paid, professional jobs also fearful of job upheaval.

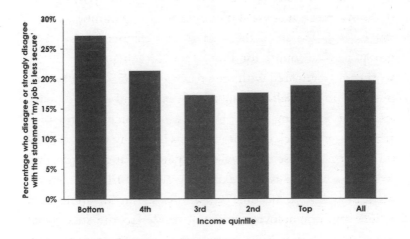

Figure 19: Job insecurity, UK: 2012
(Disagree or strongly disagree with
statement: 'my job is secure')

Not only are good jobs scarce, but Britain has become an increasingly low-paid economy, with the proportion of the workforce on low wages (by the standard measure of those earning less than two-thirds of the national median hourly wage) almost doubling over the last thirty years. It now stands at twenty-one percent, up from twelve percent in the early 1980s. As shown in Figure 20, the UK now takes second place – behind the US – in the global low-paid league table for rich nations.

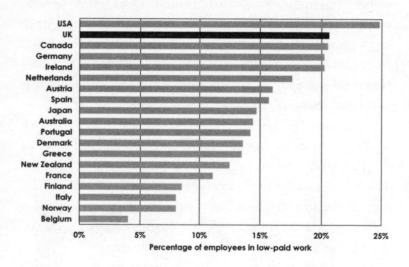

Figure 20: Proportion of employees in low-paid work, by country: 2010[10]

Of course, not all of the low paid are in poor households, especially where other adults are in work. But the strength of the labour market, the pattern of job opportunities and the level of employment protection have a critical influence on levels of poverty. One of the results of decades of unrelenting change has been a steady polarisation of jobs. While there has been a growth of well-paid, high-skill, high-productivity professional and managerial jobs towards the top, there has been a steady loss of secure, middle-income jobs and a rise in the number of routine and poorly paid jobs towards the bottom.[11]

One of the most enduring trends of the twentieth century had been the expansion of a middle social group, not just in the UK but across much of the globe. In the immediate post-war decades, this meant more of a continuum in jobs and wages with more intermediate, middle-skill, middle-income employment that filled the gap between semi- and unskilled blue-collar and higher paying professional jobs. This growth helped build a ladder for pay and job advancement and became the stepping stone for social progression and the reduction of poverty.

In the mid 1950s, the celebrated sociologist C. Wright Mills wrote that American society had become 'less a pyramid with a flat base than a fat diamond with a bulging middle'. By the 1960s, the social pattern of the United Kingdom was also conforming to a 'diamond shape' with a small group of the rich and the poor and a large middle. Sociologists talked of 'embourgeoisement' and declared the class war to be over.

In recent decades, as this middle group has been steadily hollowed out, that 'bulge' has been disappearing. In the UK – as well as in the US and a rising number of other rich nations – the social shape of the workforce has come to resemble a distorted hourglass with a small bulge of the super-rich at the top, a much larger bulge at the bottom and an increasingly thin stem in the middle.[12]

It is a trend that is set to continue. Of those jobs created since 2009, some are in highly paid sectors like business activities, but most have been in low-paid sectors such as catering, retail, office cleaning and residential care.[13] Meanwhile, the number of middle-income jobs – in sectors such as retail banking and local- and central-government administration – is continuing to contract, driven by an ongoing process of automation, outsourcing and business and government restructuring.[14] Britain is riddled with examples of 'bumping down' and downward 'absolute' job mobility – of ex-retail managers applying for jobs as coffee baristas, of former skilled factory workers cleaning cars or working as airport baggage handlers, of trained draughtsmen and IT specialists forced into temporary work in retail or taxi-driving, often with long gaps of unemployment in between.[15] The squeeze on job opportunities has brought rising levels of skills under-utilisation with significant numbers unable to find work appropriate for their skills and experience and having to moderate their job and pay aspirations.[16] The risk of poverty has, as a result, been extending up the income and class scale, threatening those who have formerly enjoyed a comfortable standard of living closer to the middle than the bottom of the income ladder.

The Institute for Employment Research at Warwick University predicts that up to a million skilled and semi-skilled jobs in sectors like secretarial and manufacturing will have been lost by 2020.[17] The stem of the wages hour glass is set to become a good deal thinner and the bulge at the bottom considerably bigger.

Despite the much-heralded end of the recession, average wage rises have continued to lag behind prices until the autumn of 2014. The Resolution Foundation think-tank predicts that those of working age in the bottom half of the income distribution will still be worse off in 2020 than they were at the start of the crisis. 'A typical low income household in 2020 is set to have an income 15 per cent lower than an equivalent household in 2008 . . . A typical middle income household in 2020 is set to have an income 3 per cent below that of 2008.'[18]

What these trends have created is a growing 'aspirations gap'. At one level, the replacement of factory by clerical and white-collar service jobs in the UK has led to an apparent upward shift in the class structure. In the four decades to 2007, the proportion of the population classified as 'working class' fell from seventy to forty-four percent, while the 'middle class' rose from thirty-one to fifty-five percent.[19] But this is largely an illusion. If the workforce is ranked by incomes, the social shape of Britain looks very different than if it is ranked by nominal class position. This reclassification up the class ladder has not been matched by a parallel rise in relative wages and opportunities and the jobs themselves are often routine. As the late cultural critic and historian Richard Hoggart wrote in his 1989 introduction to George Orwell's *The Road to Wigan Pier,* 'Class distinctions do not die: they merely find new ways of expressing themselves . . . Each decade, we shiftily declare we have buried class; each decade the coffin stays empty.'

A more aggressive model of capitalism

Britain's jobs and pay crisis has multiple causes. It is in part the product of long-term industrial decline going back at least to the 1960s, with the accelerating process of de-industrialisation during the 1980s one of the principal drivers of the rise in

poverty through that decade.[20] The brunt of the loss of manufacturing jobs – four million between 1966 and 1990 – was
borne by middle-aged and older men who had worked all
their lives in the industrial heartlands. By the late 1980s, some
700,000 people who failed to find alternative work had been
transferred from unemployment to invalidity or sickness
benefit, a deliberate policy designed to lower the headline
unemployment figures.

The period took a high psychological and social toll on
individuals, families and whole communities. As studies in
subsequent years showed, many of those losing their jobs in
the 1980s never worked again, and the victims were often left
with deteriorating health, depression and growing debt.
'Day-to-day living becomes marked by: inadequate diet; reliance on second-hand clothing; insufficient furniture;
inefficient heating systems; inability to participate in active
forms of social life and corresponding reliance on passive
forms of social contact such as television; social isolation and
monotony; and fragile money management, where even relatively minor "crises" cannot be accommodated, carrying with
it high levels of stress and anxiety.'[21]

As well as being fuelled by Britain's manufacturing decline,
essentially external factors such as globalisation, technical
change and high levels of immigration have also been at work.
The opening up of Western economies to new sources of
competition has led to a shift of jobs to developing economies
and brought downward pressure on wages, though some
mature economies have proved more successful at resisting
such pressures. The emergence of global markets has made
labour much more plentiful internationally, strengthening the

bargaining power of domestic employers. The speeding up of technological change has, by increasing the demand for skilled workers and depressing it for those without skills, also contributed to the changing patterns of work, pay and opportunity. High rates of immigration have added to the pressure, increasing the supply of labour and the level of competition for work in some sectors of the economy, while filling skill gaps in others.

But these factors are only part of the story. Deteriorating opportunities are also the direct product of an about-turn in the country's political economy. At the end of the 1970s, fighting the rising rate of inflation became the number-one economic goal, displacing the former priority given to maintaining full employment. The instruments used – tight monetary and fiscal policies and a strong pound – accelerated long-term de-industrialisation, while triggering mass unemployment. The critical decision in the 1980s to adopt a more aggressive, market-oriented model of capitalism led to the sweeping away of regulations, the favouring of finance over manufacturing, the outsourcing of public sector jobs, relentless pressure on companies to cut labour costs and, critically, an assault on labour's bargaining power.

Cabinet papers for 1983 reveal that Mrs Thatcher admonished Norman Tebbit for being too timid on trade union reform, telling him we 'should neglect no opportunity to erode union membership'.[22] In Britain the proportion of the workforce covered by collective bargaining has fallen from around eighty percent in 1979 to below twenty-five percent today (fifteen percent in the case of private sector workers). This is one of the lowest levels of coverage among rich nations, adding to the heavily skewed and economically unhealthy concentration of corporate power.[23] The UK stands at twenty-first place out of twenty-seven countries in the European Union in terms of workplace representation, though parts of the European continent are also seeing more recent falls in the level of coverage, though from a much higher base.

Britain's much-vaunted 'flexible labour market', engineered during the 1980s to give business greater freedom to hire and fire, was necessary, it was claimed, to enable domestic firms to compete in an increasingly globalised economy. Such freedom for employers has continued to be championed by subsequent governments. Yet, just as over-restrictive labour laws can be bad news for dynamism, so can underrestrictive laws.

Britain's low-wage, high-unemployment economy is as much the product of these internal, political forces as of external, economic ones. Indeed, it was later admitted by one of Mrs Thatcher's top economic advisers that one of the government's central aims was the taming of labour. 'The nightmare I sometimes have about this whole experience runs as follows ... there may have been people making the actual policy decisions ... who never believed for a moment that this was the correct way to bring down inflation. They did, however, see that it would be a very, very good way to raise unemployment.' This was how Sir Alan Budd, chief economic adviser at the Treasury in the 1980s, summed up – in 1992 – the multilayered assault on inflation and the unions. He continued: 'And raising unemployment was an extremely desirable way of reducing the strength of the working classes ... what was engineered there, in Marxist terms, was a crisis of capitalism which created a reserve army of labour and has allowed the capitalists to make high profits ever since.' [24]

The steering of bargaining power away from labour in favour of capital has been a key factor in the steady erosion of wages and conditions of employment, especially among those in the bottom half of the earnings distribution, and the main driver of the growing income gap of the last three decades. Between the war and the early 1970s, the share of income going to wages in the UK settled at an historic high – an average of fifty-nine percent – with business having to settle for lower profits and a better-paid workforce. After 1980, the share of national income going in wages began to fall, and it stands at some fifty-three percent today, with the workforce receiving around £90 billion less (some six percent of national income) than if the wage share had held its post-war average. [25]

This shift has been reinforced by a growing wage divide. Between 1979 and 2008, real gross earnings for those at the top grew almost four times as fast as those at the bottom. As a result, most of this fall in the wage share has been borne by those on middle and low earnings, with the bottom third facing a sustained double-edged squeeze – a shrinking share of a diminishing pool. These shifts have had major repercussions for the shape of the earnings distribution and the extent of poverty pay.

In parts of the UK – outside the prosperous belts such as parts of London and the South-East where the top part of the hourglass is concentrated – economic choices have become more and more limited. Former factories have been replaced by little more than car parks, cut-price retail outlets and warehouses. In Stoke, the once thriving Staffordshire Pottery is now a B&Q. In the Brierley Hill area of the West Midlands, the Marsh and Baxter's meat processing plant, once the biggest in Europe, is now a shopping centre.

Because of the concentration of joblessness and low pay, some areas have become hollowed out, with families lacking the purchasing power to sustain much private-sector activity, contributing to localised decline. In 2007, Barnsley had 274 VAT-registered businesses per 10,000 adults, Liverpool 241 and Plymouth 233, compared to a national average of 415.[26] Although other factors have also been at work, the weakness of spending power has played an important role in the decline of the high street, a much greater problem in poorer parts of Britain, contributing to the rise of local 'food deserts' – neighbourhoods where cheap, healthy food is often absent. Some of Britain's poorest areas have high streets that are dominated by loan shops, pawnbrokers, charity shops, and discount/pound stores. Even McDonald's fled Rochdale's high street in 2011, followed by other household names.

The shift to an increasingly low-paid economy has been tempered in part by the introduction of the national minimum wage in 1999. Today, just over a million workers are paid the national minimum, £6.50 an hour for those over 21 (from October 2014), concentrated in industries such as tourism, retail and food processing. But with widespread non-compliance and few prosecutions, an estimated 280,000 jobs in Britain are paid – illegally – less than the minimum wage especially in cash-in-hand informal sectors such as construction and catering.[27] Close to five million earn less than the 'living wage' – £8.80 an hour in London and £7.65 outside – a level calculated by The Living Wage Foundation to be needed to provide an adequate standard of living for an average household after tax and in-work benefits.[28]

When introduced, the expectation was that minimum-wage jobs would act as the first rung of a ladder but, with fewer middle-income jobs available, advancement opportunities have been drying up. In 2012, 1.9 million people (7.6% of all employees) earned within 25p of the minimum wage, twice the proportion in 2002.[29] Because of the persistence of the gender pay gap, women (and part-time workers) are especially vulnerable. Indeed the gender pay gap widened in 2012 for the first time in five years, and in 2013 stood at nearly twenty percent for median hourly earnings (excluding overtime). The World Economic Forum's annual Global Gender Gap report for 2014 finds the UK slipping down the international league, ranked forty-eighth out of 142 countries for labour-force participation and wage equality and sixty-fourth for estimated earned income.[30]

The rise of insecurity

The squeeze on pay has been compounded by the growth of 'bad jobs' offering minimal rights and security. The online retailer Amazon has become is a highly successful company in part by pushing other, traditional retailers such as HMV and the bookshop chain Borders, along with hundreds of independents, out of business. Yet it is notorious for the poor conditions of work, insecurity and low pay in its distribution warehouses. 'You're sort of like a robot, but in human form,' admitted one Amazon manager to a *Financial Times* reporter. 'It's human automation, if you like.' 'Our culture is friendly and intense,' the billionaire founder of Amazon, Jeff Bezos, told *Forbes* magazine, 'but if push comes to shove, we'll settle for intense.'[31]

Many jobs in the bottom bulge of the hourglass are found at the periphery of the labour market in what the academic Guy Standing has called 'the precariat' – marginal, precarious and irregular, offering few rights, rock-bottom wages, coercive management, intensified labour processes, unsocial hours and high rates of job turnover.[32] Indeed a mix of temporary contracts, reliance on agency staff, demanding targets and low pay are increasingly common across sectors as diverse as car manufacturing, food processing and hotels. Evidence has been growing of the widespread abuse of staff by employment agencies – including non-payment of wages and the denial of holiday and sick pay.[33]

The rapid spread of zero-hour contracts is part of this trend, another side effect of deregulation. Firms using such contracts include Cineworld, McDonald's, the retailer Sports Direct and a large number of care-home suppliers.[34] A decade ago such contracts barely existed. More than one-in-ten employers now use them. The Office for National Statistics, under intense pressure to reveal the full extent of the practice, estimated that, in the spring of 2014, 1.4 million were on such 'no guaranteed hours' contracts. This was a sevenfold rise over its much-queried 2011 estimate (one that was little more than a guess).

While some employees – including some students – are content with the flexibility on offer, most have little choice. Such contracts offer little or no guarantee of work or pay and have come to be widely abused. For firms they allow the circumvention of employment rights, leaving employees without entitlements to holiday, sick pay and other benefits.

In a number of industries the concept of a minimum wage

has also become meaningless. The hot house industry that is social care employs more than a million people, many on zero-hours contracts. Before the start of outsourcing, from the 1980s, care was mostly provided directly by local authorities with staff enjoying decent pay and conditions. With privatisation, conditions of work have deteriorated, a process that has accelerated since 2010 with the austerity-driven squeeze on council budgets.

Many care providers – a mix of private firms and voluntary sector organisations – have responded to heavy funding cuts by further eroding staff conditions and pay. In 2013, the tax authorities found that, because of deductions for items such as uniform costs and a refusal to pay travel time between jobs, half of 183 private care firms investigated had in effect been paying less than the minimum wage.[35] On a visit to care providers in the West Midlands, members of the Low Pay Commission learned that some providers forced their staff to run around 'like headless chickens'. One care worker had been given her rota for the weekend late on Friday evening. She had 25 calls to make on the Saturday and 27 on Sunday, an increasingly typical pattern.[36]

While social care is very poorly funded, the erosion of pay has also been a by-product of the privatisation of often non- or only partially unionised providers, many of them owned by private equity houses where good employment practices are a very low priority. Care services are increasingly operated in a commercial environment where profit is made through franchising, financial engineering and property deals. In the intense pressure to win contacts, firms have attempted to maintain service levels by cutting pay and offering poorer conditions of employment in areas from pensions to overtime payments. In one example, care workers at a former NHS-run home for people with severe learning difficulties in Doncaster took protracted industrial action when the company buying up the privatised home, Care UK, imposed pay cuts of up to a third on already low-paid workers, while bringing in new workers on lower rates.[37]

Companies – large and small – are constantly on the lookout for ways of paying their staff less, some employing recruitment agencies to advise on pay-cutting loopholes. Even large, highly profitable companies employ people on the basis of contracts apparently designed to cut wages.

One hundred years ago, the eminent historian and social reformer R. H. Tawney vividly described the experience of a casualised labour market: 'The havoc wrought by casual labour, the prevalence in certain industries of "blind alley" employment, the systematic exploitation of cheap juvenile labour by firms which take on successive relays of children, employ them "for their immediate commercial utility" and dismiss them, when they demand higher wages, to make room for another batch, which will be dismissed in its turn.'[38]

Tawney's description has uncanny parallels with today. Casualised labour is the norm in a growing number of industries, with employment practices that are taking us too often back to the Dark Ages, reversing many of the gains in employment rights battled for and won over decades. A study by Cambridge University of one large supermarket chain found that its 'super-flexible' working conditions had damaged the mental health of many employees. 'It is the invidious way that vulnerable people at the low end of the labour market are forced to live their lives ... People and their families are suffering enormous levels of anxiety and even mental illness because of what is fast becoming common practice.' Ever-increasing flexible working practices, they concluded, are 'creating a culture of servitude – trapping people in vicious cycles of instability, stress and a struggle to make ends meet'.[39]

The PSE research finds that the toll of current working practices on people is widespread and increasing. Figure 21 shows that the proportion of the population facing some degree of stress has risen since 1999, in some cases sharply. Just over thirty-four per cent said they felt 'constantly under strain' in 2012 compared with twenty-six per cent in 1999, while the proportion losing sleep because of worry rose from nineteen to thirty-one percent.

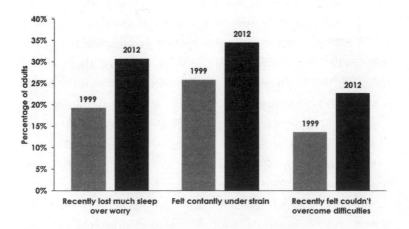

Figure 21: The extent of strain and stress among adults, Britain: 1999 and 2012

The percentage who had each problem 'rather more than usual' or 'much more than usual'

These three measures are part of a set of twelve indicators commonly used to examine mental health and with the exception of one – the ability to concentrate, for which there was little change – all show similar increases. Overall, the proportion of those who lack four or more of these twelve indicators – the level widely used as an indicator of poor mental health – has risen from 18% in 1999 to 28.6% in 2012.[40]

The hardest hit

These ongoing upheavals in work and pay have mostly been borne by those in the lower half of the income hierarchy. In the post-war, new deal, high-employment years, all groups – the high- and low-paid alike – enjoyed rising pay and opportunities roughly in line with growing prosperity. Since the 1980s, rising numbers have ended up in a wages, living standards and opportunities slow lane, leaving a growing section of the population badly behind even as the cake has continued to grow. That lane started to move even more slowly from shortly after the turn of the century, and began going backwards during the crisis years.[41]

The steady deterioration in working practices have hit those with children or other caring responsibilities, and those with disabilities, particularly hard. If you can't predict your weekly wage or when you will be working, it is very difficult to organise – and afford – the care arrangements needed to enable you to go out to work. The lack of affordable, quality childcare across all ages, compatible with unpredictable working hours – evenings, weekends and nights – means that these sorts of jobs are not just unsuitable but also often simply unobtainable.

While anti-discrimination legislation has created more employment opportunities for people with an impairment (such as lack of mobility or restricted vision) it has done little for those whose impairments are accompanied by ill health, such as fatigue or chronic pain, as well as the growing number with mental-health problems. People with impairments continue to face very high levels of disadvantage in the labour market, with significant barriers imposed by firms, even when supported in managing their illness, while the growth of insecure work is making matters far worse. As Jenny Morris, an experienced consultant on disability policy, puts it: 'Current working practices and developments in the labour market (insecure employment, long hours, low wages) are bad for people's health and are incompatible with enabling anyone with poor and/or fluctuating health to maximise their ability and opportunities to work.' [12]

In a further twist of the 'inopportunity cycle', an important consequence of these trends – the hollowing out of the middle, the earnings squeeze, the rise of precarious, low-skill, low-productivity jobs – has been the erosion of upward job and income progression. The post-war, 'new deal' era of improving pay and opportunity for almost all has been replaced by a series of new constraints on upward mobility, with a much tighter cap on aspirations and the ability to rise. For some this has meant a flattening of opportunities; for others a fall, while the routes out of poverty have been increasingly closed off. Although real wages have increased on average over the last thirty years, large numbers are in jobs offering weaker prospects and sometimes lower real pay than their parents enjoyed at a comparable age.[43]

These restricted opportunities apply in particular between generations. The group that now faces the most precarious future is the young. Through the financial crisis, youth unemployment rose at twice the average rate and during 2014 stood at nearly three times the national average. Among those who left school at sixteen without five good GCSEs, a half had no job in mid-2014. As the Prince's Trust described it: 'If we lined up Britain's unemployed young people, the job queue would stretch from London to Middlesbrough.'[44] On top of this, some 950,000 young people aged sixteen to twenty-four in the UK were, in the middle of 2014, not in employment but also not in education or training. This group, known as NEETS (not in employment, education or training), has been growing in size for the last twenty years, apparently immune to a plethora of policy initiatives. With long spells of unemployment when young often bringing perpetual disadvantage, David Blanchflower, a former member of the Bank of England's Monetary Policy Committee, has called the plight of the young 'a national disaster in the making'.[45]

When the young do get work, they are much more likely to work in low-paid sectors, while through the recession real wages fell more sharply among the young than for any other group.[46] Three times more young women were found to be employed in low-paid, low-skilled jobs in 2012 than twenty years earlier.[47] The proportion of recent graduates working in non-graduate, often low-skilled jobs rose by a fifth after 2008 to reach forty-seven percent by 2013. In the fiercely competitive hothouse of Britain's jobs market, this also means fewer jobs for non-graduates.[48]

While graduate recruitment picked up through 2014, and the overall unemployment rate continued to fall, those who left university for the dole queue still risk facing greatly restricted future choices. 'The ill-effects of economic hard times have been concentrated on one particular generation, despite the way in which they are also better qualified than their predecessors', concluded a study by the London School of Economics.[49]

Despite the urgency of the situation, many initiatives by the coalition government have hurt the young disproportionately. The educational maintenance allowance – which helped thousands of adolescents aged over 18 and from poorer households to stay on in education – was abolished; the budget for careers guidance in schools has been cut sharply, while the Future Jobs Fund, set up by the previous government, was axed. The Fund was introduced in 2009 to address long-term youth unemployment. About 100,000 people aged eighteen to twenty-four and out of work for a year (later reduced to six months) or more were guaranteed a job for six months. A short while after it was cancelled, one of the DWP's own studies found it had been a great success. 'The bottom line', concluded the independent National Institute of Economic and Social Research, 'is that the impact of the Future Jobs Fund on the chances of participants being employed and/or off benefit was substantial, significant and positive.'[50] In contrast, the replacement Youth Contract scheme, providing temporary wage subsidies to employers if they provide a six-month 'job start' for under-twenty-fives, has been branded a failure by the Social Mobility and Child Poverty Commission.[51]

The 'jinxed' or 'jilted' generation, as they have been dubbed – young people born around 1990 – are, according to the *Financial Times*, 'the first generation to see their incomes stagnate in relation to their forbears'.[52] This historic disadvantage holds even more strongly for those from poorer and middle-income backgrounds, where they are much less likely to enjoy financial support from parents, and to inherit wealth.

Blaming the victim

What is remarkable is the increasing dichotomy between the reality of the modern job market for millions of workers and the assumptions of recent policy. Despite the brittle nature of the jobs market, successive governments – of all persuasions – have viewed those of working age in poverty less as victims than as architects of their own misfortune. Ministers have mostly blamed the problems of low pay and unemployment on individuals – on a culture of worklessness, an anti-work ethic, excessive job or wage expectations and inadequate skills and qualifications – rather than on the absence of an adequate supply of secure, decently paid jobs.

There are plenty of jobs, it is argued, but the unemployed lack the motivation, skills or willingness to take them. On this interpretation, state intervention should be limited to improving the *supply of labour* through a mix of better education and training on the one hand, and benefit penalties on the other. Indeed, the thrust of recent benefits policy towards the unemployed has been one of growing harshness, built around the greatly exaggerated idea of a culture of antipathy to work.

Of course, better education and training and improved skills are vital, and there are serious skills mismatches in the UK. But as the PSE 2012 survey shows, poverty is not confined to those with the lowest qualifications. While those with GCSE grades

D to G or less make up fourteen percent of the poor, fifteen percent of the poor are graduates, twenty-two percent have A-levels or equivalent and thirty-three percent have good GCSEs. Though poor qualifications certainly raise the risk sharply (see Figure 15), poverty is far from confined to this group.

As David Webster of the University of Glasgow has shown, Whitehall has long taken the view that the 'continuing concentrations of worklessness were a supply-side, not a demand-side phenomenon'.[53] Such views were promoted by the Treasury and the DWP through the boom conditions of the Labour years. Even with the higher levels of unemployment of the post-2008 crisis years, ministers liked to argue that the aggregate number of unemployed claimants has been roughly equal to the aggregate number of job vacancies, with the implication that high unemployment is completely unnecessary.

In February 2012, Maria Miller, minister in the Department for Work and Pensions, told the BBC that the UK does not have 'a shortage of jobs'. 'If you actually look at the facts and the figures, there are 400,000 jobs at any one point in jobcentres,' she told 5 Live listeners. 'I was up in the Wirral on Friday talking to one of our local jobcentres there and there isn't a shortage of jobs. What there can be is a lack of an appetite for some of the jobs that are available.'

The facts suggest otherwise. While there were around 400,000 vacancies across the UK at the beginning of 2012, the official count of unemployed people – those actively looking for work and available to start immediately – stood at 2.69 million. At the height of the recession, when Miller claimed there was no problem, there were around six unemployed people for each job vacancy.

Moreover, job vacancies and unemployment rates are very unevenly spread. In areas such as Hartlepool in the North-East of England, and north and east Ayrshire in Scotland, for example, the ratio of unemployed to job vacancies has remained three times higher than the national average.[54] These ratios also understate the scale of the jobs shortage because the 'hidden unemployed' – a mix of the 'underemployed' and the 'economically inactive' (including those out of work on disability benefits) – are excluded. In early 2014, in addition to the official measure of 2.4 million unemployed, there were almost as many people out of the labour force (and not counting as unemployed) and wanting to work. In addition, many vacancies listed in Jobcentres are duplicates or temporary, while one investigation found that one in fifty jobs on the government's job-matching website – which it is mandatory for people on jobseeker's allowance to use – are fake.[55]

The evidence is of a strong work ethic in the UK, that most of the unemployed are desperate for a decent job, and they are persistent appliers for work. While there are undoubtedly some who would rather not work, the problem is much less one of a lack of desire than the intense competition for the jobs that are available. One late-2000s study of Middlesbrough, an area of high unemployment in the North-East of England, found a 'resilience and lasting work commitment', one 'learned across the generations'. [56]

According to the Chartered Institute for Personnel and Development, in mid-2013, there were forty-five applicants for every unskilled job vacancy in the UK – with twenty-nine applying for every medium-skilled role. Such is the competition, many employers overwhelmed with applications told the CIPD they would not even consider school-leavers or the long-term unemployed.[57] The scramble for work has been fuelled, in turn, by the way those losing better-paid jobs are competing in low-skilled sectors.

Moreover, despite the repeated claim that work is the route out of poverty, a job too often fails to provide a solution. Half of all children in poverty (lacking two or more child necessities) are in families where at least one adult works full-time while a further fifteen percent are in families where adults work but only part-time. In particular, part-time working does not substantially reduce the risk of poverty, which for children in families where the adults work part-time is almost as high as it is for those in families in which most adults are unemployed.

The poverty risk also rises sharply for those in routine or semi-routine jobs. Figure 22 from the PSE study shows the relative risks for those in managerial and professional work compared with those in routine and semi-routine work by the length of time spent unemployed.[58] For those in routine and semi-routine jobs, twenty-seven percent are in poverty (lacking three or more necessities) even if they have not been unemployed within the last five years. This rises to thirty-five percent for those unemployed for under twelve months, and to forty-eight percent for those with a period of unemployment of over twelve months in the last five years. For all types of work, experience of long periods of unemployment raises the poverty rate, even for those currently in managerial and professional work.

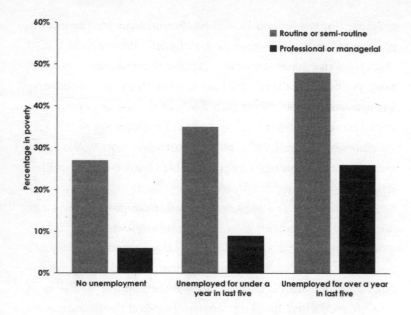

Figure 22: Risk of poverty for the employed, by type of work and experience of unemployment, UK: 2012

The frailties of today's labour market mean that many of those dependent on low-paid, insecure jobs, especially those with poor qualifications and skills, move in and out of work in a 'low-pay, no-pay' cycle, increasingly locked-in at the bottom. Because of the precariousness of many low-paid jobs, men at the bottom of the earnings distribution are nearly three times as likely, and women twice as likely, to leave work within a year as compared with those at the top. In addition, such jobs mostly offer few prospects.

The growth of 'recurrent poverty' is a direct product of the steady deterioration in economic prospects and Britain's increasingly polarised labour market. As a study by Chris

Goulden for the Joseph Rowntree Foundation, on the unemployment and low-pay cycle, finds: 'People's personal characteristics have some impact on the risks of recurrent poverty but structural labour market factors remain the strongest influence.'[59] Another study, of the job experience of young men in Scotland, concludes: 'Employment insecurity tended not to reflect negative attitudes . . . it was almost entirely a consequence of the "flexible" nature of low skilled employment in modern Britain.'[60]

A study for the DWP found that a third of poor families (on the official sixty percent of median measure) who moved into work in the period from 2001–06 did not manage to escape poverty by doing so, and some of those that did escape subsequently ended up back in poverty at some point in the next three years.[61] The Middlesbrough study found that, 'contrary to the view that "employment is the best route out of poverty", the sorts of work available to the interviewees kept them in poverty rather than lifting them out of it . . . individuals and households would repeatedly experience poverty both when in work and out of it.'[62]

Britain's increasingly entrenched 'cycle of inopportunity' is trapping rising numbers of people of working age in or close to poverty, moving in and out of low-paid work. Over relatively short periods of time, there are only limited movements between income levels with few people raising their incomes substantially. An analysis by the Work Foundation compared changes in earnings of the same group between 2001/02 and 2008/09. It found that one-third of those who were in the bottom tenth of earners in 2001/02 remained there seven years later, while around sixty percent stayed in the bottom third of earners: 'a sizeable proportion of low-earners are finding themselves trapped at the bottom-end of the labour market and are unable to increase their earnings significantly even over a relatively long period.'[63] The occupations that saw the least movement out of the bottom were sales and customer service, elementary occupations (involving routine tasks requiring minimal skill or qualifications) and personal services (such as care of the elderly and childcare). For those who do rise out of poverty, most do not rise very far above it.

On current trends, the post-recession era is likely to leave large sections of the workforce trailing any increase in prosperity, and increasingly vulnerable to forces outside their control. Despite this, Britain's system of social security has been the subject of a series of fundamental reforms that will open up bigger holes in the social safety net.

5

Punishing the poor: Benefits 'big bang'

---

*Don't push me in a statistic before you get to know
me, like learn about my aspirations before you make an
assumption about me.*
Young unemployed, Birmingham 2013[1]

During the 2010 general election campaign, the Conservative
party launched an anti-welfare poster campaign in marginal
constituencies. Focused on the unemployed, one poster –
shown in Figure 23 – featured the party's leader, David Cameron,
with the caption 'Let's cut benefits for those who refuse to
work'. While negative portrayals of benefit claimants are far
from new, they have become more frequent and more strident.
Following the election, new coalition ministers began to talk
of too many getting 'something for nothing', while the old
distinction between the 'deserving' and 'undeserving' poor was
dressed up in new language: 'workers and strivers' versus 'shirkers and skivers'. Here was a new 'them-and-us' approach to
policy, one that blamed the unemployed themselves for lacking
a job, and those with disabilities for not trying hard enough. As

Iain Duncan Smith, the secretary of state for Work and Pensions, had put it, 'the nature of the life you lead and the choices that you make have a significant bearing on whether you live in poverty.'[2]

Figure 23: Conservative party election poster, 2010

Public and official attitudes towards the poor, and especially the unemployed, tend, like other aspects of the poverty debate, to go in cycles. The most draconian law against the poor was introduced in 1547. 'In light of complaints against idleness and vagabondrie it is therefore enacted that if any man or woman able to work should refuse to labour, and live idly for three days, that he or she, should be branded with a red-hot iron on the breast with a letter V, and should be adjudged the slaves for three years of any person who should inform against the said idler.'[3]

This emphasis on punishment was eventually relaxed under the various Poor Law Acts of the Elizabethan era which introduced some minimal levels of relief. But during the early nineteenth century, policy again came to be driven by the idea that poverty was down to a failure of character and moral weakness, with the role of the state limited to encouraging people to find their own way out of destitution. The Poor Law Amendment Act of 1834 placed the workhouse at the centre of provision, with a central guiding principle of 'less eligibility' – that workhouse conditions should be worse than the lowest living standards available to a working labourer, 'that every penny bestowed which renders the lot of the pauper more eligible than that of the lowest-paid independent labourer is a bounty on indolence and vice'.[4] The workhouse imposed a harsh and monotonous life – with the separation of married couples, bad food, strict discipline and attempts to improve moral character. The aim was to prevent starvation, not poverty, and to force paupers to search for whatever employment could be found.

Today's policies towards the poor are, of course, nowhere near as harsh as those of the 1800s, but there are parallels in the tone of the debate. During the coalition years, the anti-poor rhetoric flowed, with poverty blamed on irresponsible behaviour.[5] Social security, according to the chancellor of the exchequer, George Osborne, encourages people to make a 'lifestyle choice to just sit on out-of-work benefits'.[6] At the Conservative party conference in 2012, he added spice to this idea: 'Where is the fairness, we ask, for the shift-worker, leaving home in the dark hours of the early morning, who looks up at the closed blinds of their next-door neighbour sleeping off a life on benefits.'[7] Justifying reforms to the incapacity benefit system, employment minister Chris Grayling claimed: 'We now know very clearly that the vast majority of new claimants for sickness benefits are in fact able to return to work.'[8]

While such language may have become more colourful, it is not confined to Conservative ministers. In government from 1997, Labour ministers also liked to present the party as tough on benefits and set out to create a sterner set of rules on access. As the then shadow work secretary Liam Byrne reminded Labour's annual conference in 2010: 'Let's face the tough truth – that many people on the doorstep at the last election felt that too often we were for shirkers, not workers.'[9]

In opposition during the 2000s, the Conservatives attempted to present a more 'compassionate face', adopting a more moderate stance towards the poor. 'In modern times, poverty has been a difficult issue for the Conservative Party to deal with,' wrote Duncan Smith in 2006. 'However ... it is too important an issue to be left to the Labour Party.' [10] Once in government, however, they reverted to historic type, adopting a much more punitive stance towards the poor, or one of 'tough love' as they prefer to see it.

Outside the realm of Westminster politics, the debate could not be more different. Both the Welsh Assembly and the Scottish Parliament have taken a much more sympathetic attitude towards the plight of the poor, and a positive view of welfare. In May 2013, the Welsh Assembly agreed to appoint a cabinet minister with a primary brief to tackle poverty. The first ever such appointment in the UK, the move was prompted by what the new minister, Hugh Lewis, described as an austerity wave over Wales that 'will bring hardship on a scale comparable to the 1930s and a testing of community resilience not seen since the coalmine and steel factory closures of the 1980s'.[11]

In Scotland, much of the impassioned debate in the lead-up to the independence vote on 18 September 2014 concentrated on the welfare policies of, and cuts imposed by, the Westminster government. 'The era of Tory governments unelected by the people of Scotland handing out punishment to the poor and the disabled will be gone and gone for good,' thundered Alex Salmond, first minister of Scotland and leader of the SNP.[12] Entering the debate in the weeks running up to the vote, Gordon Brown, former prime minister, appealed to Labour voters to support the pro-UK 'Better Together' campaign on the basis that independence would mean that 'inequality and poverty will survive until doomsday if Alex Salmond is all that confronts it'. The poorest would suffer, he argued, because of the loss of the UK's ability to distribute wealth across Britain to where it is most needed.[13] While independence was rejected by a narrow margin of forty-five percent Yes to fifty-five percent No, improving welfare was, throughout, a central issue of the campaign.[14]

In Northern Ireland – where the PSE research finds consistently higher levels of deprivation than the rest of the UK[15] – there has been a huge rift between the DUP and Sinn Féin on implementing the UK coalition government's welfare reforms. Sinn Féin, which has led the opposition, opposed their implementation and placed before Stormont a motion stating that a 'modern, caring society should place the protection of its most vulnerable citizens at the very top of its agenda'.[16] With the parties failing to agree to implementation, the Northern Ireland Assembly has faced the prospect of Westminster-imposed financial penalties.

Tougher sanctions

In Westminster, by contrast, the Conservatives have seen clear political gains from presenting themselves as tough and Labour as soft on welfare, as the party that rewards idleness. Getting tough on claimants was seen as striking a chord with voters reflecting an apparent hardening of attitudes towards welfare since the early 1990s.[17] Perceiving the poor themselves as the problem comes with the political bonus that it reduces the responsibility of government, with their role confined to incentivising the poor to help themselves.

During the coalition years, the level of benefits for those of working age was cut, sanctions were intensified and conditions for receipt of benefits made more restrictive. The latter is part of a long-term trend of governments choosing to exercise greater and greater control over the lives of claimants – where they live, their approach to work, how many children they have, their lifestyles. Under Labour from 1997, lone parents were required to seek work when their children were five, while disabled claimants were given new tests to check their ability to work. From 2012, penalties for unemployed and disabled claimants were severely tightened, involving a new set of fixed-period sanctions – with benefit suspensions of between four weeks and three years – for claimants on jobseeker's allowance (JSA) and for disabled people on employment and support allowance (ESA).

Sanctions fall into three categories: 'high' (such as for leaving a job voluntarily), 'intermediate' (for being deemed to be not actively seeking work) and 'low' (for example, missing a Jobcentre interview). Under the tighter rules, the number of benefit recipients being sanctioned has risen sharply. Research by David Webster of the University of Glasgow has shown that the total number of JSA and ESA sanctions in the year to September 2013 was 897,690. This is the highest for any twelve-month period since JSA was introduced in 1996 and compares with 500,000 in the last year of the previous Labour government.[18]

The most common reasons for sanctions are 'failure to attend an interview' (which in practice can mean arriving a little late, a mix-up over dates or non-delivery of an appointment letter); non-participation in a training or employment scheme, even if considered unsuitable by the claimant; and not 'actively seeking work' (which often means not applying for as many jobs as specified) Claimants subject to a sanction can apply for a discretionary 'hardship payment', but not for the first two weeks: if granted, hardship payments are sixty percent of normal JSA, or eighty percent for the 'vulnerable'. The DWP does not provide figures on what proportion of sanctioned claimants are in receipt of such payments, but one estimate suggests that no more than a quarter of those facing sanctions receive such a payment, and very few receive the higher rate.[19]

A key reason is that those given sanctions are often not told of their right to apply for such payments. A Citizens' Advice Bureau survey of 376 claimants in Greater Manchester in September 2013 found that four in ten of those sanctioned had not received a letter informing them of the sanction, while more than half had received no information about their right of appeal. The average duration of the sanction was eight weeks, with two-thirds of respondents left with no income at all after the sanction was imposed, so that those without outside help were effectively destitute, unable to buy food, pay fuel bills or bus fares, or pay for phone calls.[20] In February 2014, an internal note circulating in the DWP even suggested that those stripped of their benefit could be charged for making an appeal.

What is clear is that the sanction system is not just highly punitive, leaving growing numbers with no or very little income at all, but is also out of control. According to Webster, 'Severity is greater at times and in places where it is least productive; sanctions/disallowances are ten times more frequent in the North East than in the South East.'[21] In the three months to the end of September 2013, eighty-seven percent of sanctioned claimants taking their cases to an independent tribunal were successful. This compared with a fifth under the previous Labour government.[22] In July 2014, an independent review was undertaken by Matthew Oakley, a former economist at the centre-right think-tank Policy Exchange. It found systematic flaws in the way sanctions were imposed, with claimants often at a loss as to why their benefits had been stopped.[23]

In evidence to the review, one charity said that the department was presiding over 'a culture of fear' with examples including hostel residents with limited IT facilities told they must apply for fifty jobs a week and single parents told they needed to apply for full-time jobs.[24] In 2012, Scottish CAB reported the case of a client who, despite being dyslexic and having difficulty reading, was sanctioned for not following an official direction to use the internet to increase his chances of obtaining work. He was not warned that he might lose his benefit in this way and ended up homeless.[25]

In another case, a single, fifty-nine-year-old man with diabetes was sanctioned for four weeks despite completing two periods of unpaid work experience and a forklift truck training course. The man had worked all his life before stopping work to look after his mother who had dementia. He was waiting to hear about an application he had made to the supermarket chain Lidl, but was sanctioned for missing two appointments with the work programme officer. A few weeks later, he was found dead by his sister, with just £3.44 left in his bank account and his electricity cut off. The fridge where he kept his insulin was no longer working. The autopsy noted that he had no food in his stomach. He died from diabetic ketoacidosis, caused by a lack of insulin.

From the inception of the new tougher regime, local Jobcentres have been under considerable pressure from Whitehall to raise the number of sanctions issued. In March 2013, the *Guardian* newspaper reported that some Jobcentres had been setting targets on the number issued. This was despite assurances to parliament the same week that no such targets were being set. At a Walthamstow Jobcentre in north London, managers had threatened to discipline staff for failing to meet targets. 'Guys, we really need to up the game here,' the manager told staff in an internal email. While the DWP denied that they operated a target policy, a former Jobcentre worker in Greater Manchester claimed that the entire staff had been warned that they would be disciplined unless the number of sanctions was increased.[26] In September 2013, local Jobcentres across Britain were set to hold a week-long celebration of the tougher system of sanctions for jobseekers introduced a year earlier. In the event, what had become known internally as 'conditionality week' had to be hastily cancelled when details of the plans were made public.[27]

Poverty minus a pound

The central pillar of the government's strategy was its 'big bang' package of benefit reforms introduced in April 2013. Aimed at cutting around £20 billion from working-age benefits it was, arguably, the biggest welfare shake-up since the Beveridge reforms nearly seventy years earlier. Their principal architect, Iain Duncan Smith, called them 'one of the most aggressive programmes of welfare reform Britain has ever seen'.[28] The strategy dovetailed neatly with the 'poverty plus a pound' philosophy – that improved income levels were not the route out of poverty. Ministers liked to argue that giving extra money ended up being wasted.[29] Yet, such stereotyping of the poor is deeply misleading. The evidence is that those on low incomes budget carefully, often accounting for every pound spent. Indeed, a study by the London School of Economics found that boosting low incomes makes a big difference to deprivation levels: raising the incomes of low-income families with children 'increased their spending on children's footwear and clothing, books, and fruit and vegetables, relative to other families with children, but decreased their spending on alcohol and tobacco'.[30]

While a pound may be loose change for those further up the income range, it is anything but for those at the bottom. 'I can't minimise any more than I have,' a low-paid worker in Glasgow told the Poverty and Social Exclusion research team. 'I very rarely buy clothes because I can't afford them. Food is a bare minimum, I live on my own anyway, so I have a roll in the morning and a meal at night,' he added. 'I like to be quite organised ... I have everything written down,' a lone parent in Gloucestershire explained. 'Obviously there are things that get in the way, like emergency things, like the washing machine breaks down or things like that, I don't have anything to fall back on, I have to move it all around ... maybe cut back on the food shopping.'[31]

By cutting benefit rates the reforms were converting, at a stroke, the government's critique of 'poverty plus a pound' into a policy of 'poverty minus a pound', or 'minus many pounds'. It also fitted one of the Conservative party's most fundamental goals – to shrink the role of the state. Tim Montgomerie, editor of *Conservative Home*, put it thus in 2012: 'Iain Duncan Smith and his advisers are not tinkering at the edges of some obscure statistical issue. They are invading intellectual territory of the utmost importance ... They are saying that the war on poverty can't be won by a bigger and bigger welfare state.'[32]

For three years from 2013, nearly all working-age benefits and tax credits stopped rising in line with inflation, instead going up by just one percent a year. The real value of benefits was thus to fall in each of these years, a situation unprecedented since the war. The last deliberate political move to cut the real incomes of the poorest in this way was during the economic crisis of 1931. In that year, the attempts to cut unemployment benefits by a tenth split the cabinet and led to the collapse of the Labour government under Ramsay MacDonald.

A cap on individual benefit levels was introduced with a maximum of £26,000 a year, or £500 a week for a family of working age, the government's estimated average net household income. A 'spare room subsidy', dubbed the 'bedroom tax' by its critics, brought in a new penalty for under-occupation. Those deemed to have one spare bedroom were to lose fourteen percent of their housing benefit, and those with two or more spare rooms twenty-five percent. Council tax benefit was replaced by schemes operated by local councils in England, but with a reduction in funding of ten percent. With councils free to devise their own systems, some have reduced the maximum amount of council tax support that can be awarded from one hundred to seventy-five percent.[33] The DWP-administered social fund – which provided loans and grants for intermittent needs and crises such as broken boilers and lack of furniture – was abolished from April 2013 and its budget – cut by almost a half – devolved to 150 local councils.

Perhaps most significant of all, the government's highly complex flagship scheme, Universal Credit, is aimed at replacing six existing benefits with one monthly payment. Despite a number of detailed reservations,[34] the broad principles behind this highly ambitious scheme have been generally supported as a way of simplifying the benefits system and easing the transition from benefits to work. Nevertheless, the scheme – a Whitehall 'megaproject' – has been blighted by heated cabinet disputes, interdepartmental rifts, acute software problems and huge cost overruns. Overambitious and the subject of protracted delays – the Cabinet Office minister Francis Maude called the implementation process 'lamentable' – the scheme is years behind schedule. Just as Labour's tax credit scheme was marred by a range of serious, protracted and costly implementation problems, experts predict that once operational, universal credit will continue to be blighted by severe problems of administration.

The reformed welfare package has been targeted almost entirely at those of working age with the real value of the state pension and other benefits for the elderly fully protected. The measures – rushed, highly controversial and very poorly implemented – also came on top of a number of earlier reforms from 2010 including the freezing of the child benefit rate for three years from April 2011 and, from 2011, the change in the inflation index used to uprate benefits from the retail price index (the RPI) to the consumer price index (the CPI), a lower measure of inflation.

On top of the 'big bang' package, tougher conditionality and extended sanctions, there have been further measures aimed at tightening the benefits regime for the unemployed, such as the increase in waiting time for receipt of benefits for the newly unemployed from three to seven days. This tightening is despite the evidence that tougher conditions have a mixed record in helping the unemployed find work.[35] The government also warned that, under the new universal credit scheme, jobseekers would be penalised if they refused to take jobs coming with zero-hours contracts. A report by the Joseph Rowntree Foundation on the impact of tougher conditionality concluded that 'international evidence suggests that benefit sanctions substantially increase exits from benefits and may increase entry into short-term jobs, but with less favourable long-term results for earnings, job quality and employment retention'.[36]

Although some of the cuts have not been aimed at the poor – such as the end of child benefit for higher rate taxpayers – it is the poorest who have been hit the most by the government's austerity and welfare strategy.[37] An analysis by the Office of the Children's Commissioner for England of the tax and benefit changes and public spending cuts from 2010 found that, despite some progressive elements, the overall impact has been strongly regressive with low-income families with children losing more proportionately than high-income families and those without children.[38] Women have also been disproportionately affected.[39] A study by the New Policy Institute estimates that sixty-three percent of families affected by one of the cuts were already below the official poverty line. Close to two-thirds of those affected were in work. Hundreds of thousands have faced multiple cuts.[40] Even the Treasury's own analysis of the impact of the measures showed that in 2013/14, all households in the bottom half of the income distribution would lose a larger proportion of their income from the mix of tax, tax credit withdrawal and benefit changes than four out of five of those in the top half.[41]

Fitness-for-work

Among those most heavily affected are people with disabilities, notably through a new system of incapacity benefits affecting up to 3.7 million disabled people.[42] The DWP estimates that twenty-seven percent of planned spending on disabled people of working age will be saved through the raft of changes.[43] Analysis by the Centre for Welfare Reform in Sheffield estimates that the average amount lost per person from the combined impact of all the cuts is £467 per year, and for those in poverty an average of £2,195 per person per year, while disabled people will lose an average of £4,410 and people with severe disabilities an average of £8,832 per person per year.[44]

People with disabilities were already facing a much tougher regime as part of Labour's earlier 'welfare-to-work push'. In October 2008, a new income-replacement benefit, employment and support allowance (ESA), was introduced to replace incapacity benefit. Tougher tests – called Work Capability Assessments (WCA) – were introduced at the same time to determine entitlement to the benefit and aimed at encouraging sick and disabled people into work. The tests – based on a series of checks, ten on physical ability and ten on 'mental, cognitive and intellectual functions' – were outsourced to the French company Atos as part of the wider privatisation of service delivery. Those with low scores are deemed able to work and are likely to have their ESA withdrawn.

Despite the early evidence of the high levels of inaccuracy with the computer-based assessments, Labour moved to accelerate the process. 'We're going to go at this very fast and hard,' promised Lord David Freud in 2009. A former investment banker turned New Labour adviser, he later became the coalition's parliamentary under-secretary for welfare reform [45] Then, in 2011, the assessment process was made even more stringent leading to a surge in the number of appeals.

From the beginning, assessment has been marred by bodged administration. The 'We are Spartacus' network of disability researchers and campaigners have called the process inhumane, citing example after example of recipients being 'wrongly assessed, humiliated, badly treated', of being called and recalled for assessment, of the assessments being 'arbitrary and cruel'. 'A forty-seven-year-old man overdosed on a cocktail of drugs after he had his benefits stopped because he was not given a proper medical assessment by the DWP, an inquest heard. [He] was told his benefits of £90-a-week would be stopped on ... the same day he took to social networking site Facebook to vent his frustration at Prime Minister David Cameron and Atos ... After writing of his disapproval of the system he wrote on Facebook: "It's time to say goodbye, goodbye."[46]

The husband of a person with ill health and mental health issues recalls the reaction of his partner on having been called to an assessment for a third time, having already twice been declared unfit for work: 'It's making her ill, she just saw the envelope today and burst out in tears and had a panic attack. It's so hard for her to go to these things . . . She will literally be sleepless for days before the appointment, throwing up and breaking down.'[47]

Since their introduction, there have been 600,000 appeals against the 'fitness-to-work' tests, almost a third of all assessments. In the year to March 2013, forty-three percent of appeal cases were overturned in favour of claimants. And with the number of appeals mounting, tribunal delays have been rising, leaving claimants increasingly uncertain and stressed. The system has not just fallen into chaos, it has also been counterproductive. Many who had been making progress, for example, in tackling mental health issues, have had their progress reversed, making them less likely to get back to work.

Such was the scale of public and political anger at the mounting problems, the DWP announced in April 2014 that, although the assessment process was to continue, Atos, the lightning rod for the avalanche of criticisms, would be quitting its £500 million contract almost a year early. While charities welcomed the exit of Atos, they also warned that the entire system needed overhauling. 'The test should be more than an exercise in getting people off benefits,' said Richard Hawkes, chief executive of the disability charity Scope. 'It should make sure disabled people get the specialist, tailored and flexible support they need to find and keep a job.'[48] This was echoed by the House of Commons' Work and Pensions Committee, which called the system so full of flaws it needed a complete overhaul.[49]

On top of the fitness-to-work tests, the disability living allowance (DLA), which provided financial support for special requirements such as washing and mobility, began to be phased out from April 2013 and replaced over a three-year period by the personal independence payment (PIP). When fully implemented, some 500,000 people will lose disability benefit.[50] Those with disabilities are also being affected by the wider changes, with some hit simultaneously by up to six different reforms.

The new personal independence payment has also been spreading anxiety among many of the most vulnerable. The government claims that PIP will focus money on those who most need it, through – yet more – testing. While two-thirds of people receiving DLA qualified for an 'indefinite award', all but the terminally ill will be regularly reassessed for PIP. Its introduction – run by Atos – is also in chaos. Applicants often wait months before hearing of their entitlement. MacMillan Cancer Support reports serious delays in approving payments leaving terminally ill patients unable to claim other crucial benefits linked to PIP benefit, with some, at a time when they are especially vulnerable, turning to payday loans to get by.[51]

Targeting welfare spending
The social security budget was an easy target for one of the coalition's core political objectives, the elimination of the 'black hole' in the public finances through an 'austerity'

economic strategy. Just under a third of the targeted £63.4 billion reduction in UK public expenditure by 2015 was designated to come from benefits (excluding pensions) and tax credits, though they constituted only about twenty percent of government expenditure.[52] Cutting benefits, it was claimed, would also tackle what they called an 'overblown' social security budget. Interviewed in September 2010, the chancellor of the exchequer described welfare spending as 'completely out of control'.[53]

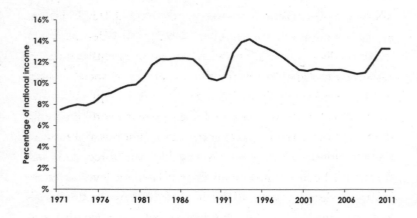

Figure 24: Social security spending as a percentage of national income, UK: 1970 to 2011[56]

In fact, the widely held view that the British social security system is excessively generous does not stand up to much scrutiny. Spending as a proportion of national income did rise in the three post-war decades, mostly down to a rise in the numbers receiving benefits, especially the basic pension, and changing family structures, notably the rise in the number of single-parent families.[54] Nevertheless, as shown in Figure 24, the spending share has remained broadly flat over the last thirty years at an average of around twelve percent. Despite the boost in the cost of housing benefit because of rising rents, the higher spending from the recession and Labour's boost to means-tested benefits for pensioners and working households, the overall social security budget as a proportion of national income was a little lower in 2010/11 than in the early 1990s.[55]

When the post-war welfare state was established, Beveridge had assumed a commitment to full employment and decent pay. In the immediate post-war period, these commitments were more effectively met than today and the role played by social security was therefore more limited. Since then, the benefit system has come to play a greatly expanded role, largely to compensate for the failure of markets to deliver decent livelihoods and housing opportunities for rising numbers of the workforce. Although there have been improvements in some benefit levels over the last three decades, such as the introduction of tax credits for working families, the growing budget has gone, for the most part, not on paying for higher benefits but on social failure – tackling the rise in unemployment, the squeeze on pay and surging rent levels. The proportionate cost of housing benefit alone has more than doubled over the last two decades to fourteen percent of the annual welfare budget. If the root causes of poverty among the workforce could be tackled, including runaway rents, by concentrating on prevention rather than cure, the social security system would have less to do, enabling either an overall fall in the budget or a rise in the level of benefits.

Current spending levels on social security are certainly not exceptional by international standards. In 2009, as a percentage of national income, the UK stood in seventeenth place among the thirty-four OECD nations and a lowly fourteenth among the EU15 with a lower proportion than in France, Italy and Germany.[57]

Despite the reality, the popular view – deliberately encouraged by government and media – remains that benefit spending is excessive. The public greatly overstate the proportion of taxes going on social security and the amount unemployed families receive. They think that almost half those on jobseeker's allowance claim it for more than a year, while the true figure is just over a quarter, and they greatly overstate the level of fraud and false claiming. In one poll the members of the public said that twenty-seven percent of the social security budget is fraudulently claimed, almost forty times higher than the official government figure of 0.7 percent. People believe that forty-one percent of the welfare budget goes on benefits to unemployed people when, in fact, the unemployed account for a fraction of the aggregate benefits bill – three percent.[58] It is the elderly who, at forty-two percent, account for the largest proportion of social security spending. The next largest proportion goes to people *in* work while sick and disabled people account for sixteen percent.[59]

Divide and rule: 'workers' versus 'shirkers'

The public and political debate around poverty is now increasingly highly charged. The government, supported by much of the press, has used language and arguments apparently designed to fuel public antagonism to the poor, thus justifying the government's argument for more punitive welfare policies, while making the poor themselves tools in the wider politics of poverty. In September 2014, the chancellor, George Osborne, announced that, if the Conservatives won the 2015 general election, they would bar childless eighteen- to twenty-one-year-olds from housing benefit and restrict their entitlement to jobseeker's allowance. In a further crackdown on the working poor, they would also impose a two-year freeze on working-age benefits, a policy that would affect ten million people, most of them in work. The goal: to axe a further £3 billion from the social security budget.

The increasingly pervasive view of social security claimants is that they are scroungers who are too lazy, or too savvy, to work. Portrayals of claimants by a succession of high-profile television series, such as Channel 4's controversial 2014 documentary *Benefits Street* and the BBC's *The Future of Welfare* presented by John Humphrys in 2011, have been highly hostile both towards the people concerned and the benefits system. As Humphrys wrote in the *Daily Mail* in the week before transmission, the welfare system leads to 'a dependency culture that has grown steadily over the past years'.[60] The programmes generated hundreds of complaints from viewers, while *The Future of Welfare* was found by the BBC Trust to have 'breached its rules on impartiality and accuracy'.

UK newspapers are also much more likely to present a negative picture than in countries such as Sweden and Denmark.[61] An analysis of press coverage of benefit claimants for the Turn2us charity found that, between 1995 and 2011, more than half of all articles concerning benefits in tabloid newspapers contained negative vocabulary, rising to seventy-five percent in the case of the *Express,* and seventy percent

in the *Daily Mail* and the *Sun*.[62] Across newspapers for which
there is consistent data, the number of times the word 'scrounger'
has been used annually in UK newspapers was four times higher
in 2010 than in any year between 1993 and 2003.[63] Newspapers
have become more likely to write about claimants in terms of
fraud, large families, and people who had never or hardly ever
worked with, as shown in Figure 25, suitably lurid headlines:
'4M scrounging families in Britain' was a headline in the *Daily
Express* on 2 September 2011; '75% of incapacity claimants are
fit to work', in the *Daily Mail,* 24 January 2012.

Figure 25: Tabloid newspaper headlines: 2010 to 2014

Such coverage perpetuates the idea that people *want* to live on benefits, that the welfare system encourages dependency by providing a disincentive to work. The incentives question – 'making work pay' – has indeed been an enduring issue in the history of the benefit system. In his blueprint for the post-war welfare state, William Beveridge argued that any social security system should aim to ensure that a person should not be better off out of than in work. He assumed that, as long as the goal of full employment could be achieved, only a small minority of those of working age would need benefits, which were set after the war at stringent levels.

While the system of unemployment benefit became gradually more generous in the post-war years, that process, in the name of boosting incentives, was set in reverse from the end of the 1970s.

In 1979, the Conservative party manifesto talked of the need for 'restoring the will to work' as if it had disappeared. 'The Government and the vast majority of the British people,' added the chancellor, Sir Geoffrey Howe, 'want hard work and initiative to be properly rewarded and are vexed by disincentives to work.'[64] The 'work must pay' concept was also central to Labour's social agenda from 1997. Policy was geared to the importance of work as a route out of poverty through a series of 'welfare-to-work' measures: raising skill levels, improved access to childcare and the introduction of 'family-friendly' policies including the right to request flexible and part-time working. The coalition government took a more strident tone. As David Cameron put it in June 2012, there was a need to end 'the nonsense of paying people more to stay at home than to get a job – and finally making sure that work really pays'.[65]

From the early 1980s, attempts to sharpen the appetite for work were mostly approached by the simple device of cutting the level of benefits available for those out of work, thereby widening the income gap between unemployment and work. In the post-war era, most benefits had been uprated in line with real earnings or prices – whichever was the greater. From the early 1980s, the earnings link was broken, while earnings-related supplements to unemployment (and sickness) benefits – introduced in the mid 1960s – were abolished in 1982. Since then out-of-work benefits have fallen sharply in relative terms, with jobless benefits halving as a percentage of average earnings from twenty percent in 1979 to less than eleven percent today.[66]

Over time, unemployment benefit – replaced by jobseeker's allowance in 1996 (and worth £72.40 for a single person over twenty-five in 2014) – has become increasingly inadequate and unreliable, weakening the protective role of the state. Cutting the value of support has had wider consequences. Cambridge economist Ha-Joon Chang argues that when unemployment benefits are set too low, workers become resistant to change, fearing the consequences of even a short time of employment. He contrasts countries with high and low unemployment benefits: 'Firms in countries such as Finland and Sweden can introduce new technologies faster than their US competitors because, knowing that unemployment need not mean penury and long-term joblessness, their workers do not resist these changes strongly.'[67]

Low benefits can also make it more difficult to return to work. The PSE 2012 survey, for example, found that twenty-one percent of the unemployed – such as Marc in Redcar – can't afford proper clothes for a job interview. Many struggle to find even the bus fare for interviews or to attend the Jobcentre. As Ha-Joon Chang points out, the British system is far less effective at returning unemployed workers into the labour force than that in Scandinavian countries.[68]

Lowering the level of benefit *has* increased the income gap between work and unemployment, but by a much greater amount than is typical across rich nations. Even when allowance is made for other benefits, the UK's 'replacement ratio' – a family's net out-of-work income as a percentage of in-work income – has fallen sharply over the last thirty years. Today it is among the meanest of any country in the developed world, and much lower than the OECD average.[69] There are strong echoes in these trends of the Victorian principle of 'less eligibility', of the state as disciplinarian, offering the jobless few rights and with benefit levels set so low that they have little choice but to take low-paid, insecure work. Allowing out-of-work benefit levels to fall, along with the wider compression of pay over the last thirty years, has simply created a downward spiral in which *neither* wages at the bottom end of the market *nor* benefit levels are adequate to provide a minimum acceptable standard of living. As the floor has been falling, benefit and pay levels have left a rising number with incomes that are short of the contemporary poverty line.

The alternative approach to tackling incentives is to improve the net incomes of those working on low pay. The most direct way of achieving this is by raising pay levels at the bottom. The introduction of the national minimum wage in 1999 – highly controversial and much criticised at the time – has raised the pay floor a little and done so without, confounding its critics, a noticeable impact on unemployment levels.[70]

Labour set out to tackle the problem of in-work poverty, low pay and incentives mostly indirectly through a generous tax credit system which, despite the early and extensive administrative problems, raised the net incomes for working families in low-paid work. This contributed to a reduction in poverty (as measured by relative income) from 2000, but also added to a long-term shift away from universal and contributory benefits to means-tested ones: for those of working age around two-thirds of benefits were means-tested in 2010/11 compared to just over a quarter in 1980.[71] In addition, tax credits also have the effect of subsidising low-paying employers.

This greater emphasis on income-related, in-work benefits has also had two separate, but contradictory, effects on work incentives, negative for those *in* work but positive for those *out of* work. Thus, because mean-tested benefits are withdrawn as wages increase, the incentive to earn *more* if already in work has been lowered, leading to a sharp rise in the 'poverty trap', with the share of any increase in earnings lost in taxes or reduced benefits standing in some cases at more than seventy percent. With growing numbers of those in poverty in low-paid jobs, this has serious consequences for people's ability to lift themselves out of poverty.

Against this, raising the incomes of the low paid through more generous tax credits has increased the incentive to *enter* work as very few people are now better off out of than in work and most are better off by some margin. As a result, one of the central and oft-repeated claims underlying the 'work must pay' strategy – that out-of-work benefits are so generous, it pays not to work – is inaccurate. As a study for the Elizabeth Finn Care charity, using the DWP's own tax-benefit model, concluded, the contention is 'overwhelmingly untrue: for the vast majority of families, taking a paid job would leave them significantly better off than receiving benefits'. It found, for example, that a single parent with two children working thirty hours a week would have been forty-five percent better off. To be better off on benefits requires having a low wage *and* a large family.[72] Despite the frequency with which the tabloid press and some television programmes feature very large families living on benefits, the DWP found only 180 claiming households with ten or more children in 2010. Ninety-one percent of claimant households have three or fewer children, and only one percent have six or more. [73]

When ministers repeatedly claim that families are better off on benefits, they have to resort to using one or more tricks. One of these is to compare *all* of the income of a family on benefits with *some* of the income of a family in work. Government statements in support of capping benefit entitlements have also compared the income of a non-working family with children with the income of a working household without children, airbrushing out of the comparison in-work entitlements for families. Such a comparison was made in a speech on welfare by the prime minister on 25 June 2012.[74]

Similarly, the often promoted view that there are deprived areas of the UK with a 'Benefits Street' culture based on generations of families choosing a life on benefits does not match the evidence. Research, funded by the Joseph Rowntree Foundation, examined two high-unemployment areas of Middlesbrough and Glasgow.[75] While families in the areas had been severely affected by unemployment, the study found none containing generations where no one had worked, none where the parents wanted their children to live a life on benefits and none where the children themselves didn't want to work. The dominant experience was one with people 'churned' in and out of low-paid work and unemployment. 'We were trying to find something that seemed mythical,' concluded Robert MacDonald, professor of sociology at Teesside University: 'families completely unemployed, who have never had jobs. It was very challenging to find anyone who even came near that model.' The DWP dismissed the research, preferring, true to form, its own anecdotal approach to policy-making: 'in areas with high concentrations of worklessness, there is a risk of it becoming entrenched and this is something which can be evidenced anecdotally,' commented a DWP spokeswoman.[76]

PSE interviews with people living on benefits across the UK have found a strong sense of disaffection and anger that their situation had been so completely misunderstood and mis-portrayed. 'Why do they just assume that we are all bad because we're single parents? It really used to get to me. It made me feel like I wasn't worth anything. Through the media you read things about it, people would be judgmental because you're on benefits,' said a single parent living in Birmingham.[77]

And a young unemployed man also from Birmingham: 'There was a programme the other day talking about the benefit cheats – how to cheat the benefits – what people do at Jobcentres. Did you interview anybody who had aspirations? Did you interview anybody who had goals that wanted to do things, that wanted to get out of the Jobcentre. No they didn't and it's all negative media. Why isn't anything positive about job searching for young people? It's just all one-sided.'[78]

In reality, the government's approach to welfare has had little to do with welfare dependency or a bloated welfare budget.

Indeed, neither is a major problem. But, under this guise, they have lowered the incomes of some of the most vulnerable in society while greatly adding to the stigma and discomfort of those claiming benefits. The spread of poverty, however, is not just down to changes in the benefit system and the rise of low pay, significant as these are. It is also intricately related to decades of failed housing policies.

6

Left on the outside: The failure of housing policy

───────

I never thought I'd be living in this situation. I thought I would have my own home. In this day and age you'd never think that people would be living this way. You may not see it on the outside, but within the heart it's very, very shocking.
Low-paid worker, London 2013[1]

In February 2014, Channel 4 News interviewed Nicky, a single mother with a five-year-old child who became homeless after her relationship broke down. Her local authority offered her a privately rented flat and told her that she would be taken off the waiting list if she refused it. 'Because it was so small, we ate on our laps. We'd put the plates down for a second, then I'd look down to find hundreds of ants crawling all over them,' Nicky – who had just been diagnosed with cancer – told the reporter. The flat was infested not just with red ants but also with mice. Despite attempts to stop the mice getting into their room at night, by morning there were still mouse droppings everywhere. 'We had to disinfect the flat every day. It was so stressful.'[2]

Her experience is far from uncommon for those housed in privately rented accommodation following a period of homelessness. In early 2014, the homeless charities Crisis and Shelter published a longitudinal study that tracked the experiences of 128 such households over nineteen months. 'Every home had a condition problem', the study found. 'Some were extremely severe and many got progressively worse.'[3]

For the first time since the late 1960s, more households are now renting their homes privately than living in social housing. Since the turn of the millennium, the number of households in privately rented accommodation has doubled from two to four million. For most, standards are adequate, and at the top end of the market often high. But for a growing number, this has meant the return of poor and, too often, grim and unfit housing conditions. Examples include water running down the walls, leaking roofs, infestations of cockroaches and, for the most vulnerable tenants, aggressive landlords and the constant fear of eviction.

Over the last thirty years, housing policy has been dominated by one overriding aim – to boost levels of home ownership. In 1980, the first Thatcher government, echoing the virtues of what Harold Macmillan had called, in the 1950s, a 'property-owning democracy', introduced the right to buy, enabling council house tenants to buy the property they lived in. The flagship 'right to buy' policy was highly popular among tenants. It enabled those of more than two years standing to buy their homes at substantial discounts – rising from thirty-two percent to sixty percent for tenants of longer standing. It was a give away bargain and, as such, a transfer of collectively owned wealth to those able to buy.

Since then, all political parties have signed up to the ambition of greater home ownership, promoting it in a myriad of ways, from the relaxation of lending rules in the 1980s to the promotion of low-cost home-ownership schemes. But while most of those able to jump on board the home-ownership drive have been the winners from this strategy, greater reliance on markets has proved increasingly dysfunctional for those left out. House prices have boomed leaving increasing numbers excluded from the home-owning dream, while those first-time buyers able to get a foot on the ladder today are often overstretched and vulnerable to interest-rate rises and stagnating incomes. Council house sales have greatly outstripped the volume of new building, leaving a greatly depleted social housing stock unable to cope with demand, so that families in need, and the young, have been left increasingly dependent on an under-regulated and expensive private rental market. The core failure of the housing system has been one of the key drivers behind the rise in poverty, restricting housing choice, trapping rising numbers in unacceptable housing conditions and putting growing pressure not just on household finances but also on the benefits system.

The ever-growing waiting list

In the post-war era meeting housing need was made a political priority leading to record rates of house building, including council-house building, and policies to limit housing costs. Creating a large stock of council homes for rent was part of the wider post-war system of enhanced social protection, designed to even up the gap in housing conditions between rich and poor. Gradually, housing standards and choices improved. But, from 1980, with the state opting for a much more back–seat role, the level of both public and private investment in housing has nosedived. The number of homes being built in the UK is down from an average 322,000 a year through the 1970s to 127,000 in 2012 while the number of units of social housing being started stood at around 33,000 in 2012 compared with an average of 135,000 in the 1970s.[4] Against this, the number of households is projected to grow by 272,000 per year until 2033. Current housing shortages, already acute, are thus set to continue to rise into the indefinite future.

In the first three decades of right to buy more than two million council properties were sold. With the rate of sales eventually falling most able to buy had done so – the coalition government relaunched the scheme in 2012, increasing discounts to tenants to seventy percent. With tenants outside London receiving discounts of up to £75,000 rising to £100,000 within London, the rate of sales accelerated once more.

The sharp fall in the stock of municipal housing has been a deliberate policy, driven by the goal of turning the UK into a nation of home owners with less dependency on the state. As Lynsey Hanley, author of *Estates*, argues: 'The dream of building a fair and equitable stake in the collective wealth of the nation – of which good housing formed a part – barely had time to bear fruit before it was punctured, without ceremony, by the idea that the only way to feel fully anchored in society, and therefore to be fully a citizen, was to own the property you lived in.'[5]

From the inception of the sales policy, councils were debarred from spending the cash on replacement housing, and instead had to use receipts to pay off housing debt. Some councils, led by

Wandsworth, the flagship Conservative borough in south London, sold off entire estates to be converted for up-market home ownership. As Mrs Thatcher explained in 1987, her aim was for the state to withdraw 'as far and as fast as possible' from the building, ownership, management and regulation of housing.[6] But the need for social housing could not be wished away. The number of households on the waiting list for social housing grew by 700,000 during the Labour years and had reached an all-time high of 1.8 million in 2012.[7]

Meanwhile, one of the long-term side effects of right to buy has been a transfer of housing stock from public ownership not – as intended – to personal ownership, but to the private rented sector. Over a third of ex-council homes in London are now privately let with rents averaging over £200 a week more than those charged by councils, an increased bill often picked up by taxpayers through housing benefit.[8] It is a system that has become widely abused. Homes sold under the relaunched 2012 right to buy scheme have already ended up in the private rented sector. Polly Toynbee of the *Guardian* reported that a Newham solicitor had helped a tenant buy a council house for £45,000: they can let it out for £700 a month and then sell it in five years for four times as much.[9] Meanwhile, in order to meet their legal requirements for rehousing, councils have ended up renting back the very houses they had been forced to sell. In Harrow, the council spent half a million pounds in 2014 renting back houses it had sold under right to buy.[10]

Another consequence of the growing shortage of homes has been the persistence of homelessness. By the end of 2013, 185,000 people in England were homeless, the figure having risen for each of the previous three years. Up-to-date figures for those sleeping rough are notoriously difficult to gather with accuracy and are known to underestimate the problem. The Homelessness Monitor, a five-year study independently monitoring the trends, estimates that while there was a gradual decline in rough sleeping during the mid 2000s, the numbers have begun to rise again, up by thirty-one percent in the two years to autumn 2012. In London the figures rose by over sixty percent.[11]

In August and September 2013, in a telling intervention, a United Nations special rapporteur stepped into the debate, ratcheting up the political controversy. On a research trip to Britain, Raquel Rolnik, a professor at the Faculty of Architecture and Urbanism of the University of São Paulo, reported that many homeless people were in 'tremendous despair'. The report, published in January 2014, and based on visits to council estates and homeless crisis centres, noted that Britain's previously good record on housing was being eroded by a failure to provide sufficient quantities of affordable and social housing.[12] 'A Marxist diatribe,' was how the finding was greeted by the housing minister Kris Hopkins.[13]

Those who experience homelessness are much more vulnerable to poverty later in life, even when they have found a place to live. PSE research is based on a household survey and therefore only interviews people currently in housing. But, as Figure 26 shows, it finds extensive experience of some form of homelessness: around five percent have lost their home, five percent have ended up in emergency or temporary accommodation while nearly fifteen percent have at some point had to stay with family or friends. But for those who are currently facing poverty (lacking three or more necessities), these figures are much higher: thirteen percent have lost their homes, twelve percent have ended up in emergency accommodation, four percent have slept rough and twenty-seven percent have been forced to stay with relatives or friends. While eight percent of those lacking *no* necessities have at some point stayed with family or friends, the proportion experiencing other forms of homelessness is statistically insignificant.

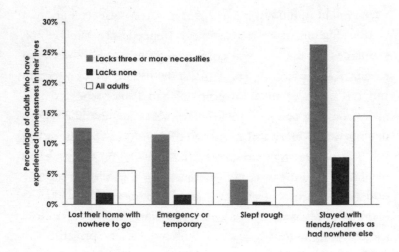

Figure 26: Experiencing homelessness at some point in their lives, UK: 2012

The retreat of the 'home-owning democracy'

For a while, through the 1990s and beyond, the decline in the quantity of social housing appeared to matter less. The sweeping away of controls over mortgage lending in the mid 1980s led to a frenzy of credit with mortgage offers on higher multiples of salary and much lower deposits. Northern Rock, the former building society converted into a bank, offered young borrowers loans equal to 125 percent of the purchase price and up to six times income. 'Sub-prime' mortgages were made available to low-income households, often with few checks and sometimes via door-to-door selling by unscrupulous lenders. While this relaxation enabled many on relatively low incomes – who previously might have turned to social housing – to enter the prized category of home ownership – it also led to the build-up of a massive debt mountain.

Boosting mortgage availability at a time when house building was in decline also led, predictably, to sharply rising house prices. The ratio of median house prices to median earnings soared: in England in 1997 it stood at 3.54; by 2013 it had risen to 6.74.[14]

Initially, the flow of credit was widely welcomed. 'Credit has democratised this country,' HBOS director Shane O'Riordain told Channel 4 News in 2005. 'And it's a good thing. When handled wisely, credit is an enabling factor that helps people to lead better lives … We're in the business of prudence.'[15] HBOS had been formed four years earlier in a merger between Halifax, the formerly mutually owned building society privatised in 1997, and the Bank of Scotland. Three years after O'Riordain's proclamations, HBOS collapsed leaving a shortfall between loans and deposits of £213 billion and a government cash injection of £46 billion.[16]

Meanwhile, the seeds of another housing transformation were being sown: from the mid 1990s, the buy-to-let revolution began to take off. Encouraged by the introduction of short hold tenancies – allowing short-term lets with no long-term security for tenants – and a proliferation of lending products geared to landlords, the number of buy-to-let mortgages soared from 58,000 in 1998 to more than a million by 2007, by then accounting for more than ten percent of all mortgages. 'Capital-rich landlords were scooping up houses, fuelling a vicious cycle of rising prices, falling supply and inevitably a plentiful supply of tenants, from those forced by a rising market to rent', concluded Graham Turner, an independent economic consultant working for some of the world's largest banks.[17] By the time the privatised building societies with the most aggressive lending policies – Bradford and Bingley and Northern Rock – went bust, they had buy-to-let mortgage liabilities of £30 billion.

Buy-to-let is, in effect, a get-rich-quick scheme for those with capital to spare – or with an existing property portfolio against which to borrow money – all heavily subsidised by the state. Landlords still enjoy tax relief on mortgage repayments (relief that had been abolished for owner-occupiers in 2000), while the Chartered Institute of Housing estimates that they benefit from a further £7 billion of tax allowances per year for deductible expenses such as repairs and maintenance, and insurance and professional fees, with no matching requirement that this relates to proper standards.[18] Since the 2008 crash, banks have seen landlords – who have assets to underpin their mortgage loans – as less risky than many first-time buyers, leaving many aspiring to home-ownership left on the outside. Across the country, first-time buyers have been going head-to-head with buy-to-let investors – and losing. Faisal Islam, former economics editor at Channel 4 News, uncovered figures that showed that sixty-five percent of buy-to-let lending in the year after the crash was from banks which had been bailed out. 'It is clearly,' he concludes, 'redistributive in the negative sense, a means of concentrating wealth where it already lies.'[19]

With more of the national housing stock being swallowed up by heavily subsidised buy-to-let landlords, the level of owner-occupation has gone into reverse. The proportion of homes in England and Wales lived in by owner-occupiers rose dramatically from just under a quarter at the end of the First World War to peak at seventy-one percent in 2003, but is now back to sixty-five percent, its lowest level for twenty-five years.[20] If the 1.3 million Britons who now have interest-only mortgages – essentially a glorified form of renting with the asset belonging to the lender and not the mortgage holder – are excluded, home-ownership figures fall to nearer fifty percent, around the level of the early 1970s.[21]

Interest-only mortgages were popular in the 1980s, taken out with endowment policies to repay the loan but fell out of favour when those endowments delivered shortfalls. Because they do not involve paying off any capital they are cheaper, and became popular in the 2000s as a way of getting into the expensive housing market; in 2007, a third of mortgages taken out were interest only. But such mortgages are effectively a gamble that house prices will have risen sufficiently to pay off the outstanding loan, and leave borrowers with the very real risk of being left with debts that they cannot repay and homes stuck in negative equity, a particular problem in Northern Ireland and, to a lesser extent, the north of England. A combination of inflated house prices, stagnating incomes and a booming rented sector has killed home-buying dreams. The average age of a first-time buyer has risen from twenty-eight at the turn of the millennium to thirty-five today. Since the mid 2000s, new home buyers have needed either an exceptionally well-paid job or well-off and home-owning parents. In 2012, sixty-three percent of new buyers received financial help from their parents.[22]

Generation rent

As a result of the acute shortage of social housing and the rising cost of home ownership, low- and middle-income families have had to turn to the most expensive and poorly regulated option of all – private renting. Increasing numbers are renting homes they would have been able to afford to buy a decade ago. With the growing pressure on social housing, councils have been writing to those on the waiting list with limited points informing them that they no longer stand a chance of getting a home from the council and advising them to rent.

With the withdrawal of rent controls in the 1980s at a time of increased demand, rent rises have outstripped general inflation, especially in urban conurbations such as London and Greater Manchester. Households who rent privately pay a higher proportion of their income on housing costs than in other tenures. According to one study, even a 'very modest rented home' is beyond the reach of a low-income household in a third of Britain, defined as rent taking up more than thirty-five percent of income.[23]

Rents in local authority and social housing have also been pushed upwards. In the past, council-house rents were heavily subsidised. The coalition government has accelerated the reduction in the level of subsidy, renamed social housing 'affordable housing' and, in a form of doublespeak, introduced a new system of 'affordable rents' to be set at eighty percent of market levels (up from nearer fifty percent under the previous system). These will apply to all new social housing lets and will gradually be phased in for existing dwellings. Despite the promise of the London mayor, Boris Johnson, that Londoners were to benefit from new housing developments, 'not oligarchs from Planet

Zog', [24] in central London, two-bedroom 'affordable' units built as part of commercial schemes carry rents of upwards of £20,000 a year. Although a quarter of the 680 new flats being built at the old Mount Pleasant Royal Mail sorting office in north London, for example, are to be 'affordable', the units will carry rents that will take them way out of reach of those on the London housing waiting list. [25]

As homes become vacant, they are switched to this new higher rent model. This has made such properties unaffordable for lower income families unless they qualify for their rent to be paid by housing benefit. Overall, since 1987, while general prices have risen about two and a half times, rents – social as well as private – have risen by three and a half times. [26]

Rising housing costs – with, in particular, rents consuming an ever-increasing proportion of budgets – have become a significant driver of the growth of deprivation and deteriorating living standards. The Resolution Foundation think-tank estimates that 1.6 million UK households – two-thirds of them working households – are spending more than half their disposable income on the ongoing costs of housing each month. This is a sharp rise over the numbers in the early 2000s. The great majority of this group are on below-average incomes, with eighty-four percent having incomes below the national median. In 2011/12 – the latest year for which data are available – the 'housing pinched' in the bottom half of incomes had an average of just £60 a week left over to spend on all other essentials (including food and bills) after paying for accommodation. [27] Unsurprisingly, rent arrears are rising.

One of the most significant effects of these trends has been a sharp rise in the number claiming housing benefit. This benefit, which came into full operation in the mid 1980s, replacing separate systems for local-authority and private tenants, is a means-tested benefit to help low-income households pay their rent, social or private. By 2014 there were a million more who could not meet housing costs than on the eve of the recession.[28] This has also meant a big jump in the numbers facing an in-work poverty trap, as housing benefit is withdrawn at 65p in the pound (compared to 41p for tax credits). Add council tax benefit withdrawal and this can rise to 85p or higher, so that an increase in pay or hours for the low paid can result in virtually no additional income. Because of higher rents and the growing number of claimants, the total housing benefit bill has risen sharply from £6 billion in the early 1990s to nearly £22 billion today, a figure that is projected to hit £25 billion by 2018.[29]

These figures reveal a central contradiction at the heart of the argument for reducing dependency. Opting out of the provision of state housing and raising rents to reduce general subsidies may reduce the state's role in providing for housing need, but only by increasing dependence on central government income support, simultaneously bringing a fundamental change in the character of the social security system.[30] One of the main effects has been a large-scale transfer of money from the taxpayer to landlords as one in five private rents is subsidised directly through housing benefit. Between 2011/12 and 2014/15, £35 billion of housing benefit went to private landlords, £13 billion more than in the previous three years.[31]

This is all the more problematic because today's 'generation rent' is concentrated among low-income families. [32] The proportion of families with young children renting privately is up from a fifth in 2001 to a third today. Not only are they increasingly likely to be trapped financially, but they are more likely to live in structurally inadequate housing than those in social housing. Figure 27, from PSE 2012, shows that private tenants are more likely to have leaky roofs, rotten window frames or floors, and to lack a proper heating system.

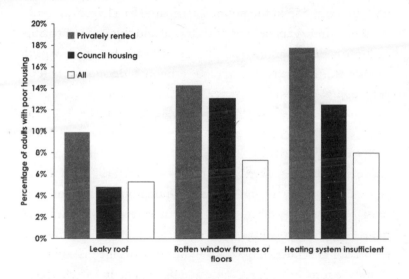

**Figure 27: Percentage of adults living in structurally
poor housing, by tenure, UK: 2012**

In 2000, a new official definition of 'decent housing' for social housing was introduced with minimum requirements for aspects such as insulation, space and adequate kitchen and bathroom facilities.[33] On this basis, the private rented sector fares even worse with a third of dwellings failing to meet these standards in 2012. By sharp contrast, standards in the social rented sector have improved – in 2012 fifteen percent of social rented homes failed to meet this decent homes standard, down from twenty-nine percent in 2006.[34]

With very limited controls, there is also evidence of growing exploitation of tenants, from harassment to illegal eviction and illicit withholding of deposits. Local authorities dealt with a twenty-two percent increase in the number of complaints about the private rented sector in the three years to 2011: more than 86,000 complaints in total.[35] The London Borough of Newham, the first local council to try to licence all its private landlords, is in the process of prosecuting 134 landlords for serious 'hazards'.[36]

The 'bedroom tax'

Compounding the rise in the cost of housing and the long-term squeeze on budgets have been a number of changes to the way the benefits system supports housing costs, all aimed at cutting the housing benefits bill. The most significant and controversial of these changes has been the under-occupation penalty (the 'bedroom tax'). The aim was to promote a more efficient use of increasingly scarce housing space and the scheme was projected to save up to £500 million in the first year from the mounting housing benefit bill. But, inflexible in design, its implementation has created prolonged disruption, stress and hardship for those affected. Jon Ashworth, MP for Leicester South, cited the example of a couple in his constituency. 'She is severely disabled following an accident at work and requires a 24 hour morphine drip, while her husband is both her full-time carer and has a full-time job of his own. He sleeps in a separate bedroom so he can get enough sleep for work. The bungalow they live in has been specially adapted to suit her needs, and they've lived there for over 20 years ... They are now faced with the "choice" of leaving their home because they can't afford to live there or finding the extra money.'[37]

The reform has been undermined by the severe lack of small properties in social housing. Aragon Housing Association, for example, with thousands of tenants across Bedfordshire, was able to move less than a tenth of the households with spare bedrooms to smaller houses. 'Nearly a quarter of those affected are disabled and have had expensive adaptations to make the home they are now under-occupying suitable. Can it really make sense to move them to a home which would need further adaptations at more cost, and then to remove the adaptations in the home they left behind?'[38]

The projected savings have not materialised. The government's own evaluation of the first six months of the scheme, carried out by independent researchers at the Cambridge Centre for Housing and Planning Research, was damning. Although one-in-five claimants had registered an interest in downsizing, shortages of smaller properties meant that just 4.5% of tenants had been able to move to a smaller home – 'a promising start' according to the DWP. As a result, the great majority of households affected have either had to move to private renting – always a more expensive option – or stay put and pay more in rent.

Four-fifths of the 523,000 tenants staying put told researchers they were finding it 'very' or 'fairly' difficult to meet the shortfalls of between £14 and £22 a week. Large numbers were forced to cut back on food and energy, and/or run up debts to meet rent payments, while rent arrears have been rising. One social landlord told researchers: 'Our customers (tenants) are in severe hardship through this reduction in housing benefit ... customers are distraught and telling us they cannot cope.' Other tenants told researchers that they now struggled to afford school uniforms or family swimming trips and had cut back on having grandchildren round for a meal.[39]

Another side effect of the scheme has been a growth in the number of large private landlords refusing to house tenants in receipt of housing benefit, though this is also an unintended consequence of the provisions of the increasingly delayed Universal Credit. For working-age tenants, support for housing costs will be paid, with a few exceptions for vulnerable tenants, direct to the tenant under the scheme, rather than, as currently, to the landlord. It is now not uncommon to see landlords stating 'No DSS' in their advertisements. Britain's largest private landlords, Fergus and Judith Wilson, have accumulated at least £100 million from their 1,000-property empire in Kent established entirely from buy-to-let loans which – for those that could be publicly traced by the *Guardian* – came from a subsidiary of Bradford and Bingley, one of the banks rescued by the taxpayer in 2008.[40] During 2013 the Wilsons issued eviction notices to all 200 of their tenants in receipt of benefit and, having announced the sale of their entire portfolio in July 2014, subsequently extended their eviction policy to those on zero-hours contracts.[41]

The housing charity Shelter has warned that, with benefit levels increasingly falling behind rents, Britain could see the emergence of 'benefit black spots' or claimant-free zones where claimants are unable to find private tenancies. This risk has been compounded by the way lower limits have been set for what is called the 'local housing allowance'. This is used to calculate the maximum amount of rent that can be assessed for benefit based on the levels of local private rents, and has reduced the level of benefit received for many families in high-rent areas.[42] Because the changes allow comparisons with the bottom third of rents only (instead of the median as previously), those in receipt of benefit seeking private accommodation are likely to be increasingly clustered at the bottom end of the market, in poor-quality and badly maintained homes and the least desirable locations.

Such was the mounting controversy and unpopularity of the bedroom tax, the government was roundly defeated – by a majority of seventy-five – in the House of Commons in September 2014, when a private member's bill was passed imposing a number of new conditions on the imposition of the under-occupation rule. While the bill has yet to reach the statute book, and did not scrap the bedroom tax, its effect would be to greatly dilute its impact with three major exemptions: disabled tenants whose home has been specially adapted; disabled tenants in receipt of disability living allowance who are unable to share a bedroom; and under-occupying tenants who have not received an alternative offer of accommodation from their landlord.

A dysfunctional market

The thrust of housing policy over the last thirty years has helped create an increasingly dysfunctional housing market, one that is unable to meet even minimal housing needs for growing numbers, while continuing to enrich one section of the population and reinforcing the fallout of the wider income divide. Extreme levels of income and wealth inequality and unregulated housing markets do not make a successful cocktail.

Increasingly, the freeing up of markets and the weakening of the state's role has led to a widening in the housing gap between rich and poor.

Britain now faces a deep-seated housing crisis, with deteriorating housing choices, runaway house prices and private rents, and a soaring housing benefit bill. There is a widening gap between owners and tenants and between the generations. While those already well housed are getting richer, the poorest in society, especially among the young, are increasingly denied access to anything resembling decent contemporary housing. The large housebuilders are sitting on landbanks large enough to enable a huge boost in building. They sit idle largely because, as the government-commissioned 2004 Barker Review of Housing Supply concluded, 'Housebuilders' profitability depends on obtaining valuable land rather than building a higher quality product in ever more efficient ways.'[43]

With a greatly overheated market, paying for a decent home is increasingly unaffordable – in particular in the South-East and London – for all but the rich and the affluent. As the leading conservative commentator Peter Oborne has written: 'To believe that those of modest means are not entitled to live in the cities, towns, villages, communities that they also serve, to assert that only wealth confers this "right" is indefensible; to believe that it is of no consequence to society when families are separated, communities and neighbourhoods uprooted and destroyed is frankly insane. It is also a betrayal of genuine Conservative values.'[44]

In London especially, housing and welfare policies, mixed in with the depression of incomes at the bottom, have caused widespread dislocation for families. The individual benefit cap has hit claimants in the capital particularly hard, forcing many families to relocate to cheaper areas and smaller homes, with children having to move schools or face long daily journeys. Many London boroughs, unable to find local affordable places which will meet the new benefit limits, are re-housing homeless families sometimes as far away as Edgbaston, Leicester and Northampton with the 'destination' boroughs complaining that the influx is placing new strains on local services, including school places, while pushing up private rents.[45] Middle- and low-income families are increasingly being forced out of central London leaving whole areas open only to those with the deepest pockets. Adding to this trend is the policy, in the name of regeneration, of a growing number of London boroughs redeveloping large local-authority estates and replacing them with mostly more expensive private housing – in essence, a form of municipal gentrification.

The fierce competition for rented accommodation in the capital has enabled some exploitative landlords to charge higher and higher rents for smaller and smaller amounts of space. One London property company charges £255 per week for what it calls 'studio apartments', measuring three metres by three metres – not much larger than a prison cell, and breaching statutory overcrowding regulations.[46] Penalties for breaking what minimal regulations exist, even if charged and convicted, are too low to act as a deterrent. In one extreme case, a landlord – subsequently taken to court by Barnet council – was charging £420 a month for a room, accessible only by a staircase, of a height less than that of an adult (between 0.7m and 1.2m) with the door to the room similarly reduced in size. The fine, including costs, was £3,000.[47]

In the capital, the impact of the growing income divide has been exacerbated by the global concentration of wealth – and widespread capital flight from countries such as Russia and Ukraine – with flows of international money adding to Britain's dysfunctional and divided property market. Some £7 billion of international money – much of it of dubious heritage and passed through multiple tax avoidance schemes – was spent on high-end central London homes in 2012, with only a fifth of prime property purchasers being from the UK. Foreign housing investment in London in 2012 was more than the entire national affordable housing budget.[48] Some of London's most expensive areas – from Knightsbridge to Mayfair – have become little more than 'ghost squares' with large numbers of homes, increasingly owned by the nomadic rich, left empty for months, sometimes years at a time.

Moreover, the issue is not confined to the top end of the market. Two out of three new-build properties in central London in the first half of 2011 were bought by overseas investors.[49] In the London borough of Islington close to three hundred new homes built in the area since 2008 still have no one on the electoral register or are marked as empty.[50]

London's property market – what gets built and where – has been increasingly determined by the economic power of the global and domestic super-rich and high-earning professionals. London property has been dubbed 'a global reserve currency' by the American *Observer* columnist and London resident, Michael Goldfarb. The market 'is no longer about people making a long-term investment in owning their shelter, but a place for the world's richest people to park their money at an annualized rate of return of around 10 per cent. It has made my adopted hometown a no-go area for increasing numbers of the middle class.'[51] Little has been built that improves the housing choices for the bulk of ordinary Londoners.

These trends have fuelled disparities in property wealth, adding to wider divisions across Britain. The small town of Elmbridge in Surrey is now worth as much as the entire residential assets of the city of Glasgow.[52] According to the Office for National Statistics: 'The share of individuals aged sixty-five or over living in households with net property wealth over £250,000 is 41% in London, 38% in the South East, 32–33% in the East of England and the South West; but only 10–15% in the North East, North West, Yorkshire and The Humber, Scotland and Wales.'[53]

Tackling the housing crisis and improving choices depends on taking the heat out of the market by controlling demand in certain areas of the country while boosting it in others through wider economic policies to regenerate the UK regions. Across the country, there needs to be a significant boost to the building of more genuinely affordable housing, and measures that will share the existing stock more equitably. Making a real difference will depend on the willingness of politicians to take on the multiple, and powerful, vested interests at play, from builders and landowners – often able to pocket huge uplifts in the sale of land – to the better off, and often elderly, owner-occupiers now sitting on artificially boosted sums of capital. The latter, along with buy-to-let landlords, have been the great winners from Britain's housing lottery. And they are determined to hang on to their windfall gains, seeing this capital as a way to help their children enter the housing market, and as an addition to their retirement pot.

Change does not seem in prospect. In the name of reducing red tape, the UK government has cut regulations governing new building in England and Wales, provoking concerns that this will lead to a reduced quality of housing and leave new homes having the meanest dimensions to be found anywhere in Europe.[54] In 2013, despite record waiting lists, ministers amended planning laws to make it easier for developers to renegotiate deals with local councils over the number of 'affordable' homes they build. While planning permission has traditionally been made dependent on providing a minimum number of social dwellings, developers are now increasingly able to cut these requirements sharply. A study by the Bureau for Investigative Journalism in 2013 found that of the eighty-two biggest housing developments in ten cities, from Birmingham to Bradford, sixty percent fell short of local affordable housing targets. There are innumerable examples of private housing schemes – from Bletchley in Buckinghamshire to Battersea in south London – in which developers have successfully reduced, on negotiation, the number of affordable homes available to a trickle.[55]

Politicians have promised time and again to boost house building, yet the rate has carried on falling. Boosting the supply of affordable homes requires a number of policy shifts: a boost to social housing budgets, a shift in the composition of new building away from the top, luxury end of the market, overcoming planning barriers and speeding up land release. Planning permission, which brings with it a rise in land prices, needs to come with far more strings attached to extract social value.

To make more equitable use of existing housing there needs to be a crackdown on the growing practice of 'buy-to-leave', along with measures to bring empty homes back into use, and a reduction in the level of under-occupation, a much bigger problem in private than in social housing. This means higher and more progressive property taxes – including new charges on vacant homes especially on foreign ownership and unoccupied homes – with the winners, including owner-occupiers, returning through taxation a portion of their gains. Council tax bands, which have not been uprated in England since 1993, need to be overhauled with the addition of more bands for higher valued properties. This would be much more effective than proposals for a mansion tax. Under the present system, those in homes worth millions of pounds are paying the same council tax as those in much more modestly priced homes.

With more than three-quarters of bank loans geared to property, thus encouraging the boom-bust cycle, new controls are needed over the flow of credit. The private rented sector is now excessively under-regulated and over-subsidised. The subsidy to buy-to-let landlords through mortgage tax relief should be phased out. Reducing the artificial stimulus to buying-to-let would help reduce house prices overall, releasing more homes for ordinary home ownership.

We need tougher regulations on the rented market, including over rent levels, and new longer-term tenancies especially for families.[56] Britain is one of the few countries in Europe where landlords are unlicenced and rents are uncontrolled. Other countries less obsessed with the virtues of markets have much more regulated systems, including control over rent rises. France, Spain, Ireland and Germany all have long-term tenancies with predictable rents while New York, where forty-five percent of people rent privately, has a policy of rent stabilisation with landlords limited to increasing rates by a certain percentage each year.

The growing gap in housing choices in Britain – with housing policy increasingly bypassing the needs of the poor, the vulnerable and the young – has been a key factor in the deteriorating living standards among those on the lowest incomes. It is also a physical expression of the wider impact of growing polarisation, one characterised by an increasing concentration of incomes in the hands of a few tens of thousands at the very top, and a growing depletion of incomes among a few millions at the bottom.

7

A problem of riches: Poverty and the distribution question

*This is how the other half live, I would like to get one
of these people and just say 'Look, this is how the
other half live.' I don't think they would last a day.
They don't realise what is happening in the real world.
They are in a little world of their own.*
Unemployed man, Gloucestershire 2013[1]

Throughout 2013 and 2014, the growing problem of low pay in Britain became the subject of an increasingly vocal national campaign. Groups like Citizens UK, a civic alliance of hundreds of community organisations – from churches to tenants' groups – were bringing growing pressure on the country's biggest employers to commit to paying their staff the living wage. Among those targeted were local councils and large supermarkets. Across university campuses, students organised protests against the pay and working conditions of cleaners employed, directly or indirectly, by their organisations. In London protestors were evicted from an occupation at the University of London headquarters, with some student leaders arrested.

With the huge chasm across the pay range in Britain, one much larger today than fifty or even fifteen years ago, the growing gap in rewards has become an increasingly hot political issue. In the 1950s, chief executives of the biggest companies would be paid twenty-five to thirty times the wage of the average employee. That ratio rose to around sixty in 1998 and to over 170 by 2012.[2] Before he resigned in 2013, Sir Terry Leahy of Tesco was paid nearly 900 times as much as the average Tesco worker while Sir Martin Sorrell of the global advertising and marketing services group WPP received nearly £30 million in 2013, 780 times his staff's average wage.[3]

In the City, the typical bonus in the 1950s and 1960s was a hamper from Harrods, not the multi-million-pound handouts that have become the norm. Even after the 2008 crash, with typical living standards sliding, the culture of entitlement within Britain's boardrooms hardly blinked, while the financial rewards enjoyed by the highest paid bankers, unlinked to performance, continued to soar, opening up an even bigger wage gap.[4] In February 2014, Barclays Bank announced it was paying £2.4 billion in bonuses to senior staff, up ten percent on 2013, despite a fall in profits of a third and plans to cut twelve thousand jobs through the year. The pay-out – more than the bank had paid out in dividends to shareholders – was a textbook case of rewards for failure, paid for by shareholders, customers and those losing their jobs.

High pay and bonuses in the City are seen by those in the financial sector as justified payments for the application of special skills in a pressurised environment, a belief that it is their skill and acumen that delivers the best results for their share-holders. Daniel Kahneman, the eminent psychologist who in 2002 won a Nobel Prize for his contribution to behavioural economics, analysed the investment outcomes for eight consec-utive years of twenty-five anonymous investment advisers for a wealth management company, outcomes that determined their end-of-year bonuses. He found no differences in skill: 'The results resembled what you would expect from a dice-rolling contest, not a game of skill.' On presenting the results to the firm's executives, the implications were 'quickly swept under the carpet'. 'Facts that challenge such basic assumptions – and thereby threaten people's livelihood and self-esteem – are simply not absorbed,' noted Kahneman.[5] If bonuses are awarded for luck not skill then a dice-rolling monkey is as deserving. Such uncomfortable truths have, despite growing political pressure for greater moderation, done nothing to interrupt the bonus and pay juggernaut that drives the culture of the wildly leveraged financial services industry on both sides of the Atlantic.

Does it matter if a small corporate and financial elite are able to command such a large and growing share of national income? Their rewards may be seen to be unmerited to many but do they have a wider impact on the rest of society? Does this runaway growth in the extremes of inequality at the top end inevitably diminish the prospects of the poor?

In the past, tighter controls were in place to ensure the gains of growth were more widely spread. From the 1930s onwards, the UK became a steadily more equal society and rewards at the top became much more modest while, crucially, tax rates on the rich were increased sharply. As a result, the concentration of income at the very top had, by the mid 1970s, fallen to its lowest level in history. As shown in Figure 28, the share of national income taken by the top one percent fell from seventeen percent in the mid 1930s to a low of 5.7% in 1978.

Figure 28: The fall and rise of the top one percent, UK: 1937 to 2011[9]
The share of net income (after income tax) received by the top one percent of taxpayers, percentages

It was not to last. Since then, the share taken by the very top has risen, moving back towards the level last seen in the 1930s. While incomes at the bottom began to rise more slowly than the wider growth in prosperity from the early 1980s, the rate of personal enrichment surged and, with a temporary step backwards in 2008, has continued to do so. Moreover, Figure 28 will underestimate the actual gains of the rich because of the growth of personal tax avoidance, and the way actual incomes at the top are understated to the tax authorities.[6] In the United States, the even greater boom in incomes at the top over the same period was dubbed an 'economic megashift' by the former Republican strategist and expert on wealth, Kevin Phillips.[7] Though they have progressed at different speeds, and from different starting points, most rich nations have experienced a similar shift from falling inequality from the 1930s to rising inequality in recent decades.[8]

The ideological divide

The relationship between inequality and poverty has long been the subject of controversy with an ideological divide between those who see reducing inequality as the solution to poverty and those who see inequality as necessary for helping the poor.

The pro-equality side argue that poverty cannot be separated from inequality, that the two are intimately linked, and that greater inequality generates greater poverty. The eminent historian and social reformer, Richard Tawney, writing a hundred years ago, argued that poverty was down to a 'problem of riches'.[10] It was the inevitable product of an excessively uneven sharing of the national pie. Challenging the mainstream thinking of the time – that poverty was the product of weak morals and idleness – Tawney pointed instead to a societal explanation where the rich gain too large a share of the nation's wealth in a way that consigns large numbers to poverty.

A similar argument was made by Peter Townsend sixty years later: 'More attention must be given to the exposure of excessive and unnecessary privilege, as much as excessive and unnecessary

power. It is impossible to raise the poor without simultaneously
diminishing the rich.'[11]

Too much at the top, according to this school, means less for
those at the bottom: reducing poverty and creating decent
opportunities for all depends on a permanent narrowing in the
huge discrepancies in wealth and power. The ways in which the
rich accumulate their wealth can lead to the impoverishment of
others, especially the weakest groups in society. Moreover,
concentrations of wealth shift what is required to properly function in a society. The Nobel economics laureate Amartya Sen has
developed these ideas through the concept of 'capabilities' –
that which enable people to lead the life they choose and
value – thereby expanding concepts of poverty from ones based
primarily on resources to other aspects of society which enable
people to function, such as health and education. Poverty is
being deprived of these capabilities and stems directly from
inequalities in society. What matters is one's relative position.
Sen puts it thus: 'being relatively poor in a rich country can be a
greater capability handicap even when one's absolute income is
high by world standards. In a generally opulent country, more
income is needed to buy enough commodities to achieve the
same social functioning.'[12]

The opponents of greater equality, in contrast, argue that
poverty is independent of the degree of inequality in society,
that the two are quite distinct. On this view, it is argued that
poverty is a quite separate, stand-alone condition, largely independent of wealth at the top or the living standards enjoyed by
others. As the American liberal philosopher Harry Frankfurt
has argued in what he calls the 'doctrine of sufficiency', what
matters is not whether one has as much as others, but whether

one has enough. He wrote: 'The egalitarian condemnation of inequality as inherently bad loses much of its force when we recognize that those who are doing worse than others may nevertheless be doing rather well ... what is of genuine moral concern is whether people have good lives, and not how their lives compare with the lives of others.'[13] 'Now that starvation and squalor are mostly avoidable, so what if somebody else has a yacht?' wrote the former chair of Northern Rock and Conservative member of the House of Lords, Viscount Ridley.[14] For this group, all that matters is that the poor are better off than in the past; once all have passed above an 'absolute' poverty line, it does not matter if the rich then colonise all the future gains from growth.

This school argued that the post-war drive to greater equality had become a drag on economic dynamism and that the way to tackle poverty was not through a narrower gap, but through growth. Too much equality, it was claimed, would simply lead to a smaller pie and lower living standards for all, including the poor. A higher level of inequality, with higher rewards at the top and a higher share going to profits, was a necessary condition for economic health and tackling poverty: under this view a rising tide lifts all boats.

For the anti-egalitarian school, the tide of greater prosperity will rise more quickly under greater inequality lifting both smaller and larger boats in the process. Some of the extra wealth at the top will 'trickle down', it is claimed, lifting the living standards of all sections of society, including the poor, by more than they would have otherwise. On this view, greater equality, far from alleviating poverty, leads to greater poverty. As the Austrian-born but New York-based economist, Ludwig von Mises, wrote in 1955: 'Inequality of wealth and incomes is the cause of the masses' well being, not the cause of anybody's distress . . . Where there is a lower degree of inequality, there is necessarily a lower standard of living of the masses.'[15] This view was later reinforced by the mainstream American economist Arthur Okun who argued in his influential book *Equality and Efficiency: the Big Trade Off*, published in 1975, that you could have more equal or more efficient economies but not both.[16]

This argument is still going strong post-2008 with, for example, the liberal philosophers Loren Lomasky and Kyle Swan writing in 2009: 'It too often presumes that solutions are to be found within the realm of distributive rather than productive justice that the poverty of the poor is to be laid at the doors of the coffers of the rich.'[17] On this view what counts is not how the pie is distributed but how big it is — it is growth that trumps all. It is an approach that comes with the added political convenience that it absolves society from direct responsibility for the poor other than creating the conditions for growth.[18]

These contrasting views have hugely different implications for the way incomes are distributed in society. It was the dominance of the egalitarian view that helped drive the narrowing income gap during the two immediate post-war decades, and the re-emergence of the counterview that did so much to fuel the rise of inequality from 1980. Gradually, the anti-egalitarian theories promoted through the 1950s and 1960s by a number of New Right thinkers began to gain ground. In 1976, Keith Joseph, one of Mrs Thatcher's closest advisers, wrote: 'Making the rich poorer does not make the poor richer, but it does make the state stronger.'[19] In 1977, during the Queen's Silver Jubilee celebrations, the Duke of Edinburgh wrote an article for the magazine *Director*, suggesting that contemporary Britain should 'not concentrate so heavily on the unfortunate, the underprivileged'.[20]

In the last thirty years, not just the UK but a number of other Anglo-Saxon countries including the US, have conducted an audacious, mass human experiment, one in which economies have been run at much higher levels of inequality. It is an experiment that was launched by Margaret Thatcher, elected in 1979, and Ronald Reagan, who was elected as US president a year later. 'Let the children grow tall,' is how Mrs Thatcher liked to express it. Moreover, although the anti-equality thrust originated with the Right, it came to be broadly accepted across much of the political spectrum including by the New Labour leadership. Throughout their term in government from 1997, Labour downgraded their traditional commitment to greater equality, dismissing claims that the growing income gap would hinder efforts to reduce poverty levels.

Despite its central role in the history of economic thought, the question of distribution – of how to divide the pie – eventually came to be dismissed as heretical by the modern market theorists who have dominated economic thinking from the 1980s. 'Of the tendencies that are harmful to sound economics, the most poisonous is to focus on questions of distribution', wrote the Chicago economist Robert E. Lucas, Nobel Prizewinner and one of the principal architects of the pro-market, self-regulating school, in 2003.[21]

So has the pro-inequality school been proved right? Has the experiment in inequality along with greater reliance on markets proved to be the solution to poverty? For success, the arguments of the pro-inequality school depend on three conditions. First, that poverty is purely an absolute concept. Second, that inequality delivers faster growth. Third, that growth will benefit, at least to some degree, the poorest in society. In practice, none of these contentions has held.

While the pro-inequality school has mostly remained wedded to an absolute concept of poverty, the debate has moved on. Indeed, the idea that poverty is relative is firmly rooted in contemporary thinking, and has come to be accepted even by conservative thinkers. As Kristian Niemietz from the pro-market think-tank the Institute for Economic Affairs has argued in *A New Understanding of Poverty*, an Institute tract published in 2011, needs are 'socially' determined: 'With rising prosperity, poverty standards need to be adjusted upwards over time to remain socially relevant.'[22] Before they came to power, leading Conservative politicians – including David Cameron – made it clear they backed the importance of relative measures of poverty even if in government they set out to distance themselves from the precise measures in use. There is thus a widespread acceptance, endorsed by public opinion on an acceptable minimum, that the line above which the boats need to be lifted is not static.

Growth, inequality and the poor

The central claim of the pro-market school, that high levels of inequality are a necessary condition for more efficient economies and faster growth, has also proved to be flawed. Most economists, from different standpoints, accept that some degree of inequality and wage disparity is necessary to promote incentives while very high levels of redistribution, via high marginal rates of taxation, can blunt incentives. But this is not an argument for unlimited levels of inequality. Too much inequality, along with too much equality, has a damaging economic effect.

Most of the many studies, especially the more recent ones, suggest that, contrary to orthodox economic theory, inequality is associated with slower growth. The evidence is that the post-1980 experiment in deregulated, unequal capitalism has failed to bring the promised pay-off of a bigger cake. Highly influential studies by the IMF have found not only that inequality slows the rate of growth but that redistribution of wealth does little to harm it. 'Lower net inequality is robustly correlated with faster and more durable growth ... redistribution appears generally benign in terms of its impact on growth; only in extreme cases is there some evidence that it may have direct negative effects on growth.'[23]

The Geneva-based International Labour Organisation (ILO) has shown that nearly all large economies – including the UK and the US – are 'wage-led' not 'profit-led'. That is, they experience slower growth when an excessive share of output is colonised by profits, with less going in wages.[24] The evidence also suggests that above a certain limit, one breached over the last two decades, income polarisation leads to more fragile economies that are more prone to crisis.[25] This evidence has led to a widespread questioning of the economic orthodoxy of the last four decades. In a powerful riposte to the established view, Christine Lagarde, head of the IMF, told delegates to the annual Davos gathering of world economic and political leaders in 2013 that 'Excessive inequality is corrosive to growth ... the economics profession and the policy community have downplayed inequality for too long.'[26] In July 2014, in a first for a central banker, the governor of the Bank of England, Mark Carney, told a London business conference on 'inclusive capitalism' that 'relative equality is good for growth.'[27]

One of the primary reasons is that excessive levels of inequality stifle purchasing power among the workforce and make growth dependent on asset bubbles. 'When almost all the gains from growth go to the top as they have for the last 30 years,' explains Robert Reich, former US secretary of labor, 'the vast middle class doesn't have the purchasing power necessary to keep the economy growing and generate lots of jobs. Once the middle class has exhausted all its coping mechanisms . . . the inevitable result is slower growth and fewer jobs.'[28]

The political solution to this problem of shrinking consumer power has been to pump economies full of private debt. In the UK, levels of personal debt rose from forty-five percent of incomes in 1981 to 157 percent in 2008. In the US debt also rose sharply to reach a third more than national income by 2009. But the personal debt explosion did not prevent recession, proving in the longer run to be unsustainable.[29]

High levels of inequality also create a number of other economic distortions that exacerbate instability. One of the key effects of the financial and industrial restructuring of the last three decades has been the diversion of wages and spending power into swollen corporate and private surpluses. Instead of boosting investment, these surpluses led to a mountain of foot-loose global capital that was used in ways that artificially inflated asset values, greatly amplifying the risk of financial crisis. But the consequent crisis did not put an end to the process. Indeed, corporate accumulation gathered pace through the crisis years.

While living standards fell sharply across rich nations from 2008, corporate cash balances – aided by tax engineering – reached new heights, with the international economy awash with such money.

In the UK, corporate cash piles stood at a record £166 billion in 2013, up a third on 2008. American corporations had cash reserves of $1.45 trillion in 2013, the equivalent of over a tenth of the output of the American economy, and up a remarkable fifty percent from 2010.[30] We can add to these the sums held in private accounts by the growing number of global billionaires. The effect, as Guy Ryder, director general of the ILO, has pointed out, is a 'dangerous gap between profits and people.'[31]

These swollen corporate and personal wealth surpluses – 'dead money' as Mark Carney has called them[32] – are the flipside of shrinking wage shares. It is no coincidence that the two nations with the largest corporate cash surpluses, the US and the UK, are also economies characterised by low pay and insecurity. When released, these surpluses are likely to be used not on a much-needed investment boom, and in ways that strengthen the economic base and promote long-term growth, but on forms of financial restructuring that deliver large, short-term, windfall gains for those masterminding the deals.

Significantly, and contrary to the predictions of market theorists, the evidence of the last thirty years is that inequality has inhibited innovation and lowered investment rates. With the exception of the economically powerful US, innovation rates have been higher in more equal countries.[33] In the UK, inequality has been associated with a much poorer record on the key drivers of growth, including investment in research and development (R&D).[34] The ratio of R&D spending as a percentage of GDP in the UK – 1.72 percent in 2012 – is below the EU average (2.06 percent).[35] This is bad news for productivity (output per worker), and thereby pay levels, jobs and economic opportunities.

The rising share taken by profits in the last thirty years has not been used to build a more productive economy but has been associated with a fall in investment in the UK, driving its economy down an increasingly low-value-added, low-skilled, low-paid path.[36] Investment in manufacturing has fallen to barely a trickle, while the finance industry has become 'the cuckoo in the nest', crowding out industries and small businesses that would otherwise have flourished, and devoting a growing share of its activity to helping tax avoidance.

Instead, growing profits have been diverted to fund much higher remuneration packages for directors, financiers and executives, and to finance a boom in corporate and financial restructuring, including a surge in mergers and acquisitions, often private equity led. Such activity, on average, redistributes existing wealth upwards at the expense of the workforce. This sort of financial deal-making has become a principal route to the accumulation of massive personal fortunes on both sides of the Atlantic.

There are other ways in which intense concentrations of wealth divert economic activity away from productive uses. The American economists Sam Bowles and Arjun Jayadev have argued that, in highly unequal societies, the rich need to protect and secure their assets, thereby using labour – mostly low paid – to do so. They estimate that, in the US, one-in-four of the workforce is employed as 'guard labour' – defined (widely) to cover jobs as diverse as security, policing, the military, surveillance and forms of IT that impose work discipline – and thus not involved directly in the production process. Today, the US employs almost as many security guards as teachers.

Bowles and Jayadev's cross-country study found that the higher the level of inequality, the greater the proportion of a workforce deployed as guard workers. Where the extremes of rich and poor are less, 'it is not necessary to devote so much effort to keeping people in line'. In the UK – a society heavily dependent on surveillance – the figure employed as 'guard labour' is close to one-in-five, but it is around one-in-ten in low-inequality countries such as Sweden and Denmark. 'The problem', Bowles and Jayadev argue, 'is that too much guard labor sustains "illegitimate inequalities," creating a drag on the economy. All of the people in guard labor jobs could be doing something more productive with their time.'[37]

The argument that growth will benefit, at least to some degree, the poorest in society is also highly questionable. Since the early 1980s, the proceeds of growth have become increasingly restricted to a small elite at the top. Over the last three decades, working-age households on low to middle incomes have seen their real incomes (that is, after allowing for inflation) rise much more slowly than those on the highest incomes.[38] Moreover, between 1999 and 2011, the Office for National Statistics shows that incomes among the poorest tenth (after deducting housing costs) fell by three percent while the top tenth were twelve percent better off.[39] This is in sharp contrast to the immediate post-war era, when the proceeds of growth were more evenly shared and came to contribute to significant improvements in the living standards of the poorest in society.

Once it is accepted that the poor have a right to a standard
of living linked to contemporary, not past standards, trends in
poverty depend on how the cake is shared. If the poor fail to
share proportionately in growth over time, even though their
absolute living standards may have improved, poverty levels
will rise.

While growth raised living standards across the board in the
1950s and 1960s, it was also accompanied by a reduction of
inequality – a rising tide lifted rowing boats more than the
super-yachts. Since that period, growth has become progressively weaker at lifting people not just out of relative, but since
the turn of the millennium, out of absolute poverty as well.

This failure to ensure that the poor benefit from growth
severely undermines one of the key claims of the New
Right – that growth fuelled by inequality is the best way to
help the poor. Not that these claims ever had any internal
coherence. If greater inequality is seen as the prerequisite for
growth, then attempts to share the proceeds of growth will be
seen as counterproductive so an assumption that the poor
will benefit from such growth is – and has been seen to
be – misplaced.

These flaws in the pro-inequality case are most dramatically
illustrated by the experience of the United States. The official
definition of poverty in the US is based on a poverty threshold
set as long ago as 1969. Aside from minor technical adjustments
and updating for inflation, it has stayed at that level ever since.
Poverty in the United States is therefore still measured according to a four-decade old standard of living, one which
government officials at the time considered the minimum
necessary to support families of different size.

Yet, despite a doubling of *average* real incomes since then, poverty on this fixed measure has actually risen from twelve percent then to fifteen percent in 2011. For children, the proportion in poverty has risen even more sharply, up from fourteen percent in 1969 to twenty-two percent in 2011. If the 1969 poverty line was updated by the growth in real US national income per capita since 1969, the proportion living in poverty would nearly double to twenty-eight percent.[40] As the American economist and former vice-presidential adviser, Jared Bernstein, has commented, growth has simply become 'a spectator sport for too many poor and middle-class households'.[41]

When growth only works for the affluent it becomes a rather distorted measure of broader well-being. Moreover changes in gross domestic product (GDP) over time say little about many aspects of the quality of life, social and environmental, or, indeed, whether or not a society is growing in any meaningful sense.[42] Attempts to devise measures of progress that more closely reflect the real world, including changes in social progress, wider environmental costs and in the distribution of income, show startling divergences in progress across countries. Many other studies have concluded that GDP is dangerously inadequate as a measure of quality of life; these include studies published by the French government's 2008 Commission on the Measurement of Economic Performance and Social Progress and the European Commission's ongoing 'Beyond GDP' initiative.[43]

Wealth extraction
The central reason why growth has become a much weaker mechanism for tackling poverty is that today's hike in personal fortunes at the top is associated less with the creation of new

products, companies and jobs than the upward extraction of existing wealth. A growing proportion of trading activities, big business deals and accountancy practices involve less a process of value creation that increases economic strength and benefits all, and more a process of value transfer. Some of this economic activity counts towards overall gross domestic product and therefore counts as 'growth' even though it is often just financial trading activity rather than something more tangible.

Today's business and financial elite have used their growing economic muscle to seize a larger share of the national and global cake for themselves, a process labelled 'rent-seeking' by economists. This leaves less to share among everyone else. Business activity built mainly on wealth diversion, rather than wealth creation, inevitably leads to greater inequality and higher levels of 'in-built poverty'.

Far from being legitimate rewards for unprecedented success, runaway executive pay, soaring City fees and record bonuses have too often been the product of reverse redistribution from those further down the income scale. The rich have, for the most part, got richer by pocketing the gains and passing on the risks and the losses elsewhere making more and more people vulnerable to poverty in the process.

Of course, some of the personal wealth boom has been the product of wealth- and job-creating entrepreneurial activity which has added to economic progress and brought wider benefits. There are plenty of business leaders, from James Dyson, the tycoon engineer and designer, to Tim Waterstone, who founded the national book chain with a £1,000 redundancy cheque in 1982, who have become wealthy by inventing new products or services and founding new companies. There are thousands of flourishing small companies, started by local entrepreneurs, which employ local labour.

But today's billionaire class are much less likely to have built their personal fortunes by taking large financial risks with their own money to pioneer new products and processes, than through financial and property speculation, private equity-led mergers and hedge-fund activity. Over the last thirty years, such extractive activity has come to permeate whole swathes of the economy. Every time a big multi-billion-pound deal is enacted, the repercussions permeate across society, affecting jobs, pay and wider opportunities.

In the driving seat has been Britain's swollen finance sector. The City's primary role should be as an intermediary, channelling savings to provide the capital for the patient organisation-building on which enduring companies and long term wealth creation are founded. Today, investing in companies of the future is an increasingly fringe activity, with banks favouring 'financial' over 'real engineering', preferring the artificial short-term gains from corporate restructuring and acquisition to more sustained long-term investment. The extended boom in merger and acquisition activity has all too often created giant conglomerates with the monopoly power to exert new pressure on suppliers, a key driver of worsening pay and conditions. This has been one of the most serious economic distortions created by the growing power of the City. Far from using the freedom offered by deregulation in the 1980s to strengthen the productive base, finance has used it to enrich a generation of bankers, financiers and executives.

In the process deregulation has become, in effect, a charter for abuse with ordinary savers in the firing line. Finance has launched wave after wave of savings and investment products – from inappropriate endowment and sub-prime mortgages to precipice bonds and payment protection insurance – which, far from providing value-for-money products of relevance to customers, have been aimed at maximising performance-related executive pay. In almost all cases savings and insurance products have come with excessively high and frequently hidden charges and are all too often backed by predatory and high-pressure selling encouraged by commission structures that would be outlawed in other sectors.

The personal private pensions system – used as a key mechanism for 'wealth extraction' – has consistently charged excessive and hidden fees – swallowing up an average of forty percent of the value of a pension – for very poor returns.[44] In the mass mis-selling of the early 1990s more than one million people were wrongly advised by their financial advisers to give up company pension schemes in favour of personal pensions. In February 2014, the Financial Conduct Authority accused pension companies of taking excessive profits, leaving pension holders seven percent worse off – £139 million a year in aggregate – on average, because of 'profiteering'.

These and other financial scandals – from the rigging of the LIBOR rate to the manipulation of the £3 trillion currency exchange market – have enriched financial and insurance company executives at the expense of millions of smaller investors, from well-off professionals to those on low incomes. Too many banks have been operating more like 'boiler rooms' than trustworthy financial institutions serving the interests of customers.

The domination of finance has been a central driver of higher levels of unemployment and low pay. As the City gained an increasing stranglehold over company boardrooms, corporate executives were persuaded that the best way to maximise the short-run share price was to shed labour and drive down the wage bill. Many of the globe's biggest corporations treat their workforces as little more than expendable 'cost centres', engaging in a constant process of restructuring and transferring the risk of economic change to the workforce.

The privatisation, from the 1980s, of the former publicly owned utilities is another example of the extractive process at work, and one that has brought a huge bonanza for corporate and financial executives at the expense of staff, taxpayers and consumers. Seventy-two state-owned enterprises were sold between 1983 and 1991 alone, with the political promise that the public-to-private transfer would raise efficiency, productivity and investment to the benefit of all. Yet such gains have proved elusive. With most of those who landed shares on privatisation selling up swiftly, the promised shareholding democracy failed to materialise. In the most comprehensive study of the British privatisation process, the Italian academic Massimo Florio, in his book *The Great Divestiture*, has concluded that privatisation failed to boost efficiency and has led to a 'substantial regressive effect on the distribution of incomes and wealth in the United Kingdom'.[45] Despite delivering little in the way of improved performance, privatisation has brought great hikes in managerial pay, profits and shareholder returns paid for by staff lay-offs, the erosion of pay and security, taxpayer losses and higher prices.

In most instances, privatisation has led to steady rises in bills, such as for energy and water. Electricity prices are estimated to be between ten and twenty percent higher than they would have been without privatisation, contributing to the rise in fuel poverty of recent years.[46] Between 2002 and 2011, energy and water bills rose forty-four and twenty-one percent respectively in real terms, while median incomes stagnated and those of the poorest tenth fell by eleven percent.[47] The winners have been largely a mix of executives and wealthy investors, while most of the costs – in job insecurity, pay among the least well skilled, and rising utility bills – have been borne by the poorest half of the population. 'In this sense, privatization was an integral part of a series of policies that created a social rift unequaled anywhere else in Europe,' Florio concluded.[48]

Ten of the twenty-three privatised local and regional water companies are now foreign owned with a further eight bought by private equity groups.[49] In 2007, Thames Water was taken over by a private consortium of investors, mostly from overseas. Since then, as revealed in a study by John Allen and Michael Pryke at the Open University, the consortium has engineered the company's finances to ensure that dividends to investors have exceeded net profits paid for by borrowing, a practice now common across the industry. By offsetting interest charges on the loan, the company will pay no corporation tax for the next five to six years. As the academics concluded: 'A mound of leveraged debt has been used to benefit investors at the expense of households and their rising water bills.'[50]

It is a similar story across other privatised sectors from the railways to care homes. The fixation with private ownership is also now increasingly out of step with other countries which have been unwinding their own privatisation programmes in response to the way the utilities have been exploited for private gain. Eighty-six cities – throughout the US and across

Europe – have taken water services back into a form of public ownership.[51]

The booming private equity revolution in the UK is another example of the way industrial and financial restructuring has delivered large-scale financial gains to the partners organising the buy-outs.[52] For those employees of companies taken over by private equity – from Boots to Debenhams – it often meant large-scale job losses. The industry claims private equity buy-outs – which peaked in the New Labour years at a rate of 150 to 200 buy-outs a quarter – bring many benefits from business mentoring and financial discipline to encouraging enterprises to realise their growth potential.[53]

While there are some success stories of failing companies turned around, and the addition of real value, research by Warwick, Loughborough and Cardiff Business Schools compared 105 institutional buy-outs by private equity companies from 1997 to 2006 with two control groups (one of industry rivals and the other with companies not bought out which had had similar performances prior to the buy-out). The study found that a far higher percentage of the private equity companies cut jobs (fifty-nine percent) than the other companies (thirty-two percent) *and* the productivity per employee of the private-equity-owned companies fell far behind those of the other companies. 'What we found was the promised productivity gains of a take-over rarely materialised. Rather, there was evidence of private-equity buy-outs reducing the number of workers and squeezing wages, without making the firm more efficient,' wrote one of the team, Professor Wood at Warwick Business School.[54]

Financed by the global cash mountain, private equity groups in the UK and the US today hold more cash than at the height of the highly damaging leveraged buy-out boom before 2007. In 2014, private equity giants the Carlyle Group and Blackstone were ready to pounce with, respectively, $50 billion and nearly $40 billion of 'dry powder'.

The question of how wealth is generated has been central to economic debate from the foundations of modern economics. Adam Smith had warned that, because of their love of quick money, 'the prodigals and projectors' could lead the economy astray. 'The efforts of men are utilized in two different ways,' said the influential Italian economist Vilfredo Pareto in his *Manual of Political Economy*, published in 1896: 'they are directed to the production or transformation of economic goods, or else to the appropriation of goods produced by others.'[55] In a modern-day equivalent, the World Bank economist Branko Milanovic has distinguished between 'good' and 'bad' inequality. While personal fortunes that arise from exceptional personal risk-taking and innovation and which help build the economic pie are examples of the former, too much of the rise in the wealth and income gap of recent times is a product of the latter – more 'trickle up' than 'trickle down'.

Power and leverage

One of the central legacies of the changing politics of distribution is found in the increasing muscle wielded by the new financial and corporate barons over domestic and global economic policy. 'At no previous time in British history have the financial and business elites been as dominant as they are today,' wrote a former adviser to the Conservative party, Hywel Williams, in 2006.[56]

While money-power was more contained in the post-war era, checked more effectively by a mix of regulation and restraining social mores, it has re-emerged, with the economic and political system working disproportionately in the interests of wealthy elites, and against those of employees, consumers and savers. The City, big corporations and their lobbying organisations exercise disproportionate leverage over the political process in ways that can undermine economic, tax and regulatory policies. Political parties have become increasingly dependent on funding from the corporate and private sector and the very rich. There is an ever-revolving door, with senior government officials, former cabinet ministers and private sector executives moving between government, Whitehall, the City and multinational companies. After leaving office, Patricia Hewitt, former Labour health secretary, became a consultant to Alliance Boots UK and an adviser to Cinven, a private equity firm that specialises in buy-outs in the health-care industry.[57] The former director-general of commissioning at the Department of Health, who had been responsible for designing the new commissioning health-care system then became global head of health care at KPMG, a company bidding – and winning – some of the consequent contracts.[58]

Despite successive promises, governments have done little to tackle the more egregious financial practices at work or to stem out-of-control City bonuses, rewards for failure and the short-termism that is slowly wrecking the productive base of the economy. Tax avoidance and evasion continues largely unabated. Increasingly, as the distinguished American economist Avinash Persaud has put it, 'the regulators have been captured by those whom they should be regulating'.[59] This process has gone furthest in the United States, a nation dubbed a 'plutonomy' by the American megabank, Citigroup. Outlining the way economic decision-making and consumption in the United States is heavily concentrated in the hands of a tiny minority, the bank described America's return to nineteenth-century levels of inequality as 'the economic disenfranchisement of the masses for the benefit of the few'.[60]

In the UK, the banking industry has run rings around the Financial Services Authority and the Bank of England, while HMRC is constantly doing deals with giant corporations over their tax bills, always, it seems, in favour of the latter. Senior representatives of Britain's big four accountancy firms, between them responsible for an array of tax-avoidance devices, also regularly sit on Treasury sub-committees established to reduce such avoidance. A senior KPMG manager was the lead adviser to the government on a new tax relief for patents – and having done so returned to KPMG advertising to clients how to get the most out of the new laws. The Treasury estimates that this new patent scheme will come at a cost of £1.1 billion in lost corporation tax.[61]

It is those in the bottom half, and the poorest among them, who have been the big losers from the long-term realignment of influence, the strengthened muscle that comes with the upward shift of money and power, and the increased competition for position. Accompanying this realignment has been a change in the political economy of poverty and the weakening collective voice of the poor. In the UK, encouraged by the media and the political classes alike, influential opinion pins the blame for poverty on the poor themselves. The poor lack the weight to counter a constant stream of misinformation about the causes and nature of poverty.

The same trends have contributed to a decline in democratic engagement. In the UK – as in the US and elsewhere[62] – falling voting rates have been greatest among those on low incomes. 'In the 1987 general election there was only a four-point gap in the turnout rate between the highest income group and the poorest', according to a study by the left-of-centre Institute for Public Policy Research (IPPR) think-tank. 'By 2010 this had jumped to 23 points.' Such a divide is also associated with preferential treatment of voters over non-voters: those who did not vote in the 2010 general election faced cuts worth twenty percent of their annual household income, compared to twelve percent for those who did vote.[63]

The distorted power nexus in the UK now has many parallels with the United States. 'Across multiple presidential administrations and a wide range of political conditions, two patterns remain constant', writes the Princeton academic Martin Gilens, author of *Affluence and Influence*. 'First, the poor never have as much influence as the middle class and the middle class never have as much influence as the affluent. Second, over the last four decades, responsiveness to the affluent has steadily increased, while responsiveness to the middle class and the poor has depended on the existence of [specific] circumstances.'[64]

Excessively skewed patterns of power ultimately bring fragmented societies. Studies have shown that excessive inequality exerts a negative influence on trust and is associated with falls in 'social solidarity' – a 'willingness to do something to improve the living conditions of other people'.[65] Despite the growth in inequality, the full scale of the income gap is greatly understated by the public.[66] Most of us have a very poor idea of where we rank in the income hierarchy, though, significantly, it is the affluent who are most at odds with reality – high earners know next to nothing about other people's incomes – while it is the poorest who have the best grasp of their position in the income hierarchy.[67] The misconception is widespread. In 2008, a report by the insurance company AXA defined 'Middle Britain' as households that 'typically earn gross household incomes of between £40,000 and £100,000, and have an average income of £62,000'.[68] The median household income in that year was a fraction over £20,000.

Britain's elite stand accused by the Social Mobility and Child Poverty Commission of running a 'closed shop at the top', one whose entry ticket favours, in particular, private-school education – preferably followed by Oxbridge.[69] The percentage of those in top professions from such backgrounds is so disproportionate that, according to the report, it could be called 'social engineering'. The result is that many of those in positions of influence have little or no experience, or understanding, of the circumstances and lives of others and, in particular, the poor.

Increasingly, the richest have insulated themselves from the realities of other people's lives, unaware of the wider capping of opportunities and diminution of life chances. Such levels of ignorance serve to shield much of society from the real scale of hardship that exists and make it easy to buy into false portrayals of what it is like to be poor. The rich like to view inequality as reflecting a natural order – that they are at the summit by right, by virtue of talent and hard work, while those at the bottom are there because of personal shortcomings. US studies have found that the rich are much more likely to subscribe to 'just world theories' – that their place in society is deserved: 'upper-class people are more likely to explain other people's behavior by appealing to internal traits and abilities, whereas lower-class individuals note circumstances and environmental forces'. [70]

Claiming that inequality merely reflects differences in talent and endeavour makes it much easier to defend the status quo. Evidence that extreme differentials in rewards mostly reflect the imbalance of power, with rewards at the top overstating economic contribution, and those at the bottom understating it, can be conveniently ignored.

Some have argued that this power-inequality nexus is no accident – that those who enjoy the benefits of being at the top also have a strong vested interest in maintaining high levels of poverty. The German-born American sociologist Herbert J. Gans has catalogued the various benefits those at the top of societies gain from the existence of a low-income population. The poor, for example, provide a low-wage labour pool that is willing – or, rather, has little choice but – to perform dirty work at low cost; by working for low wages, they subsidise a variety of economic activities that benefit the affluent; they depress wages more generally, thus allowing more income to go to capital; they help to legitimise conservative ideology by providing examples of deviance and conveniently bear the costs of economic change. [71]

There is a substantial body of evidence that the ideologically driven experiment of the last thirty years – that inequality does not matter in tackling poverty, that poverty levels are independent of how the pie is shared – has been found wanting in the real world. The much-vaunted 'trickle down' theory has been just that – a theory. As Pope Francis has observed: 'There was the promise that once the glass had become full it would overflow and the poor would benefit. But what happens is that when it's full to the brim, the glass magically grows, and thus nothing ever comes out for the poor.'[72]

The dismissal of the distribution question in the debate on poverty has been highly damaging. How the cake is divided, between wages and profits on the one hand, and across wage-earners on the other, has a profound effect on the spread of opportunities, on the scale and nature of poverty, and on economic and social well-being.[73.] Yet, the rising number of pressure groups and charities that have stepped in to press the case for firmer action to tackle poverty have found themselves at war with a political establishment intent on silencing its critics.

8

Hand-to-mouth: Turning to charity in a shrinking state

Security isn't being gradually taken, it is being ripped away.
Low-paid worker, male, Glasgow 2012[1]

In June 2012, the aid charity Oxfam launched a new campaign against poverty in modern Britain. The campaign was supported by a striking image styled like a film poster depicting a raging sea under the tagline: 'The perfect storm . . . starring zero hours contracts, high prices, benefit cuts, unemployment, child care costs.'[2] A message beneath the image said: 'Lifting the lid on austerity Britain reveals a perfect storm – and it's forcing more and more people into poverty.'

Within twenty-four hours, the poster and the campaign were under attack. 'Many people who support Oxfam will be shocked and saddened by this highly political campaigning in domestic British politics,' backbench Conservative MP Conor Burns told the *Daily Telegraph*. Burns then announced that he had asked the chairman of the Charity Commission to investigate Oxfam 'as a matter of urgency'. Other MPs shared this view. 'Oxfam is deliberately misleading people,' added Charlie Elphicke, Conservative MP for Dover and Deal.[3]

This was hardly the first high-profile international aid charity to find itself under fire over its entry into the UK poverty debate. In September 2012, the Save the Children Fund announced that it was launching a £500,000 appeal to help poor British families with the most basic of needs – from a hot meal to blankets and beds. This was the first time in its history – nearly a hundred years – that the charity, known for its work in providing aid overseas, had intervened to provide direct help domestically, and it was a decision that was soon met by a wave of denunciations.

The *Daily Mail* attacked the move as 'obscene' for implying that British children were as needy as African children and called on the charity's director to stick to its traditional role. Christian Guy, director of conservative think-tank the Centre for Social Justice – founded by the cabinet minister, Iain Duncan Smith in 2004 – proclaimed that instead of fighting poverty, 'Save the Children should be fighting family breakdown and welfare dependency.'[4]

Brooks Newmark, then minister for Civil Society, put it more bluntly still in September 2014: 'The important thing charities should be doing is sticking to their knitting and doing the best they can to promote their agenda, which should be about helping others ... We really want to try and keep charities and voluntary groups out of the realms of politics.'[5]

The foodbank explosion

British charities are no strangers to campaigning about poverty and hardship in Britain. But in recent years such high-profile interventions have led to a succession of media and political clashes. Significantly, these stand-offs have arisen not just over criticism of government policy by charities, but also over their growing involvement in the direct relief of poverty, triggered by the provision of food aid on an increasingly mass scale.

In January 2013, a primary schoolboy from Gloucester stopped attending school because he could not face the embarrassment of having no money for lunch. When the school's liaison officer visited his home, he discovered that, apart from oat cereal and milk, there was no food at all in the home. The mother of two explained that her husband had left her, and because they were in his name, all the family's benefits had been stopped because of her 'change in circumstances'. The support worker estimated that it would take two to four months for the benefits to be reassessed. Help only arrived when the local foodbank stepped in.[6]

At the forefront of the rise of food aid is the Christian charity, the Trussell Trust, founded in 1997. In 2009, the charity ran twenty-eight foodbanks. By 2014 the number had climbed to over four hundred, with the charity providing help to around 800,000 people in 2013/14 – a third of them children. A third of all councils in England and Wales have subsidised local foodbanks, in many ways the modern-day equivalent of the soup kitchens of the thirties, providing almost £2.9 million in funding over two years.

Through its network of foodbanks, the Trussell Trust provides emergency food boxes containing three days' supply of foods from tinned fruit and vegetables to pasta and cereal. Recipients must be referred by agency staff or care professionals such as social workers or police officers, and are limited to three vouchers a year. 'We're seeing people from all kinds of backgrounds turning to foodbanks,' explains the Trust's chairman, Chris Mould: 'Working people coming in on their lunchbreaks, mums who are going hungry to feed their children, people whose benefits have been delayed and people who are struggling to find enough work.'[7]

With many other organisations providing food aid, if on a lesser scale, the actual numbers receiving help are much higher. FareShare is a charity which redistributes surplus food from supermarkets and manufacturers to hostels, day centres and breakfast clubs. FoodCycle helps local communities to set up groups of volunteers to collect local produce that would otherwise be wasted, and prepare meals in unused, professional kitchen spaces to be served to those in need in local communities. Kids Company, which helps children across London, has seen rising numbers arriving at its centres, not in search of shelter or a safe haven, but a decent meal. In 2012, the Birmingham Central Mosque teamed up with other local charities to open a foodbank for the local area. There has also been a surge of school breakfast clubs and 'whip rounds' by teachers and neighbourhood groups to help feed hungry children.

The emergence of child hunger is also having much wider effects: 'Our research has highlighted the stigma associated with free school meals, trouble concentrating at school on an empty stomach and the inability to invite friends home for dinner as key issues affecting the social and health implications of living with hunger', concluded a study for the Greater London Authority by the Ipsos Mori Social Research Unit.[8] In one example, a schoolboy brought some friends home without asking. With little food in the house the mother 'had to ring their parents and explain that she couldn't feed them, it is embarrassing . . . sometimes I've had to say to my son: "I haven't got the food, he can't stay." '

Foodbanks are just one area where charities have been stepping in. In Sheffield, a charity called Baby Basics, run from a church storeroom since 2008, provides essential baby products to vulnerable new and expectant mothers. As part of its 'Sleep, Learn, Play' crisis grant programme, Save the Children has helped eight thousand children in the UK with items such as cots, beds and toys.[9] Informal networks run by faith and community groups also provide ad hoc help to meet other needs, including shoes or winter coats for children. A survey of teachers for the Prince's Trust in 2012 not only found a rise in the number of pupils coming to school 'hungry' and 'struggling to concentrate', but two-thirds of teachers said they had witnessed a rise in the number of pupils with holes in their shoes, and seventy-one percent said that they taught children who lacked a coat.[10]

The provision of food aid has become a highly charged political issue. This is, in part, because it has made visible a reality that was formerly much more hidden, helping to expose the full scale and repercussions of contemporary poverty. Initially ministers, keen to back the 'big society' at work, praised the way charities had responded to those in need. But as the government's policies – on austerity, benefits and sanctions – came to be blamed for the surging demand for help, ministers began to publicly clash with food aid charities, becoming increasingly defensive about the impact of their own policies.

Energy secretary Ed Davey told MPs in May 2013 that it was 'completely wrong to suggest that there is some sort of statistical link between the benefit reforms we're making and the provision of foodbanks'.[11] When challenged by the Bishop of Truro in the House of Lords two months later, the work and pensions minister, Lord Freud, attributed the rising numbers to a growth in supply: 'food from a foodbank – the supply – is a free good, and by definition there is an almost infinite demand for a free good'.[12] Then, in September 2013, the education secretary Michael Gove accused those who turn to foodbanks of having only themselves to blame as they are 'not best able to manage their finances'.[13]

But these assertions have been strongly challenged. 'The reality is that there is a clear link between benefit delays or changes and people turning to foodbanks,' said the Trussell Trust's Chris Mould in July 2013.[14] The Trust estimates that fifty-five percent of referrals for food help have been due to problems with benefits and sanctions. Many also struggle with debt, domestic violence or family break-up. A fifth of the Trust's users turn to help because of low earnings or underemployment.[15]

Despite the Trust's evidence, work and pensions secretary Iain Duncan Smith refused requests to meet the charity's leaders and accused them, publicly, of 'scaremongering'. In a letter to the Trust, one which echoed the wider attacks on other charities, he criticised the 'political messaging of your organisation', which had 'repeatedly sought to link the growth in your network to welfare reform'.[16] It also emerged that, almost a year earlier, a senior aide to Iain Duncan Smith had threatened to 'shut down' Britain's main provider of foodbanks, in what had become an increasingly bitter row over allegations of the 'politicisation of poverty'. Chris Mould later admitted that, as a result, the charity had decided to become less vocal about food poverty.[17]

A few days after this revelation, and shortly after the referral of Oxfam to the Charity Commission, Sir Stephen Bubb, the chief executive of the Association of Chief Executives of Voluntary Organisations, warned against 'concerted attacks' against the Trussell Trust and Oxfam. In a letter to *The Times* newspaper on 16 June 2014, Bubb described the outcry over Oxfam's campaign as 'fabricated'. 'The attacks on Oxfam and the Trussell Trust,' he wrote, 'represent an indefensible attempt to shoot the messenger and ignore the message about serious poverty in the UK.'[18] Earlier, in February 2014, the Department for Environment, Food and Rural Affairs (DEFRA) had finally published the research it had commissioned more than a year earlier into the sudden rise in 'food aid'. The report – written by experts at Warwick University – had been ready nine months earlier. But with its findings contradicting ministerial claims and making uncomfortable reading for the government, there was much speculation that the report had been suppressed. In a press release accompanying the report's publication, the authors wrote: 'We found no evidence to support the idea that increased food aid provision is driving demand. All available evidence ... points in the opposite direction. Put simply, there is more need and informal food aid providers are trying to help.' The report also cited benefit problems as a cause, while highlighting the evidence of an underlying and much wider problem of 'food insecurity'.[19]

The growing numbers of people turning to foodbanks, far from being a response to growing supply – as government ministers have claimed – reflects the steadily rising crisis in household finances. It is a symptom of a series of much more deep-seated and long-term trends that have been driving higher levels of entrenched poverty. A rising number of households – in and out of work, with and without children – face dangerously tight finances, leaving them highly exposed to sudden emergencies and often with unmanageable debts, problems that have been greatly compounded by the impact of the 'bedroom tax', the new liability (in England) for partial council tax and the extra travel costs incurred through the demand for more regular attendance for mandated activities to search for work. The tightening benefits and sanctions regime has increased the likelihood of already vulnerable families being left with little or no money, sometimes for weeks at a time or longer. Just to get by, more and more are becoming dependent for financial help on friends and family, and in desperation, on loans or pawnbrokers, and now charities.

Because of the growing crisis of food poverty, and the controversy over its causes, in early 2014, a new All Party Parliamentary Committee on Hunger and Food Poverty was established by Frank Field and Laura Sandys to investigate 'the root causes of hunger and food poverty'.[20] As one piece of evidence to the committee concluded: 'Sanctions and their associated "hardship payment" regime make poor claimants destitute, with the result that they are *inevitably* dependent on food banks and the like ... Given the huge increase in sanctions, the question is not how to explain increased need for food aid, but how it could have been possible for increased sanctions *not* to lead to it.'[21]

Some of those offered vouchers have gone without food for days. In one example, a Yorkshire school started collecting for a foodbank after discovering that a pupil hadn't eaten for an entire weekend.[22] With the number of vouchers restricted to three, people only turn to them when desperate. One manager at the

Manchester branch of Barnado's asked a single parent who had turned to them for help if she 'wanted me to refer her to a food-bank, but she said no. She wanted to save going until she was really desperate, even though she was already skipping meals.'[23] With many seeking help facing multiple financial problems, the Trussell Trust has started to offer 'kettle boxes' containing items such as instant soup and just-add-water porridge for those desperate to keep down their fuel bills. Others who can't afford heating or whose fuel supply has been turned off are given 'cold boxes' containing mainly tinned groceries.

But such 'solutions' are only ever temporary and fail to tackle, as the charities themselves recognise, the underlying problems. The growth of food poverty, while fuelled by the impact of the downturn and, in particular, the government's benefit reforms, has not just suddenly emerged. At root, it stems from height-ened levels of impoverishment and a steady rise in social and economic risk.

Stoking anxiety

Britain has turned, steadily, into a more brittle and a more fiercely competitive society. A number of trends – from the move from an industrial to a service-based economy and the much greater freedom given to markets, to the impact of globali-sation and new technology – have increased levels of insecurity. More chase fewer decent jobs and homes; personal and family incomes have become more volatile; family break-ups are more common; and social support networks are more atomised. Former certainties are being steadily eroded – the job for life, the secure occupational pension, the upward mobility ladder, a decent, affordable home.

Economic shocks have become more frequent and more severe. The last thirty years have seen three deep-seated and prolonged recessions – the early 1980s, early 1990s and post-2008. This compares with three short-lived and shallow ones in the first two post-war decades. One of the effects of the post-war new deal and its more inclusive economic strategies was what the historian Noel Annan has called, in his book *Our Age,* the 'calming of anxiety'.[24] Today, that anxiety is back. Insecurity, about work, housing, income, is increasingly widespread.

Moreover, while levels of risk have been rising, successive governments have been encouraging greater self-dependence. One of the foundation stones of the post-war welfare state and wider economic policy was the socialisation of risk. Aimed at preventing a return of the mass ills of the 1930s – when unemployment rates hit twenty percent – governments embraced a new social contract with the electorate, accepting, for the first time, responsibility for stewarding the economy and minimising the impact of economic upheaval.

Today's emphasis on greater individual responsibility is in part a response to rising affluence. But, often couched in terms of personal choice, it also reflects a change in political philosophy, one that favours a more limited state. Shifting the balance of responsibility from state to individual is a process that was promoted with the election of Mrs Thatcher in 1979. An apostle of individual responsibility, and distrustful of the state, Mrs Thatcher held a very different vision from that of the post-war social reformers. 'I came to office with one deliberate intent: to change Britain from a dependent to a self-reliant society – from a give-it-to-me to a do-it-yourself nation: to a get-up-and-go instead of a sit-back-and wait-for-it Britain.'[25]

All subsequent governments of whatever political hue have signed up to the partial shift from the collective to the private encouraging, for example, a myriad of financial products to protect against job loss, illness, accidents and death, and to shift a greater share of the provision for old age to private – rather than state – pensions. Large chunks of the welfare system – from social care to disability assessments – have been outsourced to private companies. While legislative changes – such as maternity and paternity pay – have in some respects secured improved workforce rights, firms have weakened or withdrawn many of the wider responsibilities to their work-forces that were the norm in the 1950s and 1960s. Notably, over the last decade, companies have moved away from guar-anteed fixed pensions thereby creating long-term financial uncertainty for employees while at the same time decreasing the generosity of occupational pension schemes. By depower-ing unions and empowering boardrooms, the state has handed over the question of wages, jobs and work conditions increas-ingly to market forces, quickening the pace of job destruction and raising the rate of community upheaval, while transfer-ring more of the risk of economic change from government and business to the workforce.

Accompanying these trends has been a wholly different set of values and standards: the promotion of competitive values, a new authority to the pursuit of private advantage over public accomplishment, and the downgrading of the merits of the common good. As Paul Goldberger, architectural critic of the *New York Times* described, in 1990, the identical process in the

United States: 'Today in Los Angeles and Miami, in Boston and Chicago we build great shiny skyscrapers, but they are private not public. We build enclosed arcades and shopping malls, but they too, are private. Corporate office towers but not housing, private arcades but not parks, these choices stand as the symbols of our age . . . If there is any legacy of the Reagan years, it is to have devalued completely the importance of the public realm and to have raised dramatically the value we place on the private realm.'[26]

In many ways the encouragement of greater personal responsibility and self-determination has been embraced by the public. The emphasis on individual rights and responsibilities has offered more choice and empowerment for many in diverse areas from lifestyle choices to personal relationships. Women enjoy much better job opportunities and greater economic, social and personal choice compared with their mothers or grandmothers. For many the shift has been liberating, enabling people to express themselves more openly and for some, notably those with different sexual orientations or gender identities, in ways not possible for previous generations.

Against this, there is a distinction to be drawn between a wider goal of encouraging greater individual freedom and self-expression, and its co-option – and corruption – to justify a more competitive, market-driven, economy. While encouraging greater choice can be a desirable goal, leading to a less paternalistic approach to welfare, a system that prioritises *personal* gain can equally lead to the erosion of mutual systems of public support and a weakening of the collective voice. The result, notably in areas such as housing provision and pensions, is that the marketisation of choice, sold as promoting greater freedom ends up with a significant overall diminution of real choice and opportunity.

At a time when levels of uncertainty and wider economic risks have been rising, the advent of rugged, competitive individualism may have worked for some, mostly better-off groups, but it has left large numbers, including the most vulnerable, much more poorly placed to withstand the shocks that are increasingly prevalent in modern societies. Instead of building cohesive protection, people are left, indeed encouraged, to stand on their own. As the American political scientist Joseph Hacker has written of the United States: 'All of these mounting risks add up to an ever more harrowing reality: Increasingly, all of us . . are riding the economic roller coaster. And yet most of us seem to feel that we are riding it alone.' [27]

A leaner state

Adding to these greater risks have been a number of attempts to limit the role of the state, beginning with the 1980s drive at a permanent reduction in the level of public spending. Yet, as a share of total output, public spending in the UK has not been out of line with other comparable nations. Before the 2008 crisis, this share was roughly in the middle of the major capitalist economies, above the USA, Japan and Canada though below Germany, Italy, Sweden and France.[28]

Despite this, while David Cameron initially justified the post-2010 package of spending cuts as necessary to strengthen the public finances, ministers also made it clear they favour a much smaller state. As the prime minister told his City audience at the lord mayor's banquet in November 2013, austerity is not a temporary response to the economic crisis, but 'something more profound. It means building a leaner, more efficient state. We need to do more with less. Not just now, but permanently.'[29] The austerity programme provides 'the opportunity for government to move decisively against the welfare state tradition', writes the social policy academic Peter Taylor-Gooby, 'and to entrench a radical, competitive and individualistic liberalism permanently in the national political economy.'[30]

According to projections by the International Monetary Fund, the government's spending plans have set the UK heading, by 2017, towards the lowest share of public spending among the major economies, and about on a par with the USA, the traditional home of small government.[31] Because of the prolonged nature of the recession, this projection is likely to be missed but when fully in place – and there are plenty more public spending cuts in the pipeline – the effect of the government's spending and welfare strategy will be a marked erosion of the state's social protection role. The government's welfare reforms will not be reversed as the economy gets stronger while the Labour party plans to continue cutting public spending, if less steeply, and with a longer timetable for reducing the fiscal deficit. This means a permanent dilution in the value and reach of the benefits and wider welfare system. Alongside the shake-up in benefit levels and entitlements, a range of non-cash social and public services are also facing severe and mostly unprecedented cuts in budgets. Local councils in England – the reductions in funding in Scotland, Wales and Northern Ireland have been less severe – have been disproportionately hit by the austerity programme, and will have lost, on average, close to thirty percent of Whitehall grants by 2015.

In England, the reduction in central government grants to councils has been very heavily weighted against the poorest authorities, with many richer authorities left almost unscathed. Analysis by the Audit Commission, the independent local government spending watchdog, has shown that 'councils in the most deprived areas have seen substantially greater reductions in government funding as a share of revenue expenditure than councils in less deprived areas'.[32]

'The proposed cuts distribution is based on technical manipulations of a very complex grant system,' according to Paul Woods, director of resources at Newcastle City Council. 'There is clear evidence that councils that face the largest percentage cuts are those with the highest proportions of pensioners; the highest numbers of children in need; the lowest levels of income and council tax income. Conversely, councils with the lowest proportion of cuts are generally the least deprived councils; in the wealthiest areas; with the lowest percentage of pensioners and looked-after children.'[33]

Because much local authority spending is ring-fenced, non-capped services, such as adult and child social care, which provide often critical support for the most vulnerable, are bearing the brunt of local cuts. As a result, the threshold for entitlement for help is being severely tightened, and is now increasingly restricted to those in the most severe need. Analysis by the Nuffield Trust's Quality Watch programme finds that home- and day-care services in the community for older adults in England lost £539 million – a twenty-three percent reduction in expenditure between 2010 and 2013 alone, leading to sharp cuts in the number of social care visits to the vulnerable elderly and a halving of the number of meals on wheels. 'It is highly likely that this is having a negative effect on older people's health and wellbeing and that of their carers', the report's authors concluded.[34]

In some areas community-support services are in financial crisis. Legal aid for those on benefits has been withdrawn and women's refuges have been closed, while key services for the most vulnerable, such as help for the homeless and those leaving care, are being pared back, in some cases sharply. In addition, careers services for vulnerable young people provided by Connexions offices, along with social support for families and the young, are being greatly scaled back. The number of Sure Start centres – local community centres set up from 1997 to provide a range of support services for families – has fallen by 281 since 2010.[35] Hundreds of public libraries have closed while others have been 'saved' by, controversially, handing them over to volunteers to run. With growing pressure on health and local authority budgets, a report from the Centre for Social Justice found 'repeated evidence of staggering delay and shortfalls, in some cases over many years, in the care, protection and/or support afforded to some vulnerable children and young people by some social care services', leaving teachers and schools all too often forced to pick up the pieces after cuts to the youth mental health service.[36]

Gloves off: charities versus the government

There is a direct link between the rise of social risk and the drive to a more minimal state *and* the way faith groups and charities have been stepping in to fill some of the gaps opening up in the social protection system. Charities have long played an important role in the relief of poverty. In their book *The Prevention of Destitution*, published in 1916, Sidney and Beatrice Webb distinguished between two models of support: the 'parallel bars' model involving the state and the voluntary sector working side by side, and the 'extension ladder' model, with the state guaranteeing a national minimum of a civilised life for all and voluntary help providing additional support. For most of the post-war era, the second model – one endorsed by Beveridge in accepting the central responsibility of the state – has been at work with charities working in partnership with, not as a substitute for the state.

Gradually, that balance has been shifting, with the British model of social support being steered, in part by design, in part by default, in the direction of the 'parallel bars' model which operated in the first two decades of the twentieth century. Charitable and religious groups have come to play a growing part in the system of social support, taking on the role of what the eighteenth-century British politician and philosopher Edmund Burke once called the 'little platoons' that form the basis for a secondary, but very partial safety net.[37] Although charities have long been direct providers of a range of services, this role has been expanding with the state turning increasingly to voluntary organisations to be direct providers, and funding them to do so, in areas from support for the homeless and the provision of mental health services, to residential care for the elderly.

More recently, and controversially, the voluntary sector – in response to the growth of severe hardship – has moved up several gears to provide help with meeting basic material needs. In this sense, the charitable sector is now playing a much more direct role in poverty relief.

The government may prefer charities to 'stick to knitting', as the former minister for civil society provocatively put it, but many play a dual role, helping directly with need and acting as a pressure group, lobbying on behalf of those with a weak voice and little influence, pressing the case for the unfairly sanctioned and low-income groups that are increasingly stigmatised by the media and political forces alike. With few friends in the press, in corporate Britain, or in government, and largely sidelined by the Labour party in its search for Middle England voters, the poor have – all too often – come to rely on the church, charities and pressure groups to make their case, by offering a collective voice and a corrective, if small, to the gradual erosion of effective countervailing power in Britain. This is hardly new. The Victorian founders of groups such as Barnardo's and the Children's Society may have begun with practical help, by providing homes for children, but soon realised that meeting charitable goals required entering the wider arena, campaigning for change among the public and lobbying the political classes.

Figure 29: 'Britain isn't eating' poster, 2013

At Christmas 2013, Church Action on Poverty launched its markedly political 'Britain isn't eating' poster campaign aimed at highlighting 'the scandal of hunger'.[38] The poster – shown in Figure 29 – took the famous 'Labour isn't working' Conservative campaign poster of the 1979 election, with its snaking queue of the unemployed, and turned it into one of the hungry today. The caption read: 'Thousands are going hungry because of benefit changes'.

'The fact that people are left in destitution is a disgrace' is how Archbishop Vincent Nichols, leader of the Roman Catholic Church in England and Wales, put it on the eve of his being made a cardinal.[39] Then, two months later, in a ratcheting up of the Church's anti-poverty campaign, more than forty Anglican bishops and six hundred church leaders signed a letter highlighting what they called a 'national crisis' of hunger and food poverty.[40] Not since the controversial *Faith in the City* report in the 1980s – a report dismissed as a 'load of Communist clerics' by one Conservative MP and 'pure Marxist theology' by another[41] – has the Church clashed so directly and publicly with government.

Reporting a growing flow of pleas for help and advice from those facing multiple hardship and problems with benefits and housing, charities are finding themselves increasingly in the front line of help for many of the most vulnerable in society.[42] When, in 2013, a man approached a children's centre in North Tyneside run by the children's charity Barnardo's to ask for some help with nappies, the project worker visited his home to find that all the family had to eat were a few biscuits and some packets of crisps. The parents had been skipping meals to make sure their children had something to eat. The father had not asked for help with food because he was too proud to do so. The mother worked at a call centre with the father looking after their three children. The mother's earnings were above the level for many of the means-tested benefits.[43]

When Terry, a twenty-year-old former care-leaver living in the Midlands, approached Barnardo's for help, they found he had multiple debts for rent, council tax and phone bills that dated to when he first began living independently and found budgeting difficult. He had been paying off all he could through payment plans and was just about managing to pay for bills and essentials. When an unexpected bill arrived – for £50 – and he was no longer able to get a crisis loan, he went without electricity and cut back on food.[44]

Some, if not all, of these roles have been encouraged by government. David Cameron has made the promotion of the 'big society' a central plank of his vision for Britain. 'The idea of communities taking more control, of more volunteerism, more charitable giving, of social enterprises taking on a bigger role, of people establishing public services themselves' is how he described it in a speech in Milton Keynes in February 2011.[45]

But the differing – and expanding – roles being played by charity do not always sit comfortably beside each other. Indeed there are clear conflicts of role at work. Charities which provide services with state funding *and* engage in lobbying, risk losing financial help. Those heavily dependent on national or local state funding may be less critical of the policies that lead to the gaps they are being asked to fill. Because of this conflict, and the pressure from government to 'depoliticise', charities have 'morphed', according to one critic, 'into becoming subcontractors to the state . . . instead of challenging policies that cut services and entitlements, most keep their head down with their eye on the next contract and a seat at the table'.[46]

As the experience of foodbanks has shown, charities are encouraged to step in – and help provided they don't ask too many uncomfortable questions of government at the same time. Long-established charities are warned – openly and behind closed doors – that their entry into the poverty debate in Britain is not welcomed. Large charities with extensive popular support can ride the storm, but it is less easy for smaller, less public and well-funded names. The big society, it seems, comes with strings attached, a duty of acquiescence. The model apparently favoured by government is one in which citizens are encouraged to volunteer (as long as they are not on benefits, when they should be always available for work) and do good – but to do it quietly and subject to the rules imposed by the state.

These conflicts are becoming more acute as long-established voluntary organisations are simultaneously facing sharp withdrawals in central and local government funding, forced to cut services, lay off staff, and cut levels of pay. The big society is at work but it is creaking badly. A 2013 survey by the Charities Aid Foundation found that half of all charities had been forced to dip into reserves to stay afloat, while a sixth feared they would be forced to close.[47] Scores of specialist hostels and support services for rough sleepers, care-leavers, ex-offenders and those with complex mental health problems have already been closed, despite an official report by consultants Cap Gemini finding 'huge benefits' to individuals and wider society from such services.[48] In some areas, including Nottingham and Derby, funding streams have been cut by more than sixty percent. As a result charities are falling into what one expert has described as 'survivalist mode', ever anxious about where the next grant will come from.[49]

Relying on charity to play a key role in the relief of poverty raises a number of issues. When successful, the voluntary movement risks giving a green light to government to outsource even more of the task of poverty relief, forcing the welfare system into an increasingly residual mould. Charities are only too aware of the risks of becoming a substitute for a uniform system of decent state support, yet the likelihood is that, unless there is a reversal of strategy, direct support will continue to grow and become a permanent part of the anti-poverty landscape, making the poor increasingly reliant on the uncertainties and vicissitudes of charitable aid.

Although they can and do play a vital role, charities, vulnerable themselves to the generosity of government and the public, can never do more than patch up a system frayed by slump, austerity, and the steady transfer of economic and social risks from business and state to the individual. Those in need of help are often deterred by the stigma and shame of having to plead poverty, of getting 'assessed', of satisfying tests of worthiness, not just by the agencies referring them for help but by the rest of society.

Charities themselves are also finding themselves in the firing line on other fronts. In April 2014, the *Mail on Sunday* undertook a 'special investigation' of a foodbank. 'No ID, no checks . . . and vouchers for sob stories: The truth behind those shock food bank claims', screamed its headline.[50] The newspaper claimed to have uncovered abuse of foodbanks with volunteers failing to check credentials and allowing 'scroungers' to flout the system. The 'investigation' was widely, and angrily, condemned on social media.[51]

As the Warwick University report into their rise concluded, foodbanks inevitably fail to tackle the underlying causes of food insecurity. 'Food aid has a limited impact on overall food security status even though it may provide immediate relief.'[52] Foodbanks are neither an efficient way of distributing food (centres dependent on donations can have a very skewed selection of goods), nor a particularly healthy one, with mostly non-perishable goods on offer rather than, say, fresh fruit and vegetables. The Warwick University report notes, however, that foodbanks 'can have an important and constructive role to play in terms of advocacy and lobbying, and in giving a voice to those who experience household food insecurity' – precisely the role that the government wants to clamp down on.

Of all the indicators of the rise in the spread of hardship, the growth of foodbanks is one of the most telling. The banks are, 'the most up-to-date source of data on social marginalisation in our societies – and thus hold the key to understanding the nature of poverty in developed countries', reports Olivier de Schutter, United Nations special rapporteur on the Right to Food and professor of international human rights law at the Université catholique de Louvain in Belgium. 'Access to food is the perfect bellwether for broader socio-economic inequalities. Food insecurity hotspots generally correlate not only with poverty but also with a series of factors that marginalise people and narrow their options.'[53]

The potential consequences of a growing dependency on foodbanks can be seen in Canada where such banks are an established part of emergency food provision. Canada saw a rapid rise in the numbers of banks in the early 2000s resulting from – as in the UK – a retreat from welfare provision and increasingly stringent eligibility tests. Assessing their overall impact, Graham Riches, director of social policy at the University of British Columbia, found that while recipients had come to accept foodbanks as part of a food coping strategy, many found the experience demeaning. He found little evidence 'that they ameliorate food poverty, prevent hunger or contribute to nutritional well-being'. Riches warns countries where foodbanks are in their infancy that while they do provide emergency relief, the risk is that they 'undermine the state's obligation, as ratified in international conventions, to respect, protect and fulfil the human right to food. They enable governments to look the other way.'[54]

De Schutter has issued a similar warning against such schemes becoming embedded in Europe as they have been in the United States, Canada and Australia. 'Food banks are the safety net of safety nets,' he said in a lecture in London in February 2013. 'It is only when government fails that food banks have to step in ... they are not a substitute for social policies that protect people.'[55]

The growth of in-built poverty in the UK stems from a triple strategy: an economic model that allows ever-rising inequality and low pay, an increasingly punitive social strategy towards the poor that imposes tighter and tighter controls on entitlement, and a political system intent on diminishing the role of the state with a system of social protection targeted on the poor.

The result is a growing proportion of the population dependent on the generosity of charity for help with the most basic of needs. Aimed only at dealing with the consequences and not the root causes of poverty, it is unlikely to prove socially or politically sustainable. A coherent anti-poverty strategy would need to be based more closely on universal and inclusive principles of social protection. But a system built around such values would also be much more effective if it had less work to do, operating alongside a wider strategy aimed at securing a more equal distribution of the cake before the social security system comes into play.

9

'That's my dream': How can poverty be tackled?

My dreams for my children, the foremost, is for them to be happy, to be comfortable, see that they have a good job and they can go on their merry ways and enjoy their life. That's my dream.
Single parent, London 2013[1]

On current trends, the next five years will see more people in the UK in poverty, more often and for longer. Despite falling unemployment, the combination of an increasingly polarised labour market, rising housing costs and a continuing squeeze on benefits will put further pressure on low incomes. Although such estimates are always uncertain, the Institute for Fiscal Studies predicts that relative income child poverty in the UK will increase by five percentage points between 2010/11 and 2020/21.[2] A similar prediction is made by the Social Mobility and Child Poverty Commission.[3] In their 2014 report, they predict a future 'where rising living standards will by-pass the poorest in society' and where 2020 will mark the end of the first decade since records began where 'absolute' poverty – as measured against a fixed point in time – does not fall.[4]

Different ways of running modern economies have different outcomes. In general, more market-based economies (such as the US and the UK) have higher poverty rates than more 'regulated models' as in Scandinavia.[5] The countries with the best records have poverty rates (as measured by relative income poverty) of around, or just over a tenth (Figure 1). Britain has not enjoyed such a rate since the mid 1970s. Indeed the poorest fifth in Britain are now significantly poorer than the comparable group in a range of other affluent nations: forty percent poorer than in Germany and Austria and a third poorer than in France, for example.[6]

So can the level of poverty in the UK be brought down to that of the most successful countries today, nearer to the level found in the UK in the 1960s and 1970s? Poverty and welfare have been central issues in political debates in the run-up to the 2015 general election, but at the time of writing, none of the main political parties are offering the kind of radical programme that would be needed even to prevent poverty from continuing to rise.

The extent of poverty for those of working age depends first on how market incomes are distributed, and thus on the pattern of work and wages; and second, on the generosity and coverage of the social security system. The state's role in tackling poverty can focus primarily on the second through 'redistribution', leaving the market to determine job opportunities and wages. Or it can also intervene to create the conditions for a more equal distribution of market incomes, aimed at tackling the root causes of poverty more directly before the tax and benefit system comes into play. This approach has been dubbed one of 'predistribution'; hardly a word that trips off the tongue, but nonetheless, a useful way of looking at the alternatives.

Between 1950 and the end of the 1970s, an active strategy of redistribution combined with a relatively narrow distribution of market incomes to bring historically low poverty rates. Through the 1980s and into the mid 1990s, poverty rates rose because market incomes widened *and* the anti-poverty elements of the tax and benefit system were weakened.

From 1997, Labour, though it did intervene in the market through the introduction of the minimum wage, relied most heavily on redistribution through a revamped tax credit system. While this did lead to a fall in the official income measure of child poverty, the reliance on redistribution through large-scale means-testing had clear limitations.[7] Lacking inclusivity, it failed to command widespread public support. By not addressing the root causes of low income it was costly, with the working and child tax credit budget jumping by almost sixty percent between 2003 and 2010.[8] Labour made the reduction of child poverty a central social goal but, by allowing inequality to rise rapidly, it did so with one hand tied firmly behind its back. The gains also proved to be highly vulnerable, with the benefit reforms by the incoming coalition government rolling back the progress made in the first millennium decade.

These limitations do not mean that 'redistribution' should not be a central plank of anti-poverty policy. It should. Nor does it mean that the present benefit system could not be greatly improved. Britain spends below the OECD average on benefits as a proportion of GDP. Levels of statutory sick pay, short-term incapacity benefits and jobseeker's allowance for single people have fallen so far that they have been described by the Strasbourg-based Council of Europe as 'manifestly inadequate'.[9]

Reclaiming universalism

A primary weakness of the present system of social security is its increasing reliance on means-testing in which support is only made available to the poor. Indeed, there has been a steady shift away from the founding post-war principle of universalism in which benefits were treated as an entitlement, with receipt dependent on circumstances (bringing up children, being unemployed, disabled, or elderly) not on an assessment of financial need. While the post-war years did see a rise in the role of national assistance – the means-tested safety net introduced to guarantee a minimum income – mainly because of the inadequacy of the basic pension, more recent decades have seen a sharp growth in the role of means-testing. This is because of the growing role played by housing benefit, working tax credit and the pensioner credit.[10]

Even child benefit, once the flagship of universal benefits, has now been restricted for high-income earners. This is a shift away from the principle of support for *all* families with children (on the basis that supporting children is intrinsically important) to one which distributes *between* families with children. 'Universal' credit – aimed at converting most working-age benefits into a single system – is, far from being universal, a super-means-tested system. It will also fail to solve one of the key problems of means-testing – inadequate levels of take-up which drop to just fifty-one percent for working tax credit, much lower than the ninety-seven percent reach of child benefit.[11]

The growth of means-testing – a strategy followed by all political parties – reflects a combination of the need to mitigate the impact of the rise in inequality and an increased preference for targeting as a way of keeping costs down.

Benefits, of course, are all targeted in one way or another (child benefit to families with children, pensions to the elderly) but means-tested benefits distinguish between the poor and the rest, with many, especially of working age, not benefiting at all. This is turning welfare into an increasingly residual service, another example of the 'them' (those receiving) and 'us' (those paying) divide in social provision. It represents a wholly different approach from the original Beveridge model where the welfare system acted to protect the vast majority through different phases of their life and in times of need. As the post-war social reformer Richard Titmuss warned, 'services for the poor would become poor services'.[12]

Unlike the universal provision provided in health and education, the benefits system has seen a decline in support. The annual British Social Attitudes Survey puts this down to 'a fundamental long-term change that leaves Britain looking like a more individualistic society, one in which those on benefits are judged more harshly than in the past and seen as less deserving of public assistance'.[13] But a system that is now designed to deliver to a minority, and a minority that are increasingly blamed for their own circumstances, risks producing less support.

Research by the Fabian Society across eleven wealthy countries shows that, as a way of tackling poverty, means-tested targeting is counterproductive. It finds that 'on average the amount redistributed to the poor actually decreases as welfare states become more targeted', largely because more targeted systems deliver less public support, while universal systems align the interests of low-, middle- and high-income groups, embracing the idea that 'we are all in this together'.[14] While universal systems appear to be the least distributive on paper, in practice they distribute the most.

Research at the University of Antwerp shows that what matters for poverty reduction is the share of national income devoted to social spending. That no advanced economy achieves a low poverty rate with low levels of social spending is, the research notes, 'arguably one of the more robust findings of comparative poverty research over the past decades'.[15] Countries with lower rates of poverty typically have higher rates of social investment in services – from education and training for those with low qualifications to more universal childcare provision – that enable people to improve their life chances and thereby reduce the numbers on benefit, especially those in receipt for long periods. These countries place more importance on collective provision, give higher priority to helping parents to work, offer more generous paid leave and put a greater emphasis on flexible working. Yet, in the UK, the independent Office for Budget Responsibility predicts that the share of national income spent on the day-to-day running of public services (excluding items like debt interest) is set to fall by 2019 to its lowest since at least 1948 when modern records began.[16]

The present system of social security does deliver substantial cash transfers – equivalent to around twelve to thirteen percent of the economy. Without this financial support levels of poverty would be much higher and deeper. But the present strategy has multiple weaknesses and leaves large numbers in poverty. The introduction of a lower benefit floor for those of working age, tougher sanctions on existing claimants and additional restrictions on new ones means that more people are slipping through the net, while most working-age benefits are to continue to fall in real terms until at least 2016 – with potentially more reductions to come.

Instead of building a stronger system of universal provision, Britain has adopted a strategy narrowly targeted on the poor, with tighter and tighter controls on entitlement and more and more intrusion into – and control over – people's lives. A more effective strategy would require a greater emphasis on universalism as a way of promoting well-being for all, not just the poor, with the risks that can be encountered through life – from disability to greater infirmity in old age – collectively shared. The contribution of those who take on caring responsibilities, for children, people with disabilities or the elderly, also needs to be more firmly supported. Work is too narrowly defined as paid employment, with those shouldering equally (or more) arduous and important tasks sidelined. Child benefit is a benefit not just to the recipients and their children but, like universal free education, to all of society. To tackle the high rates of poverty in households with children, it needs to be increased. The state pension – still low by European standards – despite its generous treatment compared to other benefits – needs to be understood as the bedrock not just of tackling poverty in old age but as a fundamental right. Concerns about universal benefits going to the better-off should be tackled by taxing them and by making the income tax system more progressive.

The principle of conditionality – in which those in receipt of out-of-work benefits have a reciprocal obligation, especially in their commitment to find work – is a desirable element of an effective benefit system. But it has become over-punitive, counterproductive and deeply unjust in a labour market that has a highly uneven distribution of job opportunities.

While means-testing currently offers significant additional support, there needs to be a better balance between universalism and targeting. The current model is too heavily weighted towards the latter.[17] The most extensive model of a universal system would be a 'citizen's' or 'basic income', a guaranteed and unconditional income paid to every individual as of right, administered in a similar way to child benefit. Such a scheme, advocated over time by a range of leading thinkers from Tom Paine to Bertrand Russell, would have many advantages. It would relieve many of the problems associated with income-related systems, from take-up to the poverty trap and stigma, encourage people to start businesses, while allowing much greater freedom of choice over work and wider childcare and community responsibilities. Trials in parts of the United States and in other countries have shown that such systems act as an incentive to work, while the forthcoming flat-rate pension scheme has some similarities. However, on its own it would not end the need for means-testing, especially of housing benefit. And because of the high gross cost of an effective universal system, such a scheme would also depend on the introduction of a much fairer tax system.[18]

Financing a more universal-based system – which requires higher levels of primary funding – is made difficult by the regressive character of the tax system. Until the mid 1980s, the UK tax system was mildly progressive, taking a higher proportion of high than of low incomes. Since then it has become regressive. In 1979, the top fifth paid 37.6% of their incomes in tax and the poorest fifth only 30.5%. By 2011, this pattern had reversed with the bottom paying, at 36.6%, more than all other groups including the top fifth, at 35.5%.[19] This is the result of the cut in the top rate of income tax from eighty-three to forty percent during the 1980s and a rebalancing of the tax system towards regressive taxes such as council tax and VAT.

Accompanying this process has been an explosion in personal and corporate tax avoidance schemes. Such avoidance is a big and highly lucrative business in the UK with the City employing an army of highly paid financiers and lawyers helping the domestic and global rich, and big corporations, to hide their incomes and wealth in a complex network of tax havens and low-tax jurisdictions. Many of these are British Overseas Territories, including the British Virgin Islands and the Cayman Islands.

Independent experts have put the tax loss from 'artificial' tax avoidance schemes – contrived but legal schemes aimed primarily at reducing tax bills – at at least £25 billion.[20] It is likely to be a good deal higher. The volume of global wealth held offshore, and thus hidden from national tax authorities, has been estimated at between $7.6 and $21 trillion (between eight and twenty-four percent of total global financial wealth). This is a figure that, because of the growth of the offshore industry, will also have grown, probably significantly, through time.[21]

This combination of a regressive tax system and widespread tax avoidance has proved a continuing headache for economic and social policy. It means that a disproportionate share of the cost of paying for welfare is borne by those on middle incomes, a group whose earnings are not much higher than those in receipt of benefits, contributing to the apparent hardening of attitudes to the social security system and imposing a clear political limit on the capacity of redistributive policies.

Moreover, while demands on the state for improved services have been growing, the 'tax-take' as a share of GDP has been falling since it peaked in the early 1980s leaving tax revenue – hovering between thirty-three and thirty-six percent of national income since the mid 1980s – falling short of public spending for most of the last thirty years. Though some of this shortfall is explained by the use of borrowing to fund capital spending, the pressure on Britain's public finances is as much a problem of under-taxation as overspending. It is not that too much is being spent on the poor but too little is being raised from those with the deepest pockets.

Britain's current political economy – a social strategy dominated by targeting, an economic system that feeds the rich and a tax system that allows mass tax avoidance – is always going to leave large numbers in poverty. A key element of a new strategy geared to cutting poverty must be a more progressive tax system. It was Adam Smith who first made the case for progressive taxation. 'It is not unreasonable that the rich should contribute to public expense not only in proportion of their revenue but in something more than that proportion', he wrote in *The Wealth of Nations* more than two and a half centuries ago.[22] The principle that tax should be progressively related to 'ability to pay' was later endorsed by the new Select Committee on Tax established in 1906 and enshrined in Lloyd George's budget of 1909, which introduced a set of graduated income tax rates. It was a view also embraced by the 1993 Ontario Fair Tax Commission which concluded: 'after sifting through the arguments, we have concluded that a fair tax system is one primarily based on the ability-to-pay principle, and that in turn requires the overall tax system to be progressive'.[23]

The progressive tax systems of the post-war era played a critical role in the trend towards greater equality, while the switch to regressive tax systems from the mid 1980s has helped fuel the 'great widening'. It is accepted among economists of all persuasions that there is a point at which an increase in tax rates would reduce incentives and thus revenue. But the latest evidence on the 'optimum tax rate' on the rich – the one that maximises revenue – from a paper by the influential economists Thomas Piketty, Emmanuel Saez and Stefanie Stantcheva, finds that the optimum could be much higher than the prevailing average rate across rich nations.[24]

The lesson is clear. Creating more equal societies and tackling poverty will require wholescale tax reforms that deliver a much larger contribution from the rich. As the secretary general of the OECD, Angel Gurría, argued in 2011, it is time for rich nations to reform 'their tax systems to ensure that wealthier individuals contribute their fair share of the tax burden'.[25]

Tackling wage contraction

Any reformed system of social security would be much more effective and less costly if core inequalities could be reduced and poverty tackled at source, leaving less work for the benefit system to do. Two of the most significant drivers of rising poverty since the early 1980s have been the rise in the level of unemployment along with sustained wage contraction among the bottom half of the workforce caused by both the fall in the share of national income going in wages and the widening gap between top and bottom earnings. A fundamental attack on endemic poverty among the working-age population would require boosting the share of national income going to wages (the wage share), a narrowing of the pay gap between the top and the bottom, and a fall in unemployment.

Boosting wage levels at the bottom would need to start with a rise in the minimum wage combined with policies to cut the numbers below the living wage. These two measures would raise the wage floor and lift wages for millions of low-paid workers. But, because of the sheer scale of wage contraction over the last thirty years, such measures, desirable as they are, would only lead to a relatively modest increase in the total pool of wages at the bottom.[26] Moreover, because poverty depends on many other factors – such as the number of wage earners, security of employment, the number of children and other dependants and housing costs – a substantial reduction in poverty levels among those who are in work would require a range of other measures.

Running the economy at a higher level of employment, provided the extra jobs are not concentrated, as currently, at the bottom end of the wage range, would also help boost wages as well as impact on poverty levels through a reduction in unemployment. Today the real rate of unemployment – including everyone who would be willing to work if jobs were available – is more than double the official headline figure of around six percent and much higher than in the immediate post-war era. While achieving the much lower post-war levels would be difficult in a more globalised world, it is now being increasingly accepted by global leaders that macroeconomic policy needs to be more strongly geared to employment generation than in the past and that reinstating the long-abandoned goal of full or near-full employment would both help create more jobs and be an important instrument in securing decent wage growth.[27]

Perhaps the most effective, and radical, measure for boosting the total wage pool at the bottom would be a rebalancing of bargaining power in favour of the workforce. Another would be a more concerted attempt to reduce the significant pay gap between men and women by raising women's wages. Both measures would raise the share of national income going in pay and would be critical elements of an effective strategy for cutting poverty levels among the workforce.

Far from being a strength, the sustained decline in workforce bargaining power in the UK is an economic and democratic weakness. Because of the 'wage premium' associated with collective bargaining, this erosion of labour's bargaining power has played a big role in wage contraction. Evidence across sixteen rich countries has shown that the higher the level of trade union membership, the lower the degree of inequality.[28] Further, it is likely that the erosion may have encouraged British employers to move down a low-pay and productivity road. By being able to minimise pay and rely on casualised labour, British employers – unlike say their German counterparts – have had few incentives to improve skills and introduce more productive processes.[29]

Phased in over time, such a policy mix – a boost to the minimum wage, a reduction in the numbers on less than the living wage, wider collective bargaining coverage and lower unemployment – would put the thirty-year-long trend of a shrinking wage share into reverse, and make an important contribution to reducing poverty among the low-paid, while taking some of the strain off the benefit system.[30]

So just how feasible are such strategies? A modest increase in the minimum wage – in mid-2014 still a tenth lower in real terms compared with 2007 – would have a minimal effect on jobs, while a phased and partial move on the living wage is feasible for large firms.[31] Indeed, those companies and organisations which have introduced the living wage – around a thousand by the autumn of 2014 – have enjoyed compensating benefits including improved retention and lower recruitment costs.[32] Even a small proportion of the record corporate cash balances held by large companies, both in money terms and as a percentage of the economy, precisely because wages are low, could help fund a wage rise across many parts of the economy.[33] But large companies are supremely unlikely to make any such moves without pressure being placed on them to do so. Moreover, as Howard Reed of Landman Economics has shown, raising *everybody* below the living wage to that level over time would – contrary to orthodox thinking – not necessarily have a detrimental effect on the overall level of employment. While such a move would lead to a loss of jobs in some sectors, this would be offset by a boost to demand sufficient to raise the level of employment across the economy.[34]

Although it would be more difficult for some industries and small firms, international experience shows that it is possible to raise pay in traditionally low-paid sectors like food retailing and hotel work. There are big cross-country variations in pay rates for less killed jobs. In the UK, basic supermarket work is associated with low skill and minimal training, with firms competing on pay rates. In Germany, in contrast, frontline workers are given some vocational training and greater responsibility and discretion for several stages of supermarket work from stocking to merchandising. In Denmark, many employers in food processing have responded to competitive pressures from globalisation by increasing the capital intensity of production, raising productivity sufficiently to pay above the low-wage threshold.[35] Other countries have chosen strategies that have not involved a race to the bottom. The key factor explaining these cross-country differences is the level of collective bargaining. In the UK, low pay is too often down to the lack of proactive unionisation in these sectors.

Delivering better-paid jobs and slowing the pace of substitution of low- for middle-income jobs requires, ultimately, a long-term strategy for raising productivity (output per worker) through an economy geared much more to innovation than to wealth diversion. The UK, along with the US, has a record of weak productivity growth largely as a result of low levels of private investment and R&D, excessive reliance on using low pay to be competitive and too big an emphasis on short-termism. These are the product of one of the central goals of market fundamentalism – the maximisation of shareholder value. The result is that the US and parts of Europe most wedded to the market model fail to prioritise policies that drive innovation and productivity.[36]

Achieving this depends on a much more active – and long-term – industrial strategy aimed at rebalancing the economy towards sectors that can support higher-waged employment, and moving the UK away from its increasingly 'low-road' economy towards a 'higher road' – a higher-skilled, higher-productivity, higher-waged model.

Currently, growth potential of this sort is centred in a number of 'hot spots' – around Heathrow, Gatwick, Stansted and Cambridge and, to a lesser extent, Manchester and Leeds airports – where there has been what the economic commentator and principal of Hertford College, Oxford, Will Hutton, has called 'a burgeoning network of high growth, innovative, knowledge intensive small or medium sized firms clustered in knowledge towns'.[37] While this offers some hope of a 'higher road' strategy in a few parts of the country, notably London and the South-East, to make such a strategy work for the UK as a whole, higher levels of regional investment are needed. Transport infrastructure programmes, in particular, have been – and are projected to be – very heavily weighted to London, with the capital receiving £2,731 per head spending on projects in the pipeline in 2012 compared to £5 per head in the North East.[38]

A more progressive political economy

Achieving substantial and sustained reductions in poverty and inequality will ultimately require a very different economic and business model built around a shift in social and cultural norms and new forms of intervention by the state. It would require more effective regulation, the spreading of power as a counter to big business – to town halls, consumers, the workforce and small businesses – and the dispersal of capital ownership more widely through encouraging alternative business models based around partnerships, co-operatives and social enterprise. This would come with tougher boardroom constraints to end corporate abuse; new cultural norms antipathetic to excesses in pay and which more effectively check rent-seeking activity; and the weakening of the economic grip still held by the City. In short a major departure from the existing Anglo-Saxon model of capitalism.

Central to a more radical anti-poverty strategy would be a new 'social contract', one suited to the post-industrial age and aimed at commanding comprehensive public support. Since 1980 many of the risks associated with corrosive economic change have been transferred from the state and corporations to families and individuals. To lower the rate of poverty, more of these risks need to be collectively shared. As the American sociologist David Brady has put it, poverty is less the inevitable product of deindustrialisation, globalisation and social change than the 'consequence of society's failure to collectively take responsibility for ensuring the economic security of its citizens.'[39]

A progressive social contract built around greater collective responsibility is integral to more egalitarian models of capitalism including those that operated from 1945. Different levels of poverty found across nations ultimately depend on political choices about how wealth is shared. 'Those born into egalitarian countries are much more likely to be economically secure in their youth, sickness and old age', writes Brady. 'In other countries, a much larger share of the population will be poor at some point in their life ... these differences in poverty are principally driven by politics.'[40]

Embedded in the new contract would be recognition of the centrality of the distribution question – of how the cake is divided. 'The principal problem in Political Economy', wrote David Ricardo, one of the founding fathers of classical economics, in 1821, is to determine how the 'produce of the earth ... is divided among ... the proprietor of the land, the owner of the stock or capital necessary for its cultivation and the labourers by whose industry it is cultivated.'[41] In recent

decades, including under the three post-1997 Labour governments, the issue of distribution has been almost totally ignored
by Westminster and Whitehall. Yet how we share the cake has
a huge impact not just on the course and level of poverty but
also on economic stability and durability. High levels of
inequality reduce social mobility and social cohesion; and, as
the epidemiologists Richard Wilkinson and Kate Picket have
shown, undermine the well-being of not just the poor but all
other groups.[42]

Any radical strategy aimed at building a more progressive
political economy would inevitably face a number of political
and economic constraints, external and internal. Wider economic
forces, including globalisation, will impose limits on the management of change while big business interests and the global
billionaire class will continue to exercise disproportionate power
to preserve their privileges, power and wealth.[43] Nowhere is this
muscle used more destructively than in the US and the UK, the
countries with the widest income gaps and deepest poverty.
Despite his sustained and outspoken attacks on inequality, one
he has called 'the defining issue of our time', President Obama
remains in many ways the prisoner of a Wall Street that paid for
his campaign, and of a political system biased to the rich.[44] In the
UK, with the dice loaded heavily in favour of those with
economic power, most of the political forces are for inertia. This
concentration of power has had a toxic impact, creating what
the leading political scientist David Runciman has called 'a
growing sense of impunity among small networks of elites. As
British society has become more unequal it has created pockets
of privilege whose inhabitants are tempted to think that the
normal rules don't apply to them.'[45]

The world is also much more open and competitive than during the post-war era, and globalisation will continue to bring pressure on pay while contributing to the loss of middle-income jobs in Western nations.[46] On the other hand, while such external factors are important, the likelihood is that the wage gap between nations will gradually close as developing economies such as China allow more of the gains from growth to flow to wages. In addition, a growing number of UK companies are switching back to domestic production, while a number of small and medium-sized UK companies have chosen to maintain production in the UK even though they could have moved overseas. Founded in 1985, the Emma Bridgewater pottery in Stoke-on-Trent manufactures in the UK, for example. Another family-run Stoke pottery, Dudson, that supplies tableware for the Dorchester Hotel and Virgin trains, employs five hundred people in its two local factory sites, and exports more than seventy percent of its production.

In addition, the falling wage share, rising pay gap and entrenchment of capital have been driven not just by globalisation but by the politically driven processes of financialisation and the erosion of alternative sources of influence. These trends can be tackled, with the political will, by appropriate measures.[47] Other countries subject to the same external forces of globalisation and automation have maintained more protected labour markets, kept a lid on the power of finance and achieved lower levels of poverty as a result as well as more balanced economies and societies.

The epoch-changing decision of the 1980s to take Britain down the market-led, union-busting, deregulation road, with its disinvestment in public housing and rolling privatisation of the delivery of many public services, is now being widely viewed as one of history's great political blunders. A great leap in the dark, it has weakened the productive base of the economy, spread social recession and plunged millions, unnecessarily, into poverty. Yet despite its evident and destabilising flaws, the post-1980 model with its bias to capital and rentier activity is still very much intact. Keynes's warning during the slump of the 1930s of the continuing grip of old thinking, 'practical men ... are usually the slaves of some defunct economists', is only too applicable today.[48]

The last century has seen two seismic shifts in the way societies have been managed. The first was triggered by the Great Depression and the economic convulsions of the 1930s which eventually led to the post-war managed model of capitalism with its emphasis on Keynesian planning, comprehensive state welfare and the greater sharing of risk. The second came forty years later, sprung by the economic crisis and turmoil of the 1970s, a period of political, industrial and labour upheaval that eventually ushered in the age of market domination.

There is now a growing consensus across some of the most powerful leaders on the planet that tackling inequality is an urgent political priority. Yet the verbal war against the mounting income gap has made little impact at a domestic or global level. To date, the collapse of Lehman Brothers, the shrinking of the world economy and the prolonged nature of the post-2008 crisis have failed to create an unstoppable momentum for change. Though the epochal shifts of earlier times took many years before they were finally embedded, today's parallel economic shock has yet to trigger a similar rupture in political and economic thinking.

What is now at work is, arguably, a deep failure of democracy. Achieving significant change will depend on the renewal of Britain's increasingly broken democratic system. The public across the rich world may have acquiesced by default – at least initially – in the inequality surge, but is now overwhelmingly in favour of reversing it. The United States – and increasingly Britain – have political systems that are heavily skewed against employees, consumers and savers, who are denied much of a say in the decisions that affect key aspects of their lives. Instead, favoured wealthy elites have been able to block even the modest change that majority opinion now accepts is critical to a more robust economic future. Modest measures such as boardrooms steering surpluses to productive use, the rich paying their due taxes, caps on corporate pay, tighter regulations on Wall Street and the City with a smaller finance sector doing its job have proved beyond national and global government. As the American historian John Buenker has argued, 'With globalization, outsourcing, off-shore schemes, and "free trade" agreements, today's "masters of the universe" operate virtually beyond the reach of even the most progressive of governments and powerful of unions.'[49]

Transnational corporations are able to dictate terms of trade with governments apparently all too willing to acquiesce. The Transatlantic Trade and Investment Partnership (TTIP) treaty, which is being negotiated in secret between the European Union and the USA, aims to remove a range of 'regulatory barriers' that currently protect labour rights, social standards and even new banking safeguards introduced to prevent a repeat of the 2008 financial crisis.[50]

Because of the undoubted economic and political constraints impeding change, some are arguing that a strategy aimed at creating more equal market incomes will be difficult to deliver. Lane Kenworthy, professor of sociology at the University of Arizona and a leading expert on poverty, fears that the haemorrhaging of better-paid manufacturing jobs, the long squeeze on wages and the rise of low-paid service jobs are set to continue. If so, the post-1980 relationship – with profit growth outstripping wage growth first in the US, then in the UK and increasingly elsewhere – is likely to be the 'new normal' rather than a temporary blip. As a result, Kenworthy argues that most of the strain for limiting the slide in living standards will have to be borne by 'good old fashioned public insurance' – state subsidies to low earners through more generous tax credits.[51]

The French economist Thomas Piketty, the author of the bestselling and highly influential book *Capital in the Twenty-First Century*, argues that the great narrowing across Western nations – from the early 1930s to the mid-1970s – was an exception to the more deeply rooted historical pattern of high inequality. The reining in of capital after the war – he argues – was made possible by the fallout from the destructive effect of two world wars and the Great Depression. The owners of capital – those at the top of the pyramid of wealth and income – faced a series of blows from the market crash of 1929, and a loss of political credibility which enabled a new pro-labour social consensus, the raising of top tax rates and the nationalisation of major industries.[52]

The post-war era – 'the golden age' of equality and inclusive growth, known as 'les trente glorieuses' in France and 'Wirtschafts-wunder' in Germany – was, Piketty argues, an historical aberration, the product of circumstances that are unlikely to be repeated at least in the immediate future. Instead, he predicts that, left to its own devices, capital will continue to follow what he calls 'a fundamental force for divergence', leading to an ever-increasing concentration of wealth in the hands of the few. 'The speed at which the inequality gap is growing is getting faster and faster ... It means in the first instance a deterioration in the economic well being of the collective, in other words the degradation of the public sector.'[53] Piketty's solution is radical: a war on inherited wealth through a series of punitive taxes – from an eighty percent income tax rate for those earning more than £300,000 a year to an internationally coordinated progressive wealth tax. This might be desirable and effective – and similar rates operated in the US and the UK in the post-war decades – but as Piketty admits such a strategy today is seen as 'utopian'. It would certainly require a new global political consensus that is not even part of the current debate.

A momentum for change

Yet, the historical process may not be quite as deterministic. As recognised by Piketty, models of capitalism are not set in stone. Social and political forces are dynamic and do change direction, as they did in the 1930s and 1970s. There are signs that the political and intellectual tide may be on the move. The market orthodoxy of the last thirty years may still be in place, but it has a decreasing number of friends. Public opinion in the United States is increasingly intolerant of the ability of the rich to accumulate without restraint. The issue of inequality is set to stay at the top of the global debate, capturing the attention not just of President Obama and the Pope, but even former cheerleaders for the market revolution, from the *Financial Times* and the *Economist* to the World Bank. 'The scale and breadth of this squeeze are striking. And the consequences are ugly', is how the *Economist* magazine has described the shrinking slice of the pie going in wages.[54]

One of the most powerful forces for change is the growing acceptance that extreme levels of inequality will, by entrenching economic distortions and squeezing the dominant component of demand – that from wages – promote sustained instability and threaten economic viability. In that sense, sustained inequality will add to the pressure for a correction. The economic risks of persistent inequality have been focusing minds. 'In the next phase of capitalism', the leading Société Générale financier, Albert Edwards, warned in 2012, 'labour will fight back to take its proper share of the national cake, squeezing profits on a secular basis'. Christine Lagarde, head of the IMF, has joined others in warning that creating more economic stability and more sustained economic growth depends on securing 'a more equal distribution of income'.[55] In its annual survey of seven hundred global opinion formers in 2013, the World Economic Forum – the organisers of the annual gathering of business and political leaders at Davos in Switzerland – identified inequality as the 'greatest economic risk of the next decade'.[56]

In May 2014, speaking at a conference on 'inclusive capitalism' organised by the City, the Bank of England governor, Mark Carney, warned his audience – one that included among others, former US president Bill Clinton, and Christine Lagarde – that capitalism risked destroying itself if it ignored its moral obligations: 'Just as any revolution eats its children, unchecked market fundamentalism can devour the social capital essential for the long-term dynamism of capitalism itself.'[57] This is strong stuff from a central banker, but, too often, such condemnations remain empty rhetoric.

To date, these concerns amongst world leaders have yet to be translated into the kind of programme that would deliver a more equal society. Indeed without sustained pressure from below fundamental change will not take place.

In the UK, the United States, and elsewhere, there has been a surge in the number of high-profile and community-based groups formed in opposition to the status quo. Across the UK, grass-roots pressure groups – from Citizens UK to the Living Wage Campaign – have launched high-profile campaigns. Several local authorities – from Sheffield to Islington – have established local poverty and fairness commissions, while groups such as the North East Child Poverty Commission have brought together representatives from the public, private and voluntary sectors, all of which have highlighted the growing plight of those on low incomes while pressing for alternative policies.[58] In 2009, people living in deprived areas of Glasgow were invited to take part in a new Scottish initiative called the Scottish Truth Commission. This set out to give local people the chance to 'bear witness' publicly to their experiences of poverty and social injustice with the ultimate aim of influencing policy and practice in the city.

Decision-makers were invited to listen to the findings and respond to participants in the project. 'The deep-set problems and far reaching consequences of poverty will not be truly tackled until those living this reality are seen as part of the solution – not as part of the problem,' explained one of the participants in the Commission, Ghazala Hakeem. 'We believe that people affected must participate in the policy-making process from beginning to end. Only by doing this do we believe that real and lasting change is possible.'[59]

In 2013, the PSE research team worked with the Community Foundation for Northern Ireland to help local groups conduct their own research that could be linked into the national findings.[60] The participating groups – from Belfast, Ballymena, Londonderry and Lurgan, Catholic and Protestant, rural and urban, representing all ages – documented what was happening locally, the first time many people from the communities felt they had been listened to. The films and community reports stemming from this project have been presented to Stormont, opened the lord mayor of Belfast's convention on poverty, and even reached the European Parliament in Brussels. 'We are sitting with the big people now,' is how one participant put it.[61]

Pressure from below is a precondition for forcing the hand of the 'big people' – for moving beyond what the playwright David Hare has likened to a mood of 'quietism'.[62] As the American labour journalist Sam Pizzigati has argued in his book *The Rich Don't Always Win*, the creation of a more equal and fairer society after the war depended on the way 'America's egalitarians had battled, decade after decade, to place and keep before us a compelling vision of a more equal – and better – society'.[63]

Hare's 'quietism' is getting louder. Grassroots groups such as UK Uncut have launched high-profile action against a number of tax-dodging companies such as Vodafone and HSBC while other citizen-based organisations, such as 38 Degrees, have used the new media to generate opposition to a wide range of issues from zero-hours contracts to austerity measures.

In both the US and the UK there is mounting public pressure to raise the wage floor. The United States has been the outrider for the revival of capital's historic dominance and after decades of stagnant wages and opportunities, one-in-seven Americans now depends on food stamps, while the long-term decline of 'Middle America' has been eating away at a number of the country's enduring social values, including its belief in the 'American dream'. But gradually a backlash has been building. There have been waves of coordinated industrial walkouts by staff from fast food chains to retail outlets demanding the right to unionise and calling for a rise in the $7.25 federal minimum wage, a level unchanged since 2007. While the call has been backed by President Obama but ignored by Congress, the protests have been more successful at the state and local level. California, Connecticut, Rhode Island and New Jersey have all raised the local minimum, while in Maryland the minimum has been raised, via legislation, to $10.10 across the state.[64]

In the UK, the number of employers agreeing to pay the living wage has been on the rise – including big names such as Nestlé, HSBC and Google – while in 2012 Islington Council became the first accredited Living Wage council to include this requirement in its procurement process. All the main political parties favour a modest hike in the national minimum wage. The 'living wage campaign' has a number of influential backers, including the London mayor, Boris Johnson, while there have been a number of high-profile individual campaigns including the celebrity-backed battle by staff at the Picturehouse cinema chain to force the company, which owns a number of art-house cinemas across the country, to pay it. In July 2014, a fake book even appeared (for less than a day) on Amazon's listings: *A Living Wage For All Amazon Workers!*, a move that generated a good deal of publicity.

To date, mounting community pressure, telling as it is, has yet to be translated into a sustained mass popular movement on the scale, say, of the hunger marches of the 1930s, which is perhaps necessary to trigger more fundamental change. What *can* be achieved is evident from the way the 2014 Scottish referendum campaign spawned a wave of political involvement – and of radicalism – leading to public debates on foodbanks, poverty levels and even TTIP, not just in campaign meetings but in pubs, on street corners and on internet forums.[65] Such pressure proved sufficiently powerful to exact substantial commitments on further devolution from Westminster.

Never before has the once-entrenched market model been under such intense scrutiny, with big question marks over its social and economic sustainability. A system which condemns close to thirty percent of the population to live in deprivation carries clear social, political and economic risks. Depending on charity to pick up the pieces is neither effective nor fair. Finding ways of building more equal societies is, increasingly, an economic and social imperative. As a result, today's huge imbalance, between 'people and profits' built around poverty wages and huge corporate and private surpluses, is unlikely to hold indefinitely.

The PSE research over the last thirty years has found a consistent and widespread agreement that all citizens are entitled to a minimum standard of living that is contemporary and relevant to today, not some distant past, and sufficient to enable all to be full citizens. Yet British policy-makers have increasingly failed to back this consensus, instead leaving growing numbers in poverty, with slim opportunities and few prospects of escape, while repeatedly charging large sections of this group with the blame for the situation they find themselves in.

None of this is ordained. Despite the political and economic barriers, there are plenty of workable policies that could, with political will, reverse the course of the last three decades. But without a radical programme of change, many of today's poor will be left unable to fulfil their all-too-modest ambitions. As Jennie hopes for her children: 'Seeing my children have a stable place, proper food, good clothes. You know, a better life. I would want better for them.'

APPENDIX
The Breadline Britain and Poverty and Social Exclusion Surveys

———

Designing the surveys

The items and activities included in the surveys have, in each year, been based on in-depth discussions in focus groups, across a variety of different groups (low-paid workers, the unemployed and the elderly as well as middle-income earners), and different parts of the country (including, in the various years, in and around London, Newcastle-upon-Tyne, Bristol, Cardiff, Belfast and Glasgow). All the surveys have followed similar procedures, though the more recent ones have been able (due to greater funding) to undertake more comprehensive consultations with the public.[1] This has ensured that the items chosen reflect changing customs, priorities and technologies.

Ensuring continuity over time – so that trends can be identified – while also ensuring relevance to the current period at which the survey is taking place is a balancing act. Items have been added as priorities have changed – a question on fresh fruit and vegetables was added in 1990, one on being able to take part in sport or exercise in 2012 and, over time, a number relating to household finances such as on saving and household insurance.

Where possible, the wording of questions used across several surveys has been kept the same or very similar. On occasion, the wording has been adjusted but with the aim of measuring the same thing. In 1990, for example, because of the rise in the number of vegetarians, 'vegetarian equivalent' was added to the question about meat and fish every other day and to a roast joint once a week. Where sums are given (such as for savings) these have been uprated over time.

As time has passed, some items have been dropped, notably for items widely seen as necessities and where ownership had become almost universal. In 1990, an indoor toilet was seen as a necessity by ninety-nine percent of people, was lacked by only one percent and was subsequently dropped. In 1999, eighty percent thought a fridge was a necessity, and the percentage lacking one because they couldn't afford it was insignificant: it was dropped from the list in 2012. This has enabled room for other items to be introduced.[2]

In 1983, thirty-five items were tested (including six specifically for families with children) and in 1990 forty-four items were tested (including eight specifically for families with children). Of these, twenty-six were seen as necessities in 1983 and thirty-two in 1990. The 1983 and 1990 analysis of household poverty is based on these items covering household, adult and child.

In 1999, a new set of questions was introduced specifically addressing the question of necessities for children and thereby enabling more detailed analysis of child poverty. In 1999, fifty-four items were tested for households, which covered household items (such as a damp-free home) and items for adults (such as two meals a day); and a further thirty items were tested specifically for children (such as three meals a day for children). Of these, thirty-five of the household and adult items were seen as necessities and twenty-seven of the children's items. In 2012, forty-six household and adult items were tested and thirty specifically for children – with twenty-five and twenty-four being seen as necessities, respectively. In 1999 and 2012, the analysis of household poverty is based on the household and adult items and the analysis of child poverty is based on the child items.

The deprivation count

From 1999, all the items and activities seen by a majority to be necessities have been tested, using a variety of statistical measures, to ensure that they are reliable and a valid indicator of deprivation.[3] For example, the lack of each item is checked against other factors known, a priori, to be related to poverty – in particular health and self-perception of poverty. Items which are unreliable have been dropped. In 2012, a telephone, washing machine and television were excluded from the deprivation count (though including them would make virtually no difference as the percentages going without are so small).

In addition, being able to afford an unexpected expense of £500 was excluded from the index used in this book. This item is seen as a necessity by fifty-five percent of people but it was only asked as a yes or no question and therefore does not meet the criteria that people need to be offered the 'don't have, don't want' option.[4]

The full list of necessities used in this book for adults and children for the 'deprivation poverty' count for 2012 are shown in Figure A.1.

Adults:

Heating to keep home adequately warm
Damp-free home
Two meals a day
Visit friends or family in hospital or other institutions
Replace or repair broken electrical goods
Fresh fruit and vegetables every day
Celebrations on special occasions
All recommended dental treatment
Warm waterproof coat
Attend weddings, funerals and other such occasions
Meat, fish or vegetarian equivalent every other day
Curtains or window blinds
Household contents insurance
Enough money to keep your home in a decent state of decoration
Hobby or leisure activity
Appropriate clothes for job interviews
Table and chairs at which all the family can eat
Taking part in sport/exercise activities or classes
Two pairs of all-weather shoes
Regular savings (of at least £20 a month) for rainy days
Regular payments to an occupational or private pension

For children:

A warm winter coat
Fresh fruit or vegetables at least once a day
Three meals a day
New, properly fitting shoes
A garden or outdoor space nearby where they can play safely
Books at home suitable for their ages
Meat, fish or vegetarian equivalent at least once a day
A suitable place to study or do homework
Indoor games suitable for their ages
Enough bedrooms for every child of 10 or over of a different sex to have their own bedroom
Computer and internet for homework
Some new, not second-hand clothes
Outdoor leisure equipment
At least four pairs of trousers, leggings, jeans or jogging bottoms
Money to save
Pocket money
Construction toys
Celebrations on special occasions
A hobby or leisure activity
Toddler group or nursery or play group at least once a week for pre-school-aged children
Children's clubs or activities such as drama or football training
Day trips with family once a month
Going on a school trip at least once a term
A holiday away from home for at least one week a year

Figure A.1: Items used for the deprivation count, UK: 2012

A person lacking an item is only counted as deprived if they do not have an item or cannot do an activity because they 'cannot afford it'. Those who do not have an item because they 'do not want it', or do not do an activity because 'they don't want to', are excluded. This means that the deprivation count is a clear measure of the numbers who have an ***enforced lack*** of socially perceived necessities. The 2012 survey introduced a further choice of response for the *activities* included in the survey: as well as 'do', 'don't do, don't want', 'want but cannot do because cannot afford' there was an additional choice of 'want but cannot do for other reason'. This was so that other constraining factors (such as time or caring responsibilities) could be explored. Those who chose the option of 'want but cannot do for other reason' are also excluded from the 2012 deprivation count.

This means that, when comparing 2012 with past surveys, the percentages of 'can't do, can't afford' for the activities in the 2012 survey could well be lower than they would have been if this change had not been made. For example, in 2012, eight percent of adults said they wanted but didn't take part in a hobby or leisure activity because they could not afford one, and seven percent that they wanted one but couldn't take part for other reasons. In 1999, respondents were only given the choice of 'can't afford' for which the percentage was seven percent. Whether the 2012 respondents who replied that they 'couldn't take it for other reason' would, without that choice, have selected the 'couldn't afford it' option is not known. To the extent that at least some would have chosen this option, the 2012 response would have been higher than the eight percent found with this additional choice. As such the numbers for items which are activities in Figures 6 and 7 potentially underestimate the extent of the rise in deprivation since 1999.

The definition of income

Poverty measures based on income use *net* income – that is, total income minus direct taxes (income tax, national insurance and council tax) and plus the value of any social security benefits received. This is the income that people have available to buy goods and services. In addition, income after (rather than before) the deduction of housing costs, which has been found to be more closely correlated with deprivation, is used in PSE analyses by income.

For household income, rather than individual income, the total net disposable income needs to be adjusted to reflect household composition and size – to make each income 'equivalent'. Thus, a household of two adults needs more money than a one-adult household to have the same standard of living but, because of economies of scale, they do not require twice the income. Similarly, households with children need more money than those without. Which equivalence scale is used and, in particular, what weight is given to children in the scale can make a difference to how different types of household appear to fare. Many have argued that the scales used by the government give insufficient weight to the costs of bringing up children and thereby produce lower estimates of poverty than a scale that more accurately reflects the costs of bringing up children. In addition, government scales do not allow for additional costs related to disability. Therefore, the PSE research uses a scale based on the relatives implicit in the 2012 Minimum Income Standard, namely: [5]

PSE 2012 Equivalence Scale (after housing costs)

Head of Household = 0.65
Partner = 0.35
Adult couple = 1.00
Each additional adult (anyone 16 and over) = 0.40
First child = 0.30

Each additional child = 0.25

Person with limiting long-standing disability = 0.30

The household income measure used in the analyses of the PSE 2012 data is thus: net household equivalised income after housing costs.

The poverty count

In this book, a straight deprivation count has been used as a measure of poverty, taking a level of lack for adults (because they cannot afford the items) of three or more necessities. As seen in chapter 2, at this level of deprivation, people are especially likely to suffer in a severe way from other problems measured independently of this measure (in particular poor health and financial stress) and are especially likely to see themselves as poor. The deprivation poverty count for children has been based on a lack of two or more of the child necessities.[6]

Those who lack this level of necessities are strongly concentrated in the lower income groups but some have higher incomes. There are several reasons, as seen in chapter 2, why some on higher incomes are nevertheless deprived and fall below society's minimum. If those in the top fifth of incomes are excluded, the three plus item deprivation count would drop from thirty to twenty-nine percent (for households). If the top two-fifths (by income) are excluded it drops to just over twenty-five percent. If only those in the bottom half of the income scale are included the poverty count drops to around twenty-three percent.

Such adjustment makes very little difference to the overall trends as it would also reduce the poverty count for previous years. In 1983, the deduction of those in the top half of the income range reduced the poverty count from fourteen to twelve percent.[7] This is slightly less of a proportionate fall than for 2012 – financial uncertainty and rising levels of debt have had the impact of spreading deprivation up the income range – but this does not affect the trend; there is still a doubling of deprivation poverty between 1983 and 2012, with the key trend, a rise in the risk of poverty among working households, unchanged.

The PSE research team has undertaken a poverty count that combines both deprivation and income, and aims to establish cut-off points (for income and deprivation level) that distinguish four separate groups:[8]

- 'the poor' (those deprived *and* with low income);
- those 'vulnerable to poverty' (low income but not deprived);
- those 'rising out of poverty' (those deprived but with high income);
- 'the non-poor'.

For 2012, the percentage classed as 'poor' using this method was twenty-two percent.[9]

Compatibility over time

The cumulative deprivation counts in each year given in chapter 2 are based on the standards set at the time each survey was conducted. That is, items seen by the majority at the time of the survey are counted as necessities.[10] This means that although most items are common, the full list of necessities on which the count is based has changed over time. Any measure which looks at people's living standards needs to be adjusted over time to reflect changes in society. Take, for example, measures of inflation, such as the Consumer Price Index. The associated weights for such measures are based on contemporary spending patterns and are thus updated over time as such patterns change. Inflation is thus measured against a changing basket of goods. Similarly, any measure of poverty based on real incomes (that is adjusted for inflation) will therefore incorporate a changing basket of goods. Comparability across time is attained by ensuring, as is the case in the Breadline Britain/PSE studies, that the same methodology is used to determine the basket of goods (the necessities).

Here we explore the extent to which the change to the number and nature of the items on the list between 1999 and 2012 affects the count for 2012. Figure A.2 shows the 2012 count for adults on the basis of both the 2012 list of necessities and the 1999 list. The 2012 list has twenty-one items and the 1999 list twenty-two items; sixteen are common to both. The 2012 list has five new items not asked about in 1999 (such as 'all recommended dental treatment' and 'curtains or window blinds'); the 1999 list has six items that were necessities in 1999 but were not in 2012 (such as 'presents for families or friends once a year', and 'a holiday away from home'). The 2012 count based on 2012 standards therefore excludes these six items. On the other hand, the 2012 count based on 1999 standards includes these items but excludes the five items not asked about in 1999. (Figure 11 in chapter 2 compared the 2012 cumulative counts based on 1999 standards with the 1999 count; this showed that deprivation on this basis rose between 1999 and 2012.)

Figure A.2 shows that the percentages lacking three or more items are more or less identical – both around thirty percent. As we go to higher levels of deprivation the count based on 2012 standards is slightly, but only slightly, lower than the count based on 1999 standards. The change in items on the list to reflect changing priorities and contemporary views on necessities has made no difference to the overall count though a small difference to deeper levels of deprivation with – because standards were less generous in 2012 than they were in 1999 – a slight fall.

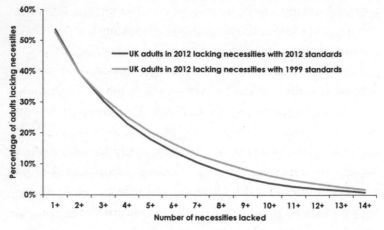

Figure A.2: Comparing the 2012 count on the 2012 standard with the 2012 count on the 1999 standard; adults, UK

Looking across all the years, two key changes take place to the lists over time. First the length of the list varies, rising in 1990 and 1999, while falling slightly in 2012. Second, the composition changes. It is the second that is most important. A longer list does not mean the count will be higher; it depends on the composition of the changes.

Changing some of the items in the list has little impact on the count. If the additional items added (or those taken out) are lacked by small percentages they have very little effect on the overall count at the three plus level and virtually none if these items are only lacked by the most deprived. So for example, in 2012, one percent could not afford the new item 'curtains or blinds'; testing the relationship between those who cannot afford an item and the severity of their deprivation, those who could not afford curtains or blinds were already likely to be severely deprived, lacking a large number of other necessities. When the count is run without this item, it makes no significant difference at all to the percentage lacking three or more necessities.

Items which are more widely lacked, however, do make a difference to the count. Over the years a number of items have been added to the list as a result of the focus group discussions and have turned out to be necessities that are widely lacked. On the other hand, others which are also widely lacked – such as holidays and replacing worn-out clothing – dropped out of the list of necessities in 2012. These changes reflect people's changing priorities. So items that were not of concern thirty years ago (and were not tested to see if they were necessities) have come to be raised as issues in later years and, in some cases, come to be seen as necessities. So, for example, dental care costs have risen sharply up the public's agenda in recent years. This item was added to the 2012 list of items tested. Similarly, rising financial insecurity has become of increasing concern, and in 2012, regular pension payments was also added to the list to be tested. Both items are seen as a necessity by a majority.

The effect of these changing priorities can make a difference to the count (sometimes up, sometimes down). For example, the addition of recommended dental treatment (lacked by seventeen percent of households) in 2012 increases the deprivation count at the three plus level by two percentage points (from twenty-eight to thirty percent). Against this, a number of items that dropped out in 2012 also had high deprivation levels – a quarter lacked a holiday because they could not afford it and fifteen percent could not afford to replace worn clothing. Excluding these items in 2012 thus lowers the deprivation count. The count therefore depends on the composition of the items seen by the public as necessities, the percentages who cannot afford these items and the extent to which the items are lacked by the most severely deprived only. But the important point is that the composition – what comes in and what falls out – is determined by public opinion.

What is being compared in these counts is the level of deprivation as measured *by the standards of the time*. The precise items on the list will change because public perceptions and ways of living change. Overall, if minimum standards rise more than the capacity of those with low incomes to keep pace, then the count will go up. This is generally what happened between 1983 and 1999. Between 1999 and 2012, in addition to the precise items changing to reflect changing priorities, the minimum standard in effect fell slightly reflecting the austere conditions in 2012. The rise in the deprivation count between these years reflects a fall in the standards of living of many people during this period even against this slightly lower standard.

Survey details

The 2012 Poverty and Social Exclusion (PSE) in the UK research was based on two surveys, funded by the Economic and Social Science Research Council (ESRC Grant RES-060-25-0052). Unlike the earlier surveys, both these surveys were also carried out in Northern Ireland.[11]

Necessities of Life survey

The Necessities of Life survey was carried out between May and June 2012 and is based on a sample of 1,447 adults aged sixteen or over in Britain and 1,015 in Northern Ireland. The survey was carried out by the National Centre for Social Research (NatCen) in Britain and by the Northern Ireland Statistics and Research Agency (NISRA) in Northern Ireland. This survey was used to determine attitudes to necessities.

Living standards survey

The Living Standards survey – used to determine levels of deprivation – was carried out between March and December 2012 by the National Centre for Social Research (NatCen) in Britain and by the Northern Ireland Statistics and Research Agency (NISRA) in Northern Ireland. The survey re-interviewed respondents to the 2010/11 Family Resources Survey (FRS) who said they could be contacted again. Every adult living at each address was interviewed.

The sampling frame was designed to give a minimum sample in Britain of 4,220 households (including 1,000 households in Scotland overall and an additional 220 households in rural Scotland) and a minimum sample in Northern Ireland of 1,000 households.[12] The final sample size achieved was 5,193 households (4,205 in Britain and 988 in Northern Ireland) in which 12,097 people were living (9,786 in Britain and 2,311 in Northern Ireland).

The 1999 Poverty and Social Exclusion research was based on two surveys. The attitudes to necessities survey was asked to a representative sample of 1,855 individuals as part of the Office for National Statistics Omnibus survey conducted in June 1999. The living standards survey was based on a random follow-up sample drawn from respondents to the 1998/99 General Household Survey using a sample design to achieve a greater probability of selection to people in lower income groups and Scotland. In total 1,534 individuals were interviewed. The main part of the fieldwork was conducted during September/October 1999. The survey was carried out by the Social Survey Division of the Office for National Statistics. See Appendix 4 *Poverty and social Exclusion in Britain:* www.poverty.ac.uk/system/files/ JRF-Full-report-Poverty-social-exclusion_0-1.pdf

The 1990 Breadline Britain survey took place in July 1990 and covered a quota sample of 1,319 adults aged sixteen and over, face-to-face in their homes. Additional fieldwork among households living in particularly deprived areas was carried out between 25 November and 9 December 1990, with 512 quota interviews conducted face-to-face in homes. Quotas were based on sex, age and working status. Aggregated data was weighted by age, household type, tenure and ACORN housing type to be representative of the population of Great Britain. The survey was conducted by MORI. See Appendix 1 of *Breadline Britain in the 1990s.* www.poverty.ac.uk/sites/default/files/attachments/ Breadline%20Britain%20in%20the%201990s%20 %28Gordon%20%20Pantazis%201997%29_0.pdf

The 1983 Breadline Britain survey took place in February 1983 and covered a quota sample of 1,174 respondents aged sixteen and over interviewed in their homes in eighty sampling points across Great Britain. The sample was designed to over represent poor people living in deprived areas using the ACORN sampling method. The survey was conducted by MORI. See www.poverty.ac.uk/system/files/poor_britain_book/poor-britain-appendices-Mack-Lansley.pdf appendix A.

Further information

The full questionnaires for all four years can be found at: www.poverty.ac.uk/pse-research/questionnaires

Details of the 2012 research development and results can be found at: www.poverty.ac.uk/pse-research/working-papers

Details of the case studies and qualitative research can be found at: www.poverty.ac.uk/living-poverty/personal-experiences; http://www.poverty.ac.uk/living-poverty/life-stories; http://www.poverty.ac.uk/community/northern-ireland; www.poverty.ac.uk/living-poverty/breadline-britain

Membership of the PSE 2012 project team, including the UK and International Advisory Boards, can be found at: www.poverty.ac.uk/pse-research/pse-uk/project-team

Acknowledgments

___

This book, even more than most, is the product of joint effort. We are indebted to the Economic and Social Research Council for funding the 2012 Poverty and Social Exclusion research (ESRC grant 060-25-0052); to London Weekend Television (now part of ITV) which funded the 1983 and the 1990 surveys; to Brian Gosschalk of MORI (now Ipsos MORI) for carrying out the 1983 and 1990 surveys; and to the Joseph Rowntree Foundation for funding the 1999 survey (and for additional funding for the 1990 survey analysis).

We would like to offer a special thanks to the scores of families and individuals who across all the years – often in difficult circumstances – have so generously shared their experiences with us. We have drawn on these for the case studies in the book. The studies are, of course, specific to the situation facing the families at the time they were conducted. Without their generous participation our understanding of the everyday realities of life for those living in poverty in a modern, affluent society would have been much diminished.

We would also like to thank the many voluntary organisations across the UK who have helped; in particular, the groups in Birmingham, Glasgow and Gloucestershire who helped with the PSE qualitative research on the experiences of low-income families during the recession and the Community Foundation for Northern Ireland for their collaborative work on their participatory Communities in Action project. We would also extend a particular thanks to Children North East and the North East Child Poverty Commission and to Poverty Alliance Scotland and the Poverty Truth Commission Scotland.

The book draws heavily on the work of others, over many decades, notably on the pioneering work of Professor Peter Townsend. Peter devoted much of his life to attempting to improve the lives of the poorest in Britain in so many ways. He developed the relative deprivation method for measuring poverty and was a key member of the bid team for the 2012 study but, sadly, he died in 2009.

The 2012 PSE project has been a collaborative effort between teams across six universities in England, Scotland and Northern Ireland: the University of Bristol (lead), Heriot-Watt University, the Open University, Queen's University Belfast, the University of Glasgow and the University of York. The academic research team has worked in close partnership with two survey organisations, the National Centre for Social Research (NatCen) in Britain and the Northern Ireland Statistics and Research Agency (NISRA).

We owe a special thanks to Professor David Gordon, head of the Townsend Centre for International Poverty Research and the lead on the 2012 study, and with whom we have collaborated closely over many years, going back to 1990. He steered the project and was a constant source of help and guidance throughout. We are heavily indebted to Dr Demi Patsios of the

University of Bristol for his generosity in giving up much of his time to help to generate many of the data sets used; without these, the book would not have appeared. We are also indebted to Dr Gill Main and Dr Shailen Nandy for their help with the analysis of the data.

We are especially grateful to Dr Simon Pemberton, who very generously read through an early draft of the book and made numerous helpful and insightful comments and who guided us through the PSE qualitative research on low-income families. Thanks too to Gabi Kent, the community engagement lead on the PSE project, whose work with the CFNI team in Northern Ireland and with numerous organisations across the UK helped immeasurably in enabling us to better understand the ways in which communities can organise for change.

The contributions made by our research colleagues and members of the PSE research team cannot be underestimated and we appreciate that many of the ideas in this book have resulted from their work and conversations with them. We would particularly like to thank: Professor Nick Bailey, Dr Karen Bell, Dr Kirsten Besemer, Professor Jonathan Bradshaw, Professor Glen Bramley, Professor Mary Daly, Dr Esther Dermott, Dr Eldin Fahmy; Maria Gannon, Dr Pauline Heslop, Nikki Hicks, Professor Paddy Hillyard, Grace Kelly, Dr Mark Livingston, Professor Ruth Levitas, Christina Pantazis, Professor Sarah Payne, Marco Pomati, Ronan Smyth, Eileen Sutton, Professor Mike Tomlinson and Lisa Wilson.

We have drawn heavily on the PSE project website – www. poverty.ac.uk – and we are indebted to our colleagues at the Open University who worked on the initial development of the site and to Steve Yates and Beverley Daley (from Xited Ltd) for its further development. A particular thanks to Pete Mitton, who throughout has generously shared his knowledge of web development and data visualisation, Ken Jones, who helped keep on top of news and reports during the period of the project research, and Sasha Laurel-Jagroo who, with great enthusiasm and dedication, has managed feedback from the website and the PSE twitter feed, enabling us to get a better understanding of the current debates. We also owe much to the very many other colleagues at the Open University – both in the Social Science faculty and in the learning and teaching centre (LTS) – who have been generous with their time, ideas and support. Thanks also go to Roshni Amin who has helped cover other work while the book was being written.

We are grateful for the feedback from a number of presentations at conferences and events including those organised by the Bristol Festival of Economics, the third Townsend Memorial Conference in 2014, the Centre for Labour and Social Studies, the ESRC Britain in 2014 launch, the Equality Trust, the Northern Ireland Council for Voluntary Organisations, the OECD, Oxfam Scotland, the Royal Society of Arts, the Scottish Council for Voluntary Organisations, the Social Policy Association, Globalnet21, the Think-Tank for Action on Social Change, Dublin, and various ESRC-funded seminars on inequalities research. Many others – from charitable organisations, pressure groups and academics involved in related research – have supported both the research project and this book. A particular thanks to the Households Below Average Income analysts (in the Department for Work and Pensions) for their help unravelling the history of poverty measurement and to Church Action on Poverty for their kind permission to use their 'Britain isn't eating' poster.

Huge thanks, too, to Andrew Lownie, our ever-supportive agent, and to Mike Harpley at Oneworld, whose determined editing has made for an immensely improved and, hopefully, more readable book.

Last, but far from least, we are grateful to Anne Rannie and Harold, Jonathan and David Frayman, for their unwarranted patience, endurance and support during the writing of this book. Anne volunteered, cheerfully, to take on the task of reading a number of early chapters and has been an immense source of encouragement and sanity throughout. Jonathan and David were throughout a source of constructive challenge and innumerable ideas. Harold, who shares with us the distinction of having been involved in this work since its conception back in 1983, still found the energy and interest for continuing our discussions on the underlying method and to comment on drafts.

This book will be just a small part of the output of the PSE project. More detailed reports by other members of the research team will be published by Policy Press at Bristol University.

Our hope is that the book will help rebalance the heavily loaded debate about the causes, nature and solutions to poverty, and contribute to a more informed and less prejudiced approach to what is now one of the most urgent policy issues in the UK.

All responsibility, of course, lies with the authors.

Notes

Preface

1 R. Tawney, 'Poverty as an industrial problem', inaugural lecture, repro-
duced in *Memoranda on the Problems of Poverty* (London: William Morris
Press, 2013).

2 These statistics, and all others in the preface, come from the only four sets
of national surveys into poverty in Britain over the last thirty years,
namely: the Poverty and Social Exclusion 2012 surveys; the Poverty and
Social Exclusion 1999 surveys; the Breadline Britain 1990 survey and the
Breadline Britain 1983 survey. Full details of the overall methodology
and results of these surveys are in chapters 1 and 2 and further technical
details are in the appendix.

Chapter 1

1 www.poverty.ac.uk/living-poverty/personal-experiences/jennie-single-
parent, film 2, *Is it fair?*

2 M. Brewer, T. Clark and A. Goodman, *The Government's Child Poverty
Target*, Commentary 88, Institute for Fiscal Studies, London, 2002, p. 2.

3 Social Policy Justice Group, *The State of the Nation Report: Economic
Dependency*, 2006.

4 D. Cameron, *Scarman Lecture*, 24 November 2006.

5 M. Brewer, 'Labour's child poverty effort was exceptional', *Guardian*, 13
June 2012.

6 The Act also contains three other targets including another income

-based target, namely a reduction in absolute income poverty taking 2010/11 as the base year.

7   The Coalition: *Our Programme for Government* (London: Cabinet Office, 2010).

8   Frank Field, *The Foundation Years: preventing poor children becoming poor adults, The report of the Independent Review on Poverty and Life Chances* (HM Government, December 2010).

9   J. Chapman, 'Benefits can do more harm than good for child poverty', *Daily Mail*, 2 December 2011.

10 www.guardian.co.uk/commentisfree/2010/nov/09/poverty-plus-pound-not-enough?CMP=twt_gu

11 *Tackling Child Poverty and Improving Life Chances* (Department for Education, December 2010).

12 Quoted in Chapman, op. cit.

13 Field, op. cit. p. 73.

14 P. Wintour, 'Coalition Government sets out radical welfare reforms', *Guardian,* 26 May 2010.

15 Frank Field, 'Poverty is about much more than money', *Daily Telegraph,* 5 June 2010.

16 These effects can be seen on interactive graphs at www.poverty.ac.uk/definitions-poverty/income-threshold-approach

17 John Veit-Wilson, 'Can Relative Poverty be Abolished?', 2013; www.poverty.ac.uk/editorial/can-relative-poverty-be-abolished

18 Iain Duncan Smith and George Osborne, 'The Conservatives' child poverty plan tackles poverty at source', *Guardian,* 26 February 2014.

19 Source: Unicef, *Measuring Child Poverty*, 2012, Report Card 10, fig 5; www.unicef.org.uk/Documents/Publications/RC10-measuring-child-poverty.pdf

20 In their early reports, the HBAI analysis adopted some absolute measures and also used a range of relative thresholds.

21 M. Dean, *Democracy Under Attack* (Bristol: Policy Press, 2013), p. 253.

22 www.ifs.org.uk/fiscalFacts/povertyStats

23 Quoted in N. Timmins, *The Five Giants* (London: Fontana Press, 1996), pp. 150–1.

24 www.ifs.org.uk/uploads/publications/bns/bn19figs.xlsx

25 R. Tunstall et al., *The links between housing and poverty* (York: Joseph Rowntree Foundation, 2013).

26 The HBAI initially used as thresholds a range of percentages (from fifty percent to ninety percent) of *mean* household income (that is, the average income calculated by dividing the sum of all incomes by the number of people in the distribution). A threshold using mean income reflects the whole income range rather than, as for the median, just the bottom half. Unlike using the median, increases in the incomes of the rich raise the target. Similarly, if the incomes of those below the threshold are raised, the target goes up unless at the same time the incomes of those above the target are reduced. In the late 1990s, the median began to be preferred over the mean because, unlike the mean, it is unaffected by a rise in the incomes of the poorest, as long as the resultant incomes stay below the median. The first HBAI report to use the sixty percent of the median income threshold as a primary low income measure was that for 1999/2000.

27 P. Spicker, 'Why refer to poverty as a proportion of median income?', *Journal of Poverty and Social Justice,* vol. 2, 2012, p. 164.

28 http://www.ifs.org.uk/uploads/publications/bns/bn19figs.xlsx, Poverty (AHC).

29 The Minimum Income Standard research sets out to try to provide such external validation for setting a minimum income level. In 2011, the research found that the income needed to keep households out of poverty went from sixty-four percent of median household income for pensioner couples to around seventy-six to seventy-seven percent for all others. See Donald Hirsch, *A Minimum Income Standard for the UK* (York: Joseph Rowntree Foundation, 2011), p. 16.

30 A more detailed version of these arguments on the difficulties of finding a measure of absolute poverty are set out in J. Mack and S. Lansley, *Poor Britain* (London: George Allen and Unwin, 1985), ch. 2, available at www.poverty.ac.uk/system/files/poor_britain_book/poor-britain-chap02-Mack-Lansley.pdf

31 Adam Smith, *Wealth of Nations* (London: Ward, 1812).

32 Karl Marx, *Karl Marx Selected Works* (London: Lawrence & Wishart, 1946).

33 J. K. Galbraith, *The Affluent Society* (London: Penguin, 1958), p. 261.

34 P. Townsend, 'The meaning of poverty', *British Journal of Sociology*, 13, 3, 1962, p. 225.

35 P. Townsend, *Poverty in the United Kingdom* (London: Penguin, 1979), p. 31. Now available at: www.poverty.ac.uk/free-resources-books/poverty-united-kingdom

36 A more detailed critique of Townsend's method is in Mack and Lansley op. cit., ch. 2.

37 D. Piachaud, 'Peter Townsend and the Holy Grail', *New Society*, 10 September 1981.

38 K. Joseph and J. Sumption, *Equality* (London: John Murray, 1979), pp. 27–8.

39 See Mack and Lansley, op. cit., ch. 2 for more detail on the development of this concept of 'socially perceived necessities'.

40 For a detailed discussion of how the items were selected see Mack and Lansley, op. cit., pp. 37–53.

41 In surveys repeating this approach in other countries which do not have universal free education or health systems, such items are included and are consistently seen to be necessities by large majorities.

42 E. Fahmy, S. Pemberton and E. Sutton, 'Public Perceptions of Poverty and Social Exclusion: Final Report on Focus Group Findings', *PSE analysis working paper No. 3*, 2012. See appendix for further details.

43 Three items in this table – namely, three meals a day, enough bedrooms for every child over 10 of different sex, and children's friends round for tea/snack fortnightly – were also asked in 1983 and 1990, for which the percentages were 82%, 77% and 37% respectively in 1983, and 90%, 82% and 52% in 1990.

44 For a fuller discussion of the results of the 2012 necessities survey see J. Mack, S. Lansley, C. Pantzasis and S. Nandy, 'Attitudes to necessities in the PSE 2012 survey: are minimum standards becoming less generous?', *PSE Analysis Working Paper No. 5*, October 2013; Gill Main and Jonathan Bradshaw, 'The Necessities of Life for Children,' *PSE Working Paper No. 6*, 2014: www.poverty.ac.uk/pse-research/pse-uk/results-analysis. For details on predecessor surveys see D. Gordon and C. Pantazis (eds), *Breadline Britain in the 1990s* (Aldershot: Ashgate, 1997); C. Pantazis,

D. Gordon and R. Levitas, *Poverty and Social Exclusion in Britain* (Bristol: The Policy Press, 2006). A PSE survey was conducted in Northern Ireland in 2002/3; see P. Hillyard, G. Kelly et al., *Bare Necessities* (Belfast: Democratic Dialogue, 2003).

45 Fahmy, Pemberton and Sutton, op. cit.

46 A more detailed discussion of the trends over time can be found in J. Mack, S. Lansley, C. Pantzasis and S. Nandy, 'Attitudes to necessities in the PSE 2012 survey: are minimum standards becoming less generous?', *PSE analysis working paper No. 5,* October 2013.

47 Median real income stood at £427 a week in 2011/12, fractionally lower than the £429 figure for 2001/2 (after adjusting for inflation): https://www.gov.uk/government/organisations/department-for-work-pensions/series/households-below-average-income-hbai--2

48 Special Eurobarometer, *Poverty and Exclusion* (Brussels: European Commission, 2007).

49 See www.poverty.ac.uk/pse-research/international-research for details of international research.

50 Shailen Nandy and Marco Pomati, *Applying the consensual method of estimating poverty in a low income African setting* (Social Indicators Research, 10.1007/s11205-014-0819-z, December, 2014).

51 See, for example, C. Snowdon, 'Poverty, taxes and the cost of living', *Prospect,* 2013.

52 See, for example, J. Flaherty, *Getting By, Getting Heard* (Glasgow: Report for the Scottish Borders Commission, 2008).

53 E. Fahmy, S. Pemberton and E. Sutton, 'Public Perceptions of Poverty and Social Exclusion: Final Report on Focus Group Findings', *PSE Working Paper Analysis No. 3,* August 2012.

54 Ibid.

55 For 2012 see Mack, Lansley, Pantzasis and Nandy op. cit.; for 1990 see D. Gordon and C. Pantazis (eds.) *Breadline Brtiain in the 1990s* (Farnham: Ashgate, 1997), pp. 71–81; for 1999 see C. Pantazis, D. Gordon and R. Levitas (eds.), *Poverty and Social Exclusion in Britain* (Bristol: The Policy Press, 2006), pp. 98–106; and for the Northern Ireland 2002/3 survey see C. McAuley, P. Hillyard, E. McLaughlin, M. Tomlinson, G. Kelly and D.

Patsios, Working Paper 1: The Necessities of Life in Northern Ireland. The 2012 results can also be explored at: www.poverty.ac.uk/pse-research/explore-data

56 M. Gannon and N. Bailey, 'Attitudes to the necessities of life in Scotland; can a UK poverty standard be applied in Scotland?', *PSE analysis working paper No. 5*, 2013.

57 To explore these differences in detail go to: www.poverty.ac.uk/pse-research/attitudes-necessities-scatterplots-uk-2012

58 J. Mack and S. Lansley, *Poor Britain* (London: George Allen and Unwin, 1985), p. 63.

59 Significance was tested using relative risk; see D. Gordon, *Why use relative risk?*, PSE statistical briefing note No. 1: www.poverty.ac.uk/pse-research /pse-uk/statistical-notes

60 Gemma Wright, *Working Paper 10: Socially Perceived Necessities in South Africa: Patterns of Possession, CASASP* (University of Oxford, 2011).

61 Mack and Lansley, op. cit., p. 86. For a debate on the strength of this finding, see S. McKay, 'Poverty or preference: what do "consensual deprivation indicators" really measure?', *Fiscal Studies*, vol. 25, note 2, pp. 201–23, and a response: C. Pantazis, D. Gordon and P. Townsend, 'The Necessities of Life' in C. Pantazis et al., op. cit., 2006.

62 *Hansard*, 28 June 1984.

63 See, for example, *Developing Deprivation Questions for the Family Resources Survey*, Working Paper Number 13, Department for Work and Pensions, 2003.

64 S. McKay and S. Collard, 'Developing deprivation questions for the Family Resources Survey', London: *DWP Working Paper No. 13*, 2004; S. McKay, 'Review of Child Material Items in the Family Resources Survey', *DWP Research Report No. 746*, 2011.

65 See, for example, Snowdon op. cit.

66 www.mirror.co.uk/news/uk-news/poverty-not-doubled-greed-grown -3738335#ixzz38UUoMK80

67 'What is poverty?', LBC, 19 June, 2014: lbc.audioagain.com/presenters/ 7-nick-ferrari/101-the-whole-show

Chapter 2

1   www.poverty.ac.uk/living-poverty/life-stories, film 1.

2   Barnardo's, *Families in need of food parcels – the food poverty crisis unwrapped,* 2013.

3   Institute for Fiscal Studies, Relative income trends: http://www.ifs.org. uk/uploads/publications/bns/bn19figs.xlsx, Income (BHC) and Income (AHC)

4   P. Townsend, *Poverty in the United Kingdom* (London: Penguin, 1979), p. 31. Available at: www.poverty.ac.uk/free-resources-books/poverty-united-kingdom

5   For a detailed discussion of the development of this approach see J. Mack and S. Lansley, *Poor Britain* (London: George Allen and Unwin, 1985), pp. 37–48. This more nuanced view of people's choices was developed further in the 2012 study by adding an additional choice when examining activities (as opposed to possessions). In this survey, for the first time, people were offered an additional choice of wanting to do the activity but not being able to do so for a reason other than lack of money. The aim of this additional choice was to examine the other pressures on people's lives that restrict their participation in key activities whether time pressures, caring responsibilities, discrimination, or some other reason. In all the surveys only those who answer that they do not have an item or do not do an activity because they cannot afford to are counted as deprived and included in the poverty count.

6   J. Mack and S. Lansley, ibid., ch. 6.

7   Sam Royston, *Behind Cold Doors* (London: Children's Society, 2013).

8   www.poverty.ac.uk/living-poverty/life-stories, film 1.

9   The Marmot Review Team, *The health impacts of cold homes and fuel poverty* (University College London/Friends of the Earth, London, 2011); Pedro Guertler and Sarah Royston, *Families and fuel poverty* (Association for the Conservation of Energy, 2013).

10   *Excess Winter Mortality in England and Wales, 2012/13*, ONS, 2013; www ons.gov.uk/ons/rel/subnational-health2/excess-winter-mortality-in-england-and-wales/2012-13--provisional--and-2011-12--final-/stb-ewm-12-13.html

11 www.poverty.ac.uk/living-poverty/personal-experiences/rosaleen-single-pensioner: film 2, *Still Campaigning.*

12 Quoted in P. Butler, 'Reports of damp soar in social housing as residents avoid turning on heating', *Guardian,* 28 December 2013.

13 'The health impacts of cold homes and fuel poverty', The Marmot Review, op.cit.; p. 28.

14 Alex Marsh, David Gordon, Christina Pantazis, Pauline Heslop, *Home Sweet Home?* (Bristol: Policy Press, 1999).

15 M. O'Kane, 'Housing crisis: did damp and crowding contribute to cot death?', *Guardian,* 19 November 2012.

16 *Choosing a better diet: a food and health action plan* (London: Department of Health, 2005).

17 Simon Pemberton, Eileen Sutton, Eldin Fahmy, Karen Bell, *Life on a low income in austere times, PSE report,* PSE, 2014.

18 See Gill Main and Jonathan Bradshaw, *Child poverty and social exclusion: Final report of 2012 PSE study,* PSE, 2014, http://www.poverty.ac.uk/pse-research/pseuk-reports

19 www.magicbreakfast.com/

20 Simon Pemberton, Eileen Sutton, Eldin Fahmy, Karen Bell, *Life on a low income in austere times, PSE report,* PSE, 2014.

21 www.poverty.ac.uk/living-poverty/personal-experiences/fiona-and-david-disabled-couple

22 'Healthy diet costs three times as much as junk food', *Daily Telegraph,* 8 October 2014.

23 *Food poverty and health,* briefing statement from the Faculty of Public Health of the Royal College of Physicians of the UK, 2005.

24 group.bmj.com/group/media/latest-news/Food%20poverty%20in%20the%20UK%20201chas%20all%20the%20signs%20of%20a%20public%20health%20emergency-201d%20warn%20experts.pdf

25 Hannah Lambie-Mumford, Dan Crossley, Eric Jensen, Monae Verbeke, Elizabeth Dowler, *Household Food Security in the UK: A Review of Food Aid* (London: DEFRA, February 2014).

26 There was a methodological change in how the lack of activities was measured in 2012 compared to previous years to enable respondents

who would like to take part in the activities (as opposed to those who did or didn't want to) to distinguish the reasons why they didn't between lack of money and other reasons (such as lack of time or caring responsibilities). The 2012 percentage for activities will be an underestimate compared to previous years as respondents in 2012 were provided with an additional choice. See appendix for further details.

27 Although being able to pay an unexpected expense of £500 is seen as a necessity, it is not included in this table as the question was asked on a yes or no basis rather than having the option of not wanting the item. Thirty -four percent of households said their household would not be able to pay an unexpected, but necessary, expense of £500.

28 www.poverty.ac.uk/living-poverty/personal-experiences/marcs-story-north-east-england

29 See 'Fairer Society, Healthy Lives', The Marmot Review, Strategic Review of health inequalities in England post-2010, London 2010, p. 13; www.instituteofhealthequity.org/projects/fair-society-healthy-lives-the-marmot-review

30 This is measured using the percentage who have a score of 4+ on the GHQ 12 questionnaire. See Sarah Payne, 'PSE methods working paper 15, Social Exclusion and Mental Health Review of Literature and Existing Surveys', January 2011, for further details. See also Sarah Payne, 'Mental health, poverty and social exclusion', in Pantazis et al., *Poverty and Social Exclusion in Britain* (Bristol: Policy Press, 2006).

31 A washing machine, telephone and TV are not included in these counts as tests found they were not valid and reliable indicators of deprivation. See appendix for further details. In fact, this makes virtually no difference to the count as the percentages lacking these items is so small. In addition, being able to afford expenses of £500 was excluded as, although a necessity and found to be valid and reliable, it was asked on a simple yes or no basis and not as with the other necessities allowing for an option to go without from choice.

32 See slide 24, *Optimal Line and poverty deprivation thresholds,* in David Gordon, *How many people are poor and how do we know?* Presentation to

The Third Peter Townsend Memorial Conference, London, 2014: www.poverty.ac.uk/take-part/events/final-conference

33 See slide 7, *Mean Income (AHC) by items lacking*, Gill Main and Jonathan Bradshaw, *Child Deprivation and Social Exclusion in 2012*. Presentation to The Third Peter Townsend Memorial Conference, London, 2014: http://poverty.ac.uk/sites/default/files/attachments/Bradshaw%2C%20Child%20deprivation%20and%20social%20exclusion.pdf

34 Slide 12, *Overlaps between household and child deprivation*, in G. Main and J.Bradshaw, *Child Deprivation and Social Exclusion*. Presentation to The Third Peter Townsend Memorial Conference, London, 2014: http://poverty.ac.uk/sites/default/files/attachments/Bradshaw%2C%20Child%20deprivation%20and%20social%20exclusion.pdf

35 C. Pantazis, D. Gordon and R. Levitas, *Poverty and Social Exclusion in Britain* (Bristol: The Policy Press, 2006), pp. 114–17 for further details of the average number of non-necessities by deprivation in the 1999 survey.

36 Demi Patios, Paddy Hillyard and Marco Pomati, *A UK living standard index*. Presentation to The Third Peter Townsend Memorial Conference, London, 2014: www.poverty.ac.uk/take-part/events/final-conference

37 See, for example, P. Townsend, *Poverty in the United Kingdom* (London: Penguin, 1979); D. Piachaud, 'Peter Townsend and the Holy Grail', *New Society*, 10 September, 1981, pp. 419–21; D. Gordon, 'The concept and measurement of poverty', in C. Pantazis, D. Gordon and R. Levitas, *Poverty and Social Exclusion in Britain* (Bristol: The Policy Press, 2006).

38 J. Mack and S. Lansley, op. cit., ch. 6.

39 Some critics, such as Christopher Snowdon, Director of Lifestyle Economics at the Institute of Economic Affairs, argue that as the necessities change over time this means that 'apples' are being compared to 'oranges' (see C. Snowdon, 'Poverty, taxes and the cost of living', *Prospect*, 2013). But all comparisons over time of people's living standards require changes to the basket of goods included in the measure precisely because society changes. The basket of goods making up the Consumer Prices Index, for example, is updated annually and hence real wages are also based on a changing basket of goods. See appendix for details of changes to the items included in the deprivation poverty count and for further discussion on compatibility over time.

40 The 1999 count also includes four items that were not asked about in 2012, namely visit to school, collecting children from school, a dictionary in the house and carpets. This will have a small effect, making the 2012 count slightly lower than it would have been if these items had been asked about, but as the percentages lacking these items in 1999 were small the effect will be marginal.

41 J. Hills, *Good Times, Bad Times* (Bristol: Policy Press, 2014), p43.

42 Institute for Fiscal Studies, *Relative income trends,* Incomes (AHC) figure bn19: www.ifs.org.uk/tools_and_resources/incomes_in_uk

43 *Consumer Price Inflation Reference Tables,* ONS, May 2014, Table 15: www.ons.gov.uk/ons/publications/re-reference-tables.html?edition=tcm%3A77-323585; see also www.jrf.org.uk/sites/files/jrf/income-living-standards-full.pdf , figure 3 .

44 House of Commons, *Payday Loans,* Business, Innovation and Skills Committee, Seventh Report of Session 2013–14, HC 789, December 2013:www.thebureauinvestigates.com/2014/03/12/uk-one-short-term-lender-for-every-seven-banks-on-the-high-street/; accessed 20 April 2014.

45 www.openwonga.com/uk/news-and-views/view/wongas-annual-report-2012#.Uy26wPl_ts4

46 G. Kent, *Hard Times: Feeling the Strain;* Communities Foundation for Northern Ireland, 2014: www.poverty.ac.uk/community/northern-ireland/cia/hard-times

47 Glen Bramley and Kirsten Besemer, *Poverty, debt and financial exclusion,* slide 6 'Problem debt and arrears'. Presentation to The Third Peter Townsend Memorial Conference, London, 2014: www.poverty.ac.uk/take-part/events/final-conference

48 M. Whittaker, *Mortgaged Future, Modelling household debt affordability and access to re-financing as interest rates rise* (London: Resolution Foundation, 2014).

49 Based on income after the deduction of housing costs: www.ifs.org.uk/fiscalFacts/povertyStats

50 The minimum basket of goods and services that comprise the Minimum Income Standard costs twenty-seven to twenty-eight percent more in 2014 than in 2008 – notably higher than the nineteen percent increase

in the official Consumer Prices Index. The Minimum Income Standard, like the Breadline Britain and PSE research, sets out to establish a minimum living standard based on the public's views though this research uses focus group discussions to do so rather than large-scale surveys. See: www.jrf.org.uk/publications/minimum-income-standard-2014

51 See, for example, K. Niemietz, *A New Understanding of Poverty* (London: Institute for Economic Affairs, 2011), p. 128.

52 Based on income after the deduction of housing costs: www.ifs.org.uk/fiscalFacts/povertyStats

Chapter 3

1 Simon Pemberton, Eileen Sutton, Eldin Fahmy, Karen Bell, *Life on a low income in austere times, PSE report,* PSE, 2014.

2 https://www.gov.uk/government/speeches/troubled-families-speech

3 DWP, *Measuring Child Poverty, A Consultation on Better Measures of Child Poverty*, p. 32, Cmnd 8483, November 2012.

4 *The lies we tell ourselves: ending the comfortable myths about poverty* (The Baptist Union of Great Britain, the Methodist Church, the Church of Scotland and the United Reformed Church, 2013).

5 R. Levitas, 'There May Be "Trouble" Ahead', *PSE Policy Response No. 3,* 2012: www.poverty.ac.uk/policy-response-working-papers-families-social-policy-life-chances-children-parenting-uk-government

6 Louise Casey, *Listening to troubled families* (London: Dept for Communities and Local Government, July 2012), p. 8.

7 Nick Bailey, *Policy based on unethical research, 2013:* www.poverty.ac.uk/news-and-views/articles/policy-built-unethical-research

8 *Measuring Child Poverty,* op. cit., p. 1.

9 DWP, *Public Views on Child Poverty: Results from the first polling undertaken as part of the Measuring Child Poverty consultation,* January 2013

10 N. Bailey and M. Tomlinson, *DWP adds to confusion over consultation on child poverty,* www.poverty.ac.uk, 4 February 2013.

11 www.dwp.gov.uk/newsroom/ministers-speeches/2013/31-01-13.shtml

12 *Homelessness: A silent killer* (London: Crisis, December 2011).

13 Susan Harkness, Paul Gregg and Lindsey MacMillan, *Poverty, The Role of*

Institutions, Behaviours and Culture (York: Joseph Rowntree Foundation, June 2012).

14 *Adult Psychiatric Morbidity in England – 2007* (London: NHS Information Centre for Health and Social Care, 2009).

15 *General Lifestyle Survey,* Office for National Statistics, GB, London, 2010, table 2.18.

16 Quoted in A. Gentleman, 'Ministers accused of downplaying the income measure of child poverty', *Guardian,* 14 February 2013.

17 J. Bradshaw et al., *Consultation on Child Poverty Measurement,* PSE policy response working paper, No. 8, 2013, p. 2.

18 Social Mobility and Child Poverty Commission, *Response to 'Measuring Child Poverty: A consultation on better measures of child poverty',* February 2013.

19 'Plans to change child poverty measures hit impasse', *Guardian* 14 February 2014.

20 *An evidence review of the drivers of child poverty for families in poverty now and for poor children growing up to be poor adults,* Cmnd 8781, HM Government, January 2014.

21 Iain Duncan Smith and George Osborne, 'The Conservatives' child poverty plan tackles poverty at source', *Guardian,* 26 February 2014.

22 DWP, *Consultation on the child poverty strategy: 2014-17,* Cmnd 8782, HMG, February 2014, p. 7.

23 www.margaretthatcher.org/document/101830

24 www.theguardian.com/politics/2013/nov/28/boris-johnson-iq-intelli-gence-gordon-gekko

25 See, for example, M. Rutter and N. Madge, *Cycles of Disadvantage,* (London: Heinemann, 1976), p. 255; S. A. Black and P. J. Devereux, 'Recent Developments in Intergenerational Mobility', in *Handbook of Labor Economics,* vol. 4, part B, 2011, pp. 1487-1541.

26 D. Gordon, 'Consultation Response, Social Mobility and the Child Poverty Review', *Policy Response Series No 2,* PSE, 2011, pp. 4-5; www.poverty.ac.uk/pse-research/pse uk/policy-response

27 Graham Allen, *Early intervention: smart investment, massive savings* (London: Cabinet Office, 2011).

28 www.theguardian.com/politics/2010/jan/11/david–cameron–nature–v
    –nurture

29 Though even prime ministers, it seems, can make parenting mistakes.
    See, for example, 'David Cameron's daughter Nancy left at pub', BBC
    online, 12 June 2012: www.bbc.co.uk/news/uk-18391663

30 Leslie Morrison Gutman, John Brown, Rodie Akerman, *Nurturing parent-
    ing capability: the early years* (University of London: Institute of Education,
    2009).

31 Kathleen Kiernan and Fiona Mensah, 'Poverty, family resources and chil-
    dren's early educational attainment: the mediating role of parenting',
    British Educational Research Journal, vol. 37, no. 2, April 2011, pp. 317–36.

32 K. Kiernan, *Poverty and Parenting: Both Matter* (University of London:
    Institute of Education, LS cohort studies newsletter, spring 2010): www.
    cls.ioe.ac.uk/library-media%5Cdocuments%5CKohort_02.10_web.pdf

33 OECD, Economic Policy Reforms: Going for growth 2010, Part II,
    chapter 5, *A Family Affair: Intergenerational Social Mobility across OECD
    Countries* (Paris: OECD, 2010).

34 Jo Blandon and Steve Gibbons, *The persistence of poverty across generations*
    (York: Joseph Rowntree Foundation, 2006), p. 3.

35 K. Hoskins and B. Barker, *Education and Social Mobility: Dreams of Success*
    (London: Trentham/Institute of Education Press, 2014).

36 Euan Holloway et al., *At What Cost: exposing the impact of poverty on school
    life,* The Children's Society, 2014: www.childrenscommission.org.uk/

37 J. Mack and S. Lansley, *Poor Britain* (London: George Allen and Unwin,
    1985).

38 In 1983, households were categorised by the work status of the 'head of
    the household' which was taken to be the person in work (if anyone in
    the household was in work). In 2012, households in work were those
    households where anyone in the household was in work.

39 The unemployed are those not working but looking and available for
    work.

40 P. Townsend, *Poverty in the United Kingdom* (London: Penguin, 1979),
    p. 819.

41 Using deprivation to measure poverty, the proportions of pensioners in

poverty is lower than using income-based measures – this is because pensioners will have accumulated a number of necessities during their lifetimes and thus have less pressure on their day-to-day incomes. But all measures show fewer pensioners in poverty with the risks of poverty having diminished sharply.

42 A. Brummer, *The Great Pensions Robbery* (London: Random House, 2010), p. 197.

43 See slide 10, *Majority of deprived were/had,* in Gill Main and Jonathan Bradshaw, *Child Deprivation and Social Exclusion in 2012.* Presentation to the Third Peter Townsend Memorial Conference, London, 2014: http://poverty.ac.uk/sites/default/files/attachments/Bradshaw%2C%20Child%20deprivation%20and%20social%20exclusion.pdf

44 www.ons.gov.uk/ons/publications/re-reference-tables.html?edition=tcm%3A77-289713 tables 3.5 – 3.7.

45 *Paying to work: child care and child poverty,* Barnardo's, 2012

46 Tania Burchardt, *Being and becoming: social exclusion and the onset of disability,* ESRC Centre for the Analysis of Social Exclusion report 21, November 2003.

47 Michaela Benzeval, Lyndal Bond, Mhairi Campbell, Mathew Egan, Theo Lorenc, Mark Petticrew and Frank Popham, *How does money influence health, (York:* Joseph Rowntree Foundation, 2014).

48 J. Morris, *Rethinking disability policy* (London: Joseph Rowntree Foundation, November 2011).

49 Data provided by Gill Main, University of York.

50 Lena Corner, 'Young black and proud to be a father', *Guardian,* 23 March 2013.

51 Institute of Race Relations, *poverty statistics:* www.irr.org.uk/research/statistics/poverty/

52 www.theguardian.com/uk/2004/nov/21/race.immigrationpolicy

Chapter 4

1 www.poverty.ac.uk/living-poverty/personal-experiences/marcs story-north-east-england

2 R. Williams, 'More than 1700 apply for just 8 jobs at Costa coffee shop', *Independent,* 19 February 2013: www.irishcentral.com/news/irelands-eye

-whats-going-on-in-the-old-sod-111103919-237728901.html; J. Griffin, '20,000 chase jobs at Jaguar factory in Castle Bromwich', *Birmingham Mail*, 4 October 2012.

3 www.poverty.ac.uk/community/northern-ireland

4 Office for National Statistics (ONS), *Labour Market Statistics*, July 2014; 'Unemployment in higher than pre-recession levels in every part of the UK', *TUC Press Release*, 14 July 2014.

5 Source: ONS, *Labour Market Statistics*.

6 *Social Justice*, Report of the Social Justice Commission, Vintage, 1994; www.ons.gov.uk/ons/publications/re-reference-tables.html?edition=tcm%3A77-296703#tab-Summary-tables

7 Of the 3.34 million extra jobs created from 1992 to 2008, as many as forty-seven percent were part-time. See D. Bell and D. Blanchflower, 'Underemployment in the UK', *National Institute Economic Review*, No. 224, May 2013.

8 www.resolutionfoundation.org/blog/2014/jul/10/omitting-earnings-one-seven-workers-jobs-data-our-/

9 ONS, *Personal Income Statistics,* 2011–12, 2014.

10 J. Schmitt, *Low-Wage Lessons* (Washington: Centre for Economic and Policy Research, 2012).

11 M. Goos and A. Manning, 'Lousy and Lovely Jobs: The Rising Polarisation of Work in Britain', *Review of Economics and Statistics*, 89, 2007, pp. 118–33.

12 P. Sissons, *The hourglass and the escalator: Labour market change and mobility* (London: Work Foundation, 2011).

13 J. Plunkett and J. P. Pessoa, *A Polarising Crisis* (London: Resolution Foundation, 2013).

14 Plunkett and Pessoa, ibid.

15 R. Crisp et al., *Work and Worklessness in Deprived Neighbourhoods* (York: Joseph Rowntree Foundation, 2009), p. 34.

16 A. Felstead et al., *Skills at Work 1986-2006* (SKOPE, 2007); D. Gallie et al., *Employment Regimes and the Quality of Work* (Oxford: Oxford University Press, 2007).

17 R. A. Wilson and K. Homenidou, *Working Futures, 2010-2020* (University of Warwick: Institute for Employment Research, 2011).

18 *Final Report of the Commission on Living Standards* (London: Resolution Foundation, 2012), p. 11.

19 S. Lansley, 'Life in the Middle', *TUC Touchstone Pamphlet,* 2009, appendix

20 A. Cairncross, *The British Economy Since 1945* (Oxford: Blackwell, 1992), p. 231.

21 E. McLaughlin, 'Employment, Unemployment and Social Security', in A. Glyn and D. Miliband, *Paying for Inequality* (London: IPPR/Rivers Oram Press, 1994).

22 www.theguardian.com/business/2014/apr/27/low-pay-recovery-working-poor; accessed 30 April 2014.

23 K. D. Ewing and J. Hendy, *Reconstruction After the Crisis* (Liverpool: Institute of Employment Rights, 2013), p. 2.

24 Interviewed in Adam Curtis, *The League of Gentlemen,* BBC2, 1992.

25 S. Lansley, *The Cost of Inequality* (London: Gibson Square, 2011), ch. 3; A. B. Atkinson, *The Economics of Inequality* (2nd edn) (Oxford: OUP, 1983), ch. 9.

26 Centre for Cities, *Public Sector Cities: Trouble Ahead,* July 2009.

27 Office for National Statistics, *Low Pay, 2013,* December, 2013; Ipsos Mori, *Non-compliance with the national minimum wage,* Low Pay Commission, February 2012.

28 www.livingwage.org.uk/ The Living Wage is based on the Minimum Income Standard research, funded by the Joseph Rowntree Foundation. See www.jrf.org.uk/topic/mis for further details.

29 Alex Hurrell, *Starting Out or Getting Stuck? An Analysis of Who Gets Trapped in Low Paid Work – and Who Escapes* (London: Resolution Foundation, 2013); Conor D'Arcy and Alex Hurrell, *Minimum Stay: Understanding How Long People Remain on the Minimum Wage* (London: Resolution Foundation, 2013).

30 *The Global Gender Gap Report 2014* (Geneva: World Economic Forum, 2014)

31 Reported in S. O'Connor, 'Amazon Unpacked', *Financial Times,* 8 February 2013.

32 G. Standing, *The Precariat* (London: Bloomsbury, 2011); P. McGovern, 'Bad Jobs In Britain', *Work and Occupations,* vol. 31, no. 2, May 2004; A. Felstead and N. Jewson, 'Flexible labour and non-standard employment',

in A. Felstead and N. Jewson (eds.), *Global Trends in flexible labour* (London: Macmillan, 1999); Commission for Vulnerable Employment, *Hard Work, Hidden Lives* (TUC, 2007).

33 O'Connor op. cit. See also, *The Invisible Workforce* (Equality and Human Rights Commission, 2014).

34 A. Lusher, 'Britain's brightest trapped on the zero-hour treadmill', *Daily Mail*, 7 August 2013.

35 publicworld.org/blog/home_care_of_older_people_the_revolution_has_started

36 S. Norris, 'Search for the low paid does not have to look far', *Guardian*, 30 November 2013.

37 D. Boffey, 'Doncaster care workers set to intensify strike in fight for living wage', *Observer*, 10 August 2014.

38 R. H. Tawney, *The school-leaving-age and juvenile unemployment* (London: Worker's Educational Association, 1934).

39 www.cam.ac.uk/research/news/zero-hours-contracts-are-tip-of-the-iceberg-of-damaging-shift-work-say-researchers

40 The 2012 PSE findings of 28.6% overall with a mental health problem is higher than that found in other studies using the GHQ indicators. See Sarah Payne, Mental Health Indicators in the 2012 PSE research for the detailed checks made on the data and possible explanations of the difference (to be published on the PSE website at www.poverty.ac.uk/pse-research/pse-uk/results-analysis).

41 L. Gardiner, *All accounted for* (London: Resolution Foundation, 2014); ONS, *Real wages down 8.5 per cent,* April 2013. See also: https://www.gov.uk/government/organisations/department-for-work-pensions/series/households-below-average-income-hbai--2https://www.gov.uk/government/organisations/department-for-work-pensions/series/households-below-average-income-hbai--2

42 Jenny Morris, *Rethinking disability policy* (York: Joseph Rowntree Foundation, 2011).

43 Lansley op. cit., p. 71.

44 www.princes-trust.org.uk/about_the_trust/headline_news/national_news_2013/1310_youth_unemployment.aspx

45   D. Blanchflower, 'The plight of the young and unemployed is truly scary', *Independent*, 12 January 2014.

46   John Hills et al., *Winners and Losers in the Crisis: The changing anatomy of economic inequality in the UK 2007–2010*, Social Policy in a Cold Climate Research Report 2 (London School of Economics: Centre for Analysis of Social Exclusion, 2013), p. 8.

47   I. Brinkley et al., *The Gender Jobs Split,* (London: The Work Foundation, 2013).

48   ONS, Graduates in the Labour Force, 2013, November 2013; www.ons. gov.uk/ons/rel/lmac/graduates-in-the-labour-market/2013/rpt---graduates-in-the-uk-labour-market-2013.html

49   Hills op. cit., p. 8.

50   niesr.ac.uk/blog/future-jobs-fund-what-waste

51   A. Grice, 'Flagship £1 billion youth unemployment scheme branded a failure', *Independent*, 22 October 2013.

52   C. Giles et al., 'The Jinxed Generation', *Financial Times*, 16 March 2012.

53   D. Webster, 'Welfare Reform: Facing up to the Geography of Worklessness', *Local Economy*, vol. 21, no. 2, 2006, pp. 107–16.

54   See: touchstoneblog.org.uk/2014/02/video-employment-trends-february-2014/; Centre for Cities, *Cities Outlook*, 2009: www.theguardian. com/news/datablog/2012/feb/06/unemployment-vacancies-ratio

55   www.channel4.com/news/why-is-government-website-carrying-fake-jobs

56   T. Shildrick et al., *Poverty and Insecurity, Life in Low-Pay, No-Pay Britain* (Bristol: Policy Press, 2012), p. 194.

57   www.cipd.co.uk/pressoffice/press-releases/employment-growth-labour-market-battleground-jobs.aspx

58   In this table those in poverty are based on a slightly different definition. See Nick Bailey and Maria Gannon, *Employment and poverty: evidence from the Poverty and Social Exclusion UK Survey 2012*, Social Policy Association conference, Sheffield, 8–10 July 2013.

59   C. Goulden, *Cycles of Poverty, Unemployment and Low Pay* (York: Joseph Rowntree Foundation, 2010).

60   A. Furlong and F. Cartwell, *Young people and social change* (Maidenhead: Open University Press, 2007).

61   J. Browne and G. Paull, 'Parents' work entry, progression and retention, and child poverty', DWP *Research Report No. 626,* 2010.

62   T. Shildrick et al., *Poverty and Insecurity, Life in Low-Pay, No-Pay Britain* (Bristol: Policy Press, 2012), p. 195.

63   Sissons op. cit., p. 28.

Chapter 5

1   www.poverty.ac.uk/living-poverty/life-stories, part 2.

2   Centre for Social Justice, *Why is the government anti-marriage?,* 2009, p. 4.

3   J, Seabrooke, *Pauperland* (London: Hurst and Co, 2013), p. 45.

4   Ibid.

5   See, for example, Iain Duncan Smith, speech to the Glasgow Welfare to Work convention, September 2012; available at www.dwp.gov.uk/newsroom/ministersspeeches/2012/19-09-12a.shtml

6   G. Osborne, *Speech by the Chancellor on the spending announcements,* 17 May 2010.

7   www.newstatesman.com/blogs/politics/2012/10/george-osbornes-speech-conservative-conference-full-text

8   www.theguardian.com/society/2011/apr/28/three-quarters-sickness-benefit-claimants-fit-work

9   www.telegraph.co.uk/news/politics/labour/8790389/Labour-Party-Conference-Liam-Byrnes-speech-in-full.html

10   The Centre for Social Justice, *The State of the Nation Report: Economic Dependency,* 2006, p. 3.

11   'Wales set for worst hardship since the 1930s', *Guardian,* 15 May 2013.

12   Alex Salmond SNP Conference Address, Saturday, 12 April 2014: www.snp.org/media-centre/news/2014/apr/first-minister-alex-salmond-snp-conference-address

13   'Gordon Brown warns Labour voters independence will only help rich', *Daily Telegraph,* 27 August 2014.

14   Gerry Mooney, 'Scotland's constitutional future: towards a Scottish welfare state?', *Policy World,* Spring 2014.

15   See *Northern Ireland: faring badly:* www.poverty.ac.uk/pse-research/northern-ireland-faring-badly. See also the report of the 2002/3 PSE

research in Northern Ireland: Paddy Hillyard et al., *Bare Necessities* (Belfast: Democratic Dialogue, 2003).

16 *Welfare reform motion tops Stormont debate*: www.bbc.co.uk/news/uk-northern-ireland-politics-29320221, accessed October 2014.

17 Elizabeth Clery, 'Are tough times affecting attitudes to welfare?' in Alison Park, Elizabeth Clery, John Curtice, Miranda Phillips and David Utting (eds.), *British Social Attitudes: The 29th Report* (London: National Centre for Social Research, 2012).

18 D. Webster, *Evidence to the Work and Pensions Committee, The role of Jobcentre Plus in the reformed welfare system*, House of Commons, Session 2013–2014, 2014.

19 D. Webster, *The role of benefit sanctions and disallowances in creating increased need for emergency food aid, Evidence to All-Party Parliamentary Inquiry into Hunger and Food Poverty in Britain*, 2014, p. 6.

20 *Punishing Poverty? A Review of Benefits Sanctions and their Impacts on Clients and Claimants* (Manchester CAB Service, 2013).

21 D. Webster, *Evidence to the Work and Pensions Committee, The role of Jobcentre Plus in the reformed welfare system*, House of Commons, Session 2013–2014, 2014.

22 D. Webster, *The DWP's JSA/ESA sanctions, statistics release*, February 2014.

23 M. Oakley, *Independent review of the operation of jobseeker's allowance sanctions* (DWP, July 2014).

24 P. Wintour, 'Jobseekers live in culture of fear', *Guardian*, 2 February 2014.

25 K. Dryburgh, *Voices from the frontline, JSA Sanctions* (CAB Scotland, 2012).

26 P. Wintour, 'Jobcentre was set targets for benefit sanctions', *Guardian*, 21 March 2013; P. Wintour, 'Report accepts mistakes were made on welfare sanctions by job centres', *Guardian*, 16 May 2013; P. Wintour, 'Whistleblower says DWP staff given targets to stop benefits', *Guardian*, 10 December 2013.

27 S. Malik, 'Ministers looking at making it harder for sick and disabled to claim benefits', *Guardian*, 30 September 2013.

28 I. Duncan Smith, 'I'm proud of our welfare reforms', *Guardian*, 28 July, 2013.

29 J. Chapman, 'Benefits can do more harm than good for child poverty', *Daily Mail*, 2 December 2011.

30 Paul Gregg, Jane Waldfogel and Elizabeth Washbrook, *Expenditure Patterns Post-Welfare Reform in the UK: Are low-income families starting to catch up?* (London: Centre for Analysis of Social Exclusion, London School of Economics, May 2005).

31 Simon Pemberton, Eileen Sutton, Eldin Fahmy, Karen Bell, *Life on a low income in austere times, PSE report,* 2014.

32 T. Montgomery, 'If compassion is no longer about how much money governments spend, Labour stops winning elections', *Conservative Home,* 14 June 2012.

33 www2.eastriding.gov.uk/housing/housing-benefit-and-council-tax-support/recent-changes/the-new-council-tax-support-scheme/

34 Fran Bennett, 'Universal Credit, the gender impact', *Poverty,* Issue 140, CPAG, London, 2011.

35 Rand Ghayad, *A Decomposition of Shifts of the Beveridge Curve* (Federal Reserve Bank of Boston, 2013); see also A. Hern, 'Punishing the poor doesn't help them find work', *New Statesman Blog,* 2 July 2013.

36 B. Watts et al., *Welfare sanctions and conditionality in the UK* (York: Joseph Rowntree Foundation, 2014).

37 Robert Joyce, 'Tax and benefit reforms due in 2012/13', *IFS Briefing Note 126,* IFS, London, 2012.

38 *A Child Rights Impact Assessment of Budget Decisions: Including the 2013 Budget, and the Cumulative Impact of Tax-Benefit Reforms and Reductions in Spending on Public Services 2010–2015* (Office of the Children's Commissioner, 2013); Howard Reed, Diane Elson and Sue Himmelweit, *An Adequate Standard of Living: A Child Rights Based Quantitative Analysis of Budgetary Decisions 2010–13* (Office of the Children's Commissioner, 2013).

39 Women's Budget Group, *The impact on women of the autumn financial statement 2012 and the welfare benefits uprating bill,* 2013, p. 2.

40 Hannah Aldridge and Adam Tinson, *How Many Families Are Affected by More Than One Benefit Cut This April?* (Rickmansworth: New Policy Institute, 2013).

41 HM Treasury, Budget 2012, Annex B; webarchive.nationalarchives.gov.uk/20130301235416/http:/cdn.hm-treasury.gov.uk/budget2012_complete.pdf

42 Press Release, *Disabled people set to lose £28.3bn of support*, Demos, April 2013

43 Peter Taylor-Gooby, *The double crisis of the welfare state and what we can do about it* (Basingstoke: Palgrave Macmillan, 2013).

44 Simon Duffy, *A Fairer Society* (Sheffield: The Centre for Welfare Reform, 2013).

45 www.ekklesia.co.uk/files/peoples_review_of_the_wca_-_further_evidence_december_2013.pdf

46 We are Spartacus, *The People's Review of the Work Capability Assessment*, November 2012, and *The People's Review of the Work Capability Assessment – further evidence*, December 2013; www.ekklesia.co.uk/node/19621

47 Ibid.

48 Quoted in H. Siddique, 'Atos quits £500m contract early', *Guardian*, 27 March 2014.

49 www.politicshome.com/uk/article/102054/work_and_pensions_committee_employment_and_support_allowance_is_not_achieving_its_aims_and_needs_fundamental_redesign_say_mps.html

50 Source: DWP, *DLA reform Impact Assessment*, May 2012; available at www.dwp.gov.uk/docs/dla-reform-wr2011-ia.pdf)

51 *Macmillan briefing on Personal Independence Payments and terminally ill cancer patients*, December 2013.

52 Simon Duffy, *A Fairer Society* (Sheffield: The Centre for Welfare Reform, 2013).

53 www.bbc.co.uk/news/uk-politics-11250639

54 James Browne and Andrew Hood, 'A Survey of the UK Benefit System', *IFS Briefing Note BN13*, 2012.

55 J. Hills, 'Social Policy in a Cold Climate', *Working Paper* (London: CASE, London School of Economics, 2013), p. 13; P. Gregg and S. Hurrell, *Creditworthy, assessing the impact of tax credits in the last decade* (London: Resolution Foundation, 2013).

56 Source: Department for Work and Pensions.

57 R. Lupton et al,, *Labour's Social Policy Record, 1997–2010*, Report 1 (London: CASE, London School of Economics, 2013), pp. 41–2.

58 *Exposing the Myths of Welfare*, Centre for Labour and Social Studies/Red

Pepper Magazine, 2012; Ambrose McCarron and Liam Purcell, *The Blame Game Must Stop: Challenging the Stigmatisation of People Experiencing Poverty* (Church Action on Poverty, 2013).

59 Browne and Hood op. cit.

60 J. Humphrys, 'How our welfare system has created an age of entitlement', *Daily Mail,* 8 August 2013.

61 Christian Albrekt Larsen and Thomas Engel Dejgaard, *The Institutional Logic of Images of the Poor and Welfare Recipients: A Comparative Study of British, Swedish and Danish Newspapers,* Working Paper 2012-78 (Centre for Comparative Welfare Studies, Aalborg University, Denmark, 2012).

62 Ben Baumberg, Kate Bell and Declan Gaffney, with Rachel Deacon, Clancy Hood and Daniel Sage, *Benefits Stigma in Britain,* 2012, Turn2us; www.turn2us.org.uk/PDF/Benefits%20stigma%20Draft%20report%20v9.pdf

63 Peter Taylor-Gooby, *A left trilemma: Progressive public policy in the age of austerity* (London: Policy Network, 2012).

64 Quoted in K. Andrews and J. Jacobs, *Punishing the Poor* (Basingstoke: Macmillan, 1990) p. 7.

65 www.number10.gov.uk/news/welfare-speech

66 J. Bradshaw, *Benefits Uprating and Living Standards* (York: SPRU, University of York, 2012); spruyork.blogspot.co.uk/2012/12/benefits-uprating-and-living-standards.html

67 Ha-Joon Chang, 'Think Welfare is spiralling out of control? You're wrong', *Guardian,* 28 March 2014; see also Ha-Joon Chang, *23 things they don't tell you about capitalism* (London: Penguin, 2012), ch. 21.

68 Ha-Joon Chang, 'Time to broaden the debate on spending cuts', *Guardian,* 19 October 2010.

69 www.oecd.org/dataoecd/52/8/42625548.xls

70 M. de Lind Leonard et al., 'Does the UK Minimum Wage Reduce Employment?', *British Journal of Industrial Relations,* vol. 52, issue 3, 2014, pp. 499–520.

71 Browne and Hood op. cit., p. 60.

72 *Read between the lines: confronting the myths about the benefits system* (London: Turn2us, Elizabeth Finn Care, 2012).

73 Ibid.

74 www.number10.gov.uk/news/welfare-speech

75 Tracy Shildrick, Robert MacDonald et al., *Are 'cultures of worklessness' passed down the generations?* (York: Joseph Rowntree Foundation, 2012).

76 'Benefits Street culture: study rubbishes '"joblessness as a lifestyle"' claim', *Guardian*, 11 September, 2014.

77 Life on a low income in austere times: Part 2; http://www.poverty.ac.uk/living-poverty/life-stories

78 Ibid.

Chapter 6

1 www.poverty.ac.uk/living-poverty/personal-experiences/renee-low-paid-worker, film 1 *Living with damp*

2 blogs.channel4.com/jackie-long-on-social-affairs/housing landlords-shelter1045/1045

3 M. Smith, F. Albanese and J. Truder, *A Roof Over My Head: The final report of the Sustain project* (London: Shelter and Crisis, 2014).

4 https://www.gov.uk/government/statistical-data-sets/live-tables-on-house-building

5 Lynsey Hanley, *Estates: An Intimate History* (London: Granta, 2007), p. 11.

6 N. Timmins, *The Five Giants,* (London: Fontana Press, 1996) p. 435.

7 Department for Communities and Local Government, *Rents, Lettings and Tenancies, Live Tables,* Table 600, 2013: www.communities.gov.uk,

8 Tom Copley, *From right to buy to buy to let* (Greater London Authority, 2014).

9 www.theguardian.com/commentisfree/2014/jan/14/housing-squalor-exploitation-where-labour-outrage-policy

10 housingnews.co.uk/index.asp?PortalID=9&cat=news&period=lastweek#461081

11 Suzanne Fitzpatrick, Hal Pawson, Glen Bramley, Steve Wilcox and Beth Watts, *The homelessness monitor: England 2013* (London: Crisis, December 2013).

12 Raquel Rolnik, *Report of the Special Rapporteur on adequate housing,* (United Nations, A/HRC/25/54/Add.2, December 2013).

13 *Minister criticises 'partisan' UN housing report,* BBC News, 3 February 2014; www.bbc.co.uk/news/uk-politics-26026021

14 data.gov.uk/dataset/ratio-of-median-house-price-to-median-earnings

15 Faisal Islam, *The Default Line* (London: Head Zeus, 2013), p. 144.

16 www.nao.org.uk/highlights/taxpayer-support-for-uk-banks-faqs/

17 G. Turner, *The Credit Crunch,* (London: Pluto Press, 2008), p. 30.

18 Philip Inman, 'Buy-to-let landlords are a disaster for Britain and the economy', *Guardian,* 23 May 2014.

19 Islam op. cit., p. 152.

20 *English Housing Survey Headline Report 2012–13* (London: Department for Communities and Local Government, February 2014).

21 Islam op. cit., p. 155.

22 www.newsroom.hsbc.co.uk/press/release/property_haves_and_have -nots

23 J. Pennington, *No Place to Call Home* (London: Institute for Public Policy Research, 2012).

24 www.telegraph.co.uk/news/politics/conservative/11130603/Ten-of-the-best-from-Boris-bricks-planet-Zog-and-Ed-Milibands-brain.html

25 H. Lewis, 'Out of the ordinary', *New Statesman,* 10–16 October 2014.

26 Consumer Price Inflation Reference tables, May 2014, Table 39, ONS: www.ons.gov.uk/ons/publications/re-reference-tables.html?edi-tion=tcm%3A77-323585

27 Laura Gardiner, *Housing pinched: Understanding which households spend the most on housing costs* (London: Resolution Foundation, 2014).

28 Declan Gaffney, *Housing crisis, what crisis?;* lartsocial.org/housingcrisis

29 These are in real terms, after adjusting for general inflation. See *housing benefit expenditure tables:* https://www.gov.uk/government/statistics/benefit-expenditure-and-caseload-tables-2014

30 Against the growth in the working-age caseload, there has been a long-term decline in housing benefit receipt among pensioners.

31 www.theguardian.com/society/2012/oct/22/working-people-housing -benefit-report?CMP=twt_fd

32 Vidhya Alakeson and Giselle Cory, *Home Truths: How affordable is housing for Britain's ordinary working families?* (London: Resolution Foundation, 2013).

33 *A Decent Home: Definition and guidance for implementation* (Department for Communities and Local Government, 2006).

34 Steve Wilcox and John Perry, *The UK housing review 2014* (London: Charted Institute of Housing, April 2014).

35 Shelter, *Asserting Authority: calling time on rogue landlords*, London, 2013.

36 www.insidehousing.co uk/legal/newham-to-prosecute-134-prs-landlords/7001532.article

37 J. Ashworth, 'Cheap, Nasty Politics', *Labour List*, 11 February 2013.

38 Aragon Housing association, *100 days of the Bedroom Tax*, July 2013.

39 DWP, *Evaluation of Removal of the Spare Room Subsidy, Interim report*, July 2014: https://www.gov.uk/government/uploads/system/uploads/attachment_data/file/329948/rr882-evaluation-of-removal-of-the-spare-room-subsidy.pdf

40 Patrick Collinson, 'Property tycoon Fergus Wilson hits back after criticism of mass evictions', *Guardian*, 10 January 2014.

41 Patrick Collinson, 'Millionaire landlords Fergus and Judith Wilson begin evicting large families', *Guardian*, 31 October 2014.

42 Hannah Aldridge and Tom MacInnes, *Multiple cuts for the poorest families* (Oxford: Oxfam, April 2014).

43 Kate Barker, *Review of Housing Supply* (London: The Treasury, 2004), p. 129.

44 P. Oborne, 'Honest work can't pay for a roof over people's head', *Daily Telegraph*, 22 April 2014.

45 A. Gentleman, 'Homeless in London', *Guardian*, 25 May 2013.

46 R. Booth, 'London flats "worse than prison cells"', *Guardian*, 5 September 2014.

47 E. Lunn, 'Landlord fined for renting room that could only be entered on all fours', *Guardian*, 22 August 2014.

48 A. Heywood, *London for Sale* (London: Smith Institute, 2013)

49 www.civitas.org.uk/pdf/FindingShelter.pdf

50 www.pgestates.com/news.dtx?c_inst={729AB58D-B7E4-43F4-836A-501DEC0263DA}

51 M. Goldfarb, *New York Times*, 12 October 2013.

52 www.opendemocracy.net/rowland-atkinson/car-parks-for-global-wealth-super-rich-in-london

53 *Wealth by region and age group*, 2008 to 2010, GB, ONS, June 2013.

54 *Housing Standards Review, Response from BRE,* October 2013; www.bre. co.uk/filelibrary/pdf/casestudies/BRE_Housing_Standards_Review_ consultation_response_22-10-13%5B1%5D.pdf ; www.theguardian.com /artanddesign/architecture-design-blog/2014/jan/27/david-cameron- bonfire-of-building-regulations-future-homes

55 www.thebureauinvestigates.com/2013/09/18/thousands-of-affordable- homes-axed/

56 See for example, J Pennington, *No Place to Call Home* (London: Institute for Public Policy Research, 2012).

Chapter 7

1 Simon Pemberton, Eileen Sutton, Eldin Fahmy, Karen Bell, *Life on a low income in austere times, PSE report,* 2014.

2 High Pay Centre, *Reform Agenda,* 2014, p. 4.

3 www.spectator.co.uk/features/7667988/class-is-back/

4 European Banking Authority, *High Earners*, 2012 Data, 2013; www.eba. europa.eu / documents / 10180 / 16145 / EBA+Report+High+ Earners+2012.pdf

5 Daniel Kahneman, 'Don't Blink! The hazards of confidence', *New York Times,* 19 October 2011.

6 C. Lakner and B. Milanovic, 'Global Income Distributions', *Policy Research Paper 6719,* World Bank, 2013; Chris Edwards, *Surveys of income distribution and their (probable) understatement,* mimeo, 2013.

7 Kevin Phillips, *Wealth and Democracy* (New York: Broadway Books, 2002), p. 109.

8 F. Alverado, A. B. Atkinson, T. Picketty and E. Saez, *The World Top Income Database* (Paris: OECD, 2014); *Divided We Stand, Why Inequality Keeps Rising* (Paris: OECD, 2011).

9 Ibid.

10 R. Tawney, 'Poverty as an industrial problem', inaugural lecture, repro- duced in *Memoranda on the Problems of Poverty* (London: William Morris Press, 1913).

11 P. Townsend, 'Forward: Democracy for the poor', in M. McCarthy,

Campaigning for the poor. CPAG and the politics of welfare (London: Croom Helm, 1986).

12 Amartya Sen, *The Idea of Justice* (London: Allen Lane, 2009), ch. 11.

13 Harry Frankfurt, 'Equality as a Moral Ideal', *Ethics* 98, 1987, pp. 21–43, p. 31.

14 www.rationaloptimist.com/blog/do-people-mind-more-about-inequality-than-poverty.aspx

15 L. von Mises, *Ideas on Liberty* (New York: Irvington, 1955).

16 Arthur Okun, *Equality and Efficiency: the Big Trade Off* (Washington, DC: The Brookings Institute, 1975).

17 L. Lomasky and K. Swan, 'Wealth and poverty in the liberal tradition', *Independent Review*, 2009.

18 See for example, C. Snowdon, 'Poverty, Taxes and the Cost of Living in Poverty in the UK', *Prospect,* 2013, p. 26.

19 K. Joseph, *Stranded on the Middle Ground?* (London: Centre for Policy Studies, 1976).

20 Quoted in D. Sambrook, *Seasons in the Sun* (London: Penguin, 2013), p. 629.

21 R. E. Lucas, 'The Industrial Revolution: Past and Future', *The Region, Annual Report of the Federal Reserve Bank of Minneapolis,* 2004, pp. 5–20.

22 K. Niemietz, *A New Understanding of Poverty* (London: Institute of Economic Affairs, 2011), p. 32.

23 J. D. Ostry, A. Berg and C. G. Tsangarides, 'Redistribution, Inequality and Growth', *IMF Discussion Paper,* 2014; see also J. C. Cordoba and G. Verdier, 'Lucas v Lucas, On Inequality and Growth', *IMF Working Paper, WP/07/17,* 2007; A. G. Berg and J. D. Ostry, 'Equality and Efficiency', *Finance and Development,* IMF, September 2011.

24 ILO, 'Wage-led growth: Concept, theories and policies', *Conditions of Work and Employment Series* No. 41, 2012.

25 S. Lansley, *The Cost of Inequality* (London: Gibson Square, 2011), ch. 6; J. Stiglitz, *The Price of Inequality* (London: Allen Lane, 2012).

26 www.imf.org/external/np/speeches/2013/012313.htm

27 www.bankofengland.co.uk/publications/Documents/speeches/2014/speech731.pdf

28 Robert Reich, 'The American right focuses on poverty, not inequality, to avoid blame', *Observer*, 23 February 2014.

29 Lansley op. cit., ch. 7.

30 A. Smith, 'Cash at record levels', *Financial Times*, 15 September 2013; A Fontevecchia 'US Companies Stashing More Cash Abroad as Stock Piles Hit a Record $1.45tr', *Forbes*, 19 March 2013.

31 www.ilo.org/global/about-the-ilo/newsroom/comment-analysis/ WCMS_234482/lang--en/index.htm

32 K. Carmichael, 'Free up "dead money"', *The Globe and Mail*, 22 August 2012.

33 J. Hopkins, V. Lapuente and L. Moller, *Low levels of inequality are linked to greater innovation in economies*, British Politics and Policies at LSE, 2013; blogs.lse.ac.uk/politicsandpolicy/archives/39215

34 *UK Gross Domestic Expenditure on Research and Development* (London: Office for National Statistics, March 2014).

35 *UK Gross Domestic Expenditure on Research and Development,* 2012 (London: Office for National Statistics, March 2014).

36 S. Lansley and H. Reed, *How to Boost the Wage-Share* (London: Trade Union Congress, 2013), chs 3 and 5; R. Jones, *The UK's Innovation Deficit and How to Repair* It, Speri Paper No. 6 (University of Sheffield, 2013).

37 S. Bowles and A. Jayadev, 'Garrison America', *Economist's Voice*, 2007.

38 *Squeezed Britain* (London: Resolution Foundation, 2010), p. 24.)

39 https://www.gov.uk/government/uploads/system/uploads/attach-ment_data/file/206778/full_hbai13.pdf , table 2.1 p. 41; this is measured after housing costs.

40 S. Babones, 'Absolute poverty in America higher than in 1969', *poverty. ac.uk*, June 2013; www.poverty.ac.uk/editorial/absolute-poverty-amer-ica-higher-1969; J. Cassidy, 'Relatively Deprived', *New Yorker*, 3 April 2006.

41 J. Bernstein, *Impact of Inequality on Growth* (Washington, DC: Centre for American Progress, 2013).

42 David Woodward and Andrew Simms, *Growth isn't working* (London: New Economics Foundation, 2006), p. 8.

43 R. Costanza, 'Development: Time to leave GDP behind', *Nature*, 15

January 2014; www.nature.com/news/development-time-to-leave-gdp
-behind-1.14499?utm_source=hootsuite&utm_campaign=hootsuite

44 Royal Society for the Arts, *Collective Pensions in the UK II*, RSA, London, 2013.

45 M. Florio, *The Great Divestiture* (Cambridge, Massachusetts: MIT Press, 2004), p. 342.

46 Quoted in A. Cumbers, *Renewing Public Ownership*, Policy Paper, London, Class, 2014, p. 10.

47 National Audit Office, *Infrastructure investment: the impact on consumer bills*, November 2013, pp. 7–8.

48 Florio op. cit., p. 363.

49 Cumbers op. cit., p. 7.

50 J. Allen and M. Pryke, 'Financialising household water', *Cambridge Journal of Regions, Economy and Society*, 2013, 6, pp. 419–39.

51 E. Lobina and D. Hall, *List of Water Remunicipalisations* (Greenwich: Public Services International Research Unit, 2013).

52 wwwf.imperial.ac.uk/business-school/research/the-centre-for-management-buy-out-research/uk-equity/; uk.reuters.com/article/2012/06/19/us-allianceboots-offer-idUSBRE85I0IT20120619

53 Paul Myners, *Insitutional investment in the UK: A review*, 6 March 2001, para 12.3.

54 G. Wood, M. Goergen, N. O'Sullivan, *Private Equity Takeovers and Employment in the UK: Some Empirical Evidence*; see www.wbs.ac.uk/news/firms-will-find-no-performance-boost-from-private-equity-buy-outs/

55 V. Pareto, *Manual of Political Economy*. (New York: Augustus M. Kelley, 1896).

56 H. Williams, *Britain's Power Elites* (London: Constable, 2006), p. 164.

57 Polly Curtis, 'Former Labour Ministers rushing to take private sector jobs, report finds', *Guardian*, 17 May 2011.

58 *Fixing the revolving door between government and business*, Policy Paper No. 2, Transparency International, London, April 2012.

59 www.gresham.ac.uk/professors-and-speakers/professor-avinash-persaud

60 Ajay Kapur et al., 'The Global Investigator: Plutonomy: Buying Luxury, Explaining Global Imbalances', *Citigroup Equity Research*, 14 October 2005.

61 Polly Toynbee, 'Accountancy big four are laughing all the way to the tax office', *Guardian*, 1 February 2013.

62 J. Stiglitz, *The Price of Inequality* (London: Allen Lane, 2012), pp. 127–31; Ulrike Guerot, 'Can politicians do anything about wages?', *Prospect*, March 2014.

63 S. Birch, G. Gottfried and G. Lodge, *Divided democracy: Political inequality in the UK and why it matters* (London: IPPR, 2013).

64 M. Gilens, *Affluence and Influence: Economic Inequality and Political Power in America* (Princeton: Princeton University Press, 2013).

65 M. Paskov and C. Dewild, 'Income Inequality and Solidarity in Europe', *GINA Discussion Paper 33*, 2012; H. Jordahl, 'Inequality and Trust', *IFN Working Paper, no. 715*, 2007.

66 Michael Norton and Dan Ariely, 'Building a Better America—One Wealth Quintile at a Time', *Perspectives on Psychological Science* 6, no. 1, January 2011, pp. 9–12.

67 www.poverty.ac.uk/articles-inequality-attitudes-income-distribution/inequality-illusion; P. Toynbee and D. Walker, *Unjust Rewards* (London: Granta, 2008), p. 25.

68 Axa, *Middle Britain* (Axa, 2008).

69 *Elitist Britain* (London: Social Mobility and the Child Poverty Commission, August 2014).

70 www.slate.com/articles/health_and_science/science/2014/01/social_darwinism_and_class_essentialism_the_rich_think_they_are_superior.single.html

71 H. Gans, *More Equality* (New York: Pantheon Books, 1973).

72 abcnews.go.com/International/pope-francis-messenger-catholic-church/story?id=21240418&page=2

73 R. Wilkinson and K. Pickett, *The Spirit Level* (London: Penguin, 2010).

Chapter 8

1 Simon Pemberton, Eileen Sutton, Eldin Fahmy, Karen Bell, *Life on a low income in austere times, PSE report*, 2014.

2 www.oxfam.org.uk/media-centre/press-releases/2012/06/work-no-longer-pays-for-britons-caught-in-perfect-storm-of-falling-incomes-and-rising-costs

3   C. Hope, 'MPs shocked by disgraceful political campaigning', *Daily Telegraph*, 10 June 2014.

4   Quoted in Nick Cohen, 'Our children go hungry for want of Tory compassion', *Observer,* 9 September, 2012.

5   www.civilsociety.co.uk/governance/news/content/18092/ brooks_newmark_charities_should_stick_to_their_knitting_and_keep_ out_of_politics

6   The Trussell Trust website, www.trusselltrust.org/real-stories, accessed July 2013.

7   www.itv.com/news/calendar/2013-04-24/charity-claims-there-is-more-demand-than-ever-for-food-banks-in-our-region/

8   IPSOS Mori, *Child Hunger in London: Understanding food poverty in the capital,* 2013; available at: www.ipsos-mori.com/DownloadPublication/ 1585_sri-ews-education-child-hunger-in-london-2013.pdf

9   www.kingscentreonline.com/baby-basics;www.savethechildren.org. uk/about-us/where-we work/united-kingdom/eat-sleep-learn-play

10   The Prince's Trust, *TES Teacher's Survey*, 2012.

11   news.uk.msn.com/uk/many people-reliant-on-food-banks-1

12   www.publications.parliament.uk/pa/ld201314/ldhansrd/text/130702-0001.htm

13   www.publications.parliament.uk/pa/cm201314/cmhansrd/cm130909/ debtext/130909-0001.htm

14   www.trusselltrust.org/resources/documents/Press/Increasing-numbers-turning-to-foodbanks-since-Aprils-welfare-reforms.pdf

15   Trussell Trust press release, *Tripling in foodbank usage sparks Trussell Trust to call for an inquiry*, 16 October 2013.

16   'Iain Duncan Smith accuses food ban charity of scaremongering', *Independent*, 22 December 2013.

17   J. Owen, 'Food bank charity threatened with closure by Iain Duncan Smith aid', *Independent,* 13 June 2014.

18   https://www.acevo.org.uk/news/acevo-responds-criticism-charity -campaigning

19   www2.warwick.ac.uk/newsandevents/pressreleases/press_briefing_ following/; Hannah Lambie-Mumford, Dan Crossley, Eric Jensen,

314 • **NOTES**

Monae Verbeke, Elizabeth Dowler, *Household Food Security in the UK: A Review of Food Aid* (DEFRA, February 2014).

20 www.frankfield.com/latest-news/news.aspx?p=102643

21 D. Webster, *The role of benefit sanctions and disallowances in creating increased need for emergency food aid,* Evidence to All-Party Parliamentary Inquiry into Hunger and Food Poverty in Britain, 2014.

22 www.itv.com/news/calendar/story/2014-01-09/sheffield-school-to-open-foodbank/

23 Barnado's, *Families in need of food parcels – the food poverty crisis unwrapped*, 2013.

24 N. Annan, *Our Age* (London: Random House, 1992).

25 Quoted in J. Rentoul, *Me and Mine* (London: Unwin Hyman, 1989).

26 Quoted in J. Chancellor, *Peril and Promise* (New York: Harper Perennial, 1990), p. 115.

27 J. Hacker, *The Great Risk Shift* (Oxford, OUP, 2008), p. 166.

28 Peter Taylor-Gooby, 'UK heading for bottom place on public spending', poverty.ac.uk, 2013; www.poverty.ac.uk/articles-government-cuts-international-comparisons-public-spending-whats-new/uk-heading-bottom-place

29 www.government-online.net/david-cameron-need-less-permanently/

30 Peter Taylor-Gooby, *The double crisis of the welfare state and what we can do about it* (Basingstoke: Palgrave Macmillan, 2013), p. 26.

31 Peter Taylor-Gooby, 'UK heading for bottom place on public spending', www.poverty.ac.uk/articles-government-cuts-international-comparisons-public-spending-whats-new/uk-heading-bottom-place

32 The Audit Commission, *Tough Times, 2012,* 2012, p. 16.

33 opinion.publicfinance.co.uk/2013/08/council-cuts-there-is-an-alternative/

34 Sharif Ismail, Ruth Thorlby and Holly Holder, *Focus On: Social care for older people* (London: Nuffield Trust, March 2014).

35 www.daycaretrust.org.uk/pages/281-fewer-sure-start-children-centres-since-2010-worrying-new-figures-show-.html

36 A. Eastman, *Enough is Enough* (Centre for Social Justice, 2014), p. 15.

37 Edmund Burke, *Reflections on the French Revolution* (London: J.M. Dent & Sons Ltd, 1955) (Everyman edn), p. 44.

38 Church Action on Poverty, Walking the Breadline campaign, www. church-poverty.org.uk/walkingthebreadline/act/poster

39 www.telegraph.co.uk/news/religion/10647064/People-being-left-in-destitution-is-a-disgrace-says-Archbishop.html

40 www.theguardian.com/society/2014/apr/16/million-people-britain-food-banks-religious-leaders-faith-groups

41 John Campbell, *Margaret Thatcher: The Iron Lady* (London: Jonathan Cape, 2003), p. 390.

42 E. Dugan, 'Soaring numbers need urgent help from Citizens Advice Bureau after welfare changes drive people to despair', *Independent*, 7 June 2103.

43 Barnardo's op. cit.

44 Ibid.

45 https://www.gov.uk/government/speeches/pms-speech-on-big-society

46 Penny Waterhouse, 'Charities are failing the poor', *New Statesman* insert, 2–8 May 2014.

47 www.lgiu.org.uk/briefing/challenges-faced-by-the-voluntary-and-community-sector in supporting-local-services-and-developing-resilient-communities/

48 webarchive.nationalarchives.gov.uk/20120919132719/www.communities.gov.uk/publications/housing/supportingpeoplefinance, accessed 3 March 2014.

49 Barry Knight, 'Climbing the ladder', *New Statesman* insert, 2–8 May 2014.

50 www.dailymail.co.uk/news/article-2608606/No-ID-no-checks-vouchers-sob-stories-The-truth-shock-food-bank-claims.html; accessed 24 April 2014.

51 Roy Greenslade, 'The Mail on Sunday food bank backlash exposes a media power struggle', *Guardian,* 21 April 2014.

52 Lambie-Mumford et al. op. cit.

53 Quoted in HoC Library, *Food Banks and Food Poverty*, December 2013, p. 10.

54 Graham Riches, 'Food Banks and Food Security: Welfare Reform, Human Rights and Social Policy. Lessons from Canada?', *Social Policy & Administration,* vol. 36, no. 6, December 2002, pp. 648–63.

55 Quoted in HoC Library, op. cit.

Chapter 9

1 http://www.poverty.ac.uk/living-poverty/personal-experiences/renee-low-paid-worker, film 2 *Well, we're not rich.*

2 J. Browne, A. Hood and R. Joyce, *Child and working-age poverty in Northern Ireland over the next decade: an update* (London: Institute for Fiscal Studies, January 2014).

3 The Social Mobility and Child Poverty Commission, *Response to the UK government's consultation on the draft Child Poverty Strategy 2014 to 2017*, June 2014: https://www.gov.uk/government/publications/response-to-the-consultation-on-the-child-poverty-strategy

4 *State of the Nation 2014: Social mobility and child poverty in Great Britain* (HMSO: Social Mobility and Child Poverty Commission, October, 2014).

5 Peter Hall (ed.), *Varieties of Capitalism* (Oxford: OUP, 2001).

6 www.oecdbetterlifeindex.org/topics/income/

7 Malte Luebker, 'A tide of inequality: what can taxes and transfers achieve?' in N. Pons-Vignon and P. Ncube (eds.), *Confronting Finance,* (Geneva: ILO, 2012).

8 blogs.channel4.com/factcheck/factcheck-ids-tax-credit-claims-discredited/12160, accessed 1 May 2014.

9 *European Social Charter: European Committee of Social Rights – Conclusions XX-2 (2013)/(Great Britain)/Articles 3, 11, 12, 13 and 14 of the 1961 Charter,* Council of Europe, 2014.

10 James Browne and Andrew Hood, 'A Survey of the UK Benefit System', *IFS Briefing Note BN13,* 2012.

11 Carol Walker 'For and against the means test', in A. Walker, A. Sinfield and C. Walker, *Fighting poverty, inequality and injustice* (Bristol: Policy Press, 2011), p. 140.

12 R. M. Titmuss, *Essays on the Welfare State* (London: Allen and Unwin, 1963).

13 Elizabeth Clery, 'Are tough times affecting attitudes to welfare?', in Alison Park, Elizabeth Clery, John Curtice, Miranda Phillips and David Utting (eds.), *British Social Attitudes: The 29th Report*), (London: National Centre for Social Research, 2012).

14 Andrew Harrop, *The Coalition and Universalism* (London: Fabian Society, 2012).

15 Ive Marx and Tim Van Rie, *Growing Inequalities' Impacts (GINI),* Work package 6: Policy analysis, GINI research, October 2012.

16 budgetresponsibility.org.uk/wordpress/docs/BriefGuide_020511.pdf

17 For the case for greater universality, see T. Horton and J. Gregory, *The Solidarity Society* (London: Fabian Society, 2009).

18 For more details of how such a scheme might work, see citizensincome.org/

19 ONS, *Effect of taxes and benefits on household incomes,* 2013, p. 7; www.ons. gov.uk/ons/rel/household-income/the-effects-of-taxes-and-benefits-on-household-income/2011-2012/etb-stats-bulletin-2011-12.html

20 Richard Murphy, 'The Missing Billions – the UK Tax Gap', *TUC Touchstone Pamphlet,* 2008: www.tuc.org.uk/sites/default/files/documents/1missingbillions.pdf

21 G. Zucman, 'The Missing Wealth of Nations: Are Europe and the US Net Debtors or Net Creditors?', *Quarterly Journal of Economics,* 2013, pp. 1321–44; N. Shaxson, J. Christensen and N. Mathiason, *Inequality: you don't know the half of it* (London: Tax Justice Network, 2012).

22 Adam Smith, *An Inquiry into the Nature and Causes of the Wealth of Nations* (London: Methuen and Co., Ltd, 5th edn, 1904).

23 *Fair Taxation in a Changing World,* Report of the Ontario Fair Tax Commission (Toronto: University of Toronto Press, 1993), p. 45.

24 T. Piketty, E. Saez and S. Stantcheva, *Taxing the 1%,* 2013; at http://www.voxeu.org/article/taxing-1-why-top-tax-rate-could-be-over-80

25 www.oecd.org/newsroom/societygovernmentsmusttacklerecordgapbe-tweenrichandpoorsaysoecd.htm

26 S. Lansley and H. Reed, *How to boost the wage share* (TUC Touchstone pamphlet, London, 2013).

27 L. Mishel et al., *The State of Working America* (Ithaca: Cornell University Press, 12th edn, 2012), p. 3; P. Gregg and S. Machin, *What a drag: the chilling impact of unemployment on real wages* (London: The Resolution Foundation, 2012), see also: https://in.finance.yahoo.com/news/g-20-vows-boost-world-081415141.html

28 B. Gustafsson and M. Johansson, 'In search of smoking guns: What makes

income inequality vary over time in different countries?', *American Sociological Review,* 1999, pp. 585–605.

29 K. D. Ewing and J. Hendy, *Reconstruction After the Crisis* (Liverpool: IES, 2013), p. 2.

30 Lansley and Reed op. cit., pp. 44–5.

31 M. Pennycook, *What Price a Living Wage?* (London: Resolution Foundation, 2012).

32 S. Lansley and H. Reed, *How to boost the wage share* (London: TUC pamphlet, 2013), pp. 29–33.

33 http://blogs.reuters.com/macroscope/2014/01/24/why-are-us-corporate-profits-so-high-because-wages-are-so-low/

34 Landman Economics, *The Economic Impact of Extending the Living Wage to all Employees in the UK* (London: Unison, 2013).

35 J. Gautié and J. Schmitt, *Low-wage work in the wealthy world* (New York: Russell Sage Foundation, 2010).

36 R. D. Atkinson, *Falling behind in the innovation race* (London: Policy Network, May 2014).

37 W. Hutton, 'George Osborne's economic recovery is built on sand', *Observer,* 26 January2014.

38 *Differences in public sector transport spending across England*, UK Parliament Scrutiny Unit, March, pp. 2012.

39 D. Brady, *Rich Democrats, Poor People* (Oxford: Oxford University Press, 2009),

40 Ibid., pp. 1–3.

41 D. Ricardo, *On the Principles of Political Economy and Taxation* (London: JM Dent, 1817).

42 Richard Wilkinson and Kate Pickett, *The Spirit Level: Why more equal societies almost always do better* (London: Allen Lane, 2009).

43 T. Dolphin and D. Nash, *All Change, Will There be a Revolution in Economic Thinking in the Next Few Years* (London: IPPR, 2011).

44 http://www.nytimes.com/2014/01/10/opinion/krugman-the-war-over-poverty.html?nl=todaysheadlines&emc=edit_th_20140110&_r=1

45 http://www.ippr.org/juncture/171/11631/the-crisis-of-british-democracy-back-to-the-70s-or-stuck-in-the-present

46 S. Rattner, 'The Myth of Industrial Rebound', *New York Times*, 25 January 2014.

47 Lansley and Reed op. cit.; L. Mishel, H. Shierholz and J. Schmitt, *Don't Blame the Robots* (Washington, DC: Economic Policy Institute, 2013).

48 J. M. Keynes, *The General Theory of Employment, Interest and Money* (London: Macmillan, 1936, reprinted 2007), ch 24.

49 Quoted in http://www.washingtonspectator.org/index.php/The-Income -Tax-and-the-Progressive-Era.html

50 John Hilary, *The Transatlantic Trade and Investment Partnership* (Brussels: War on Want, 2014).

51 L. Kenworthy, 'What's wrong with predistribution?', *Juncture*, 20 September 2013.

52 Thomas Piketty, *Capital in the Twenty-First Century* (Harvard: Harvard University Press, 2014).

53 http://www.theguardian.com/books/2014/apr/13/occupy-right-capi talism-failed-world-french-economist-thomas-piketty, accessed 1 May 2014.

54 'A Shrinking Slice', *The Economist,* 2 November 2013.

55 http://www.imf.org/external/np/speeches/2013/012313.htm

56 http://www.weforum.org/reports/global-risks-2013-eighth-edition

57 http://www.reuters.com/article/2014/05/27/britain-boe-carney -idUSL6N0OD55220140527

58 See for example: http://www.nechildpoverty.org.uk/blog

59 See http://povertytruthcommission.org/index.php?id=8

60 http://www.poverty.ac.uk/community/northern-ireland

61 Gabi Kent, *'We are sitting with the big people now'*, final report of the PSE's pilot community engagement project in Northern Ireland, 2013.

62 Quoted in D. Aitkenhead, 'The security services are running the country, aren't they?', *Guardian*, 21 February 2014.

63 S. Pizzigati, *The Rich Don't Always Win* (New York: Seven Stories Press, 2012), p. 8.

64 http://www.reuters.com/article/2014/05/21/mcdonalds-protests -idUSL1N0O718220140521

65 See for example: http://wingsoverscotland.com/the-nhs-and-the-ttip- trap/

Appendix

1 For 2012 see Eldin Fahmy, Simon Pemberton and Eileen Sutton, 'Public Perceptions of Poverty, Social Exclusion and Living Standards: Preliminary Report on Focus Group Findings', *PSE Methods working paper No. 12,* April 2011; and E. Fahmy, S. Pemberton and E. Sutton, 'Public Perceptions of Poverty and Social Exclusion: Final Report on Focus Group Findings', *PSE Working Paper Analysis No. 3,* August 2012. See http://www.poverty.ac.uk/pse-research/pse-uk/methods-development for a full list of the methods working papers for the 2012 survey.

2 Full lists of all the items tested and classed as necessities can be found in the annotated questionnaires, four each year, available at: http://www.poverty.ac.uk/pse-research/questionnaires

3 For full details of the validity and reliability tests see: Gill Main and Jonathan Bradshaw, *Child deprivation and social exclusion in 2012,* slides 4 and 5, http://poverty.ac.uk/sites/default/files/attachments/Bradshaw%2C%20 Child%20deprivation%20and%20social%20exclusion.pdf; and David Gordon, *The extent of poverty in the UK,* slides 16, 17 and 18, http://www. poverty.ac.uk/sites/default/files/attachments/Gordon%20-%20 How%20Many%20People%20are%20Poor%20in%20the%20UK.pdf

4 This item is included on the PSE website cumulative count and raises the percentage of households lacking three or more necessities to thirty-three percent: http://www.poverty.ac.uk/pse-research/falling-below -minimum-standards

5 http://www.jrf.org.uk/sites/files/jrf/income-living-standards-full.pdf

6 Gill Main and Jonathan Bradshaw, *Child deprivation and social exclusion in 2012,* presentation to PSE final conference: http://poverty.ac.uk/sites/ default/files/attachments/Bradshaw%2C%20Child%20deprivation%20 and%20social%20exclusion.pdf

7 J. Mack and S. Lansley, *Poor Britain* (London: George, Allen and Unwin, 1985), pp. 175–6.

8 For further details see D. Gordon, 'The concept and measurement of poverty', in C. Pantazis, D. Gordon and R. Levitas (eds.), *Poverty and Social Exclusion in Britain* (Bristol: Policy Press, 2006).

9 See David Gordon, *The extent of poverty in the UK,* PSE presentation,

http://www.poverty.ac.uk/sites/default/files/attachments/Gordon%20
-%20How%20Many%20People%20are%20Poor%20in%20the%20UK.
pdf; and for children, Gill Main and Jonathan Bradshaw, *Child Poverty and
Social Exclusion*, PSE final report, http://www.poverty.ac.uk/pse-research/
pseuk-reports

10 Others have examined the use of a proportional index which weights
those who cannot afford a necessity by the proportion of the population
regarding it as a necessity, by sex, age and family type. As there was found
to be considerable overlap between this and the consensual measure with
very similar estimates of the characteristics of the poor, this method has
not been adopted further. See: 'Adapting the consensual definition of
poverty' by Bjørn Halleröd, Jonathan Bradshaw and Hilary Holmes
(from *Breadline Britain in the 1990s*, Gordon and Pantazis, 1997) and B.
Halleröd, *A New Approach to the Direct Consensual Measurement of Poverty*
(New South Wales Social Policy Research Centre, 1994).

11 In 2002/3, a Poverty and Social Exclusion survey was conducted in
Northern Ireland, so the 2012 PSE survey allows comparison within
Northern Ireland back to 2002/3. See http://www.poverty.ac.uk/
pse-research/pse-uk/pse-northern-ireland and http://www.poverty.ac.uk/
pse-research/past-uk-research/pse-northern-ireland-20023 for further
details.

12 D. Gordon, *The main PSE UK sampling frame,* PSE methods working
paper No. 21, 2011.

Index

This index covers major topics and themes and significant figures.
Locators in *italics* indicate figures and diagrams.